Global Justice and Recognition Theory

In the light of intense international focus on ongoing forms of world poverty, this book examines the potential of the concept of recognition in contemporary political philosophy to respond morally to this dire condition.

This book uses recognition theories to develop a two-tiered response to the problem of global poverty. First, it highlights non-degradation, non-humiliation and the avoidance of social suffering as essential components to the agency of the very poor. This runs counter to liberal arguments that focus only on the deficit of basic material interests. Second, even if universal conditions of agency are met, many of the world's extreme poor may still suffer domination. The book argues that empowering the world's poor to resist domination is an essential response to global poverty. By conceiving poverty in terms of agency and empowerment, this book highlights the transnational relevance of recognition theory to one of the most crucial problems affecting a rapidly globalising world.

Global Justice and Recognition Theory will be of interest to scholars and advanced students working in social and political philosophy, political theory, and global justice.

Monica Mookherjee is a Senior Lecturer in Political Philosophy at Keele University, Staffordshire, UK. She has previously published in the fields of contemporary political philosophy, especially in the fields of recognition theory, feminist philosophy and multiculturalism. She is the author of *Women's Rights as Multicultural Claims* (2009).

Routledge Studies in Contemporary Philosophy

Conservatism and Grace
The Conservative Case for Religion by Establishment
Sebastian Morello

The Ethics of Interpretation
From Charity as a Principle to Love as a Hermeneutic Imperative
Pol Vandevelde

The Nature and Practice of Trust
Marc A. Cohen

A Plea for Plausibility
Toward a Comparative Decision Theory
John R. Welch

Living with the Dead
On Death, the Dead, and Immortality
J. Jeremy Wisnewski

Free Will's Value
Criminal Justice, Pride, and Love
John Lemos

Emotional Self-Knowledge
Edited by Alba Montes Sánchez and Alessandro Salice

Global Justice and Recognition Theory
Dignifying the World's Poor
Monica Mookherjee

For more information about this series, please visit: https://www.routledge.com/Routledge-Studies-in-Contemporary-Philosophy/book-series/SE0720

Global Justice and Recognition Theory

Dignifying the World's Poor

Monica Mookherjee

Routledge
Taylor & Francis Group
NEW YORK AND LONDON

First published 2023
by Routledge
605 Third Avenue, New York, NY 10158

and by Routledge
4 Park Square, Milton Park, Abingdon, Oxon, OX14 4RN

Routledge is an imprint of the Taylor & Francis Group, an informa business

ISBN: 978-0-367-48798-0 (hbk)
ISBN: 978-1-032-43820-7 (pbk)
ISBN: 978-1-003-04503-8 (ebk)

DOI: 10.4324/9781003045038

Typeset in Sabon
by Deanta Global Publishing Services, Chennai, India

Contents

Acknowledgements

Writing this book has taken much time and concerted effort. It is a task which would not have been possible but for the generous and supportive assistance of individuals who either contributed by commenting on draft chapters or by offering general moral support and conversation on the themes of the book. I owe special thanks to the following individuals: Linda Ahall, Andrea Baumeister, Rowan Cruft, Lynn Dobson, Jane Krishnadas, Moran Mandelbaum, Michal Krumer-Nevo, Charlotte Newey, Shane O'Neill, Luis Rodrigues, Gottfried Schweiger, Jonathan Seglow, Nick Smith, Alison Stone and Kerri Woods.

Early versions of draft chapters were presented at colloquia and workshops at Keele, Reading and Stirling Universities in the UK, and at the Centre for Ethics and Poverty Research at Salzburg University, Austria. I am extremely grateful to the audiences of these seminars for sharing their thoughts and feedback and for highly supportive dialogue about the themes raised in the book.

Parts of Chapter 2 draw from my 2020 article, 'On Axel Honneth's Cosmopolitanism: The "Forgetfulness" of Global Poverty as a Form of Reification', which was first published in *Social Theory and Practice*. I am grateful to Springer for permission to reproduce parts of my earlier arguments concerning global poverty and social suffering in Gottfried Schweiger (ed.), *Poverty, Inequality and the Critical Theory of Recognition* (2020) in Chapter 3.

Special thanks are also due to Andrew Weckenmann at Routledge for so enthusiastically supporting the initial book proposal, and to two anonymous reviewers who commented constructively and positively on the early draft of a sample chapter. Equally, I owe much gratitude and many thanks to Rosaleah Stammler, as the Philosophy Editorial Assistant at Routledge, whose patience and support have been ongoing and highly appreciated. Additionally, Bharath Selvamani at Deanta provided excellent support and assistance at the copyediting stage.

Finally, I am as ever incredibly appreciative of friends and family members, who have been so understanding in terms of the time and mental space needed for a project of this length and scope.

Monica Mookherjee,
Keele University, December 2022.

Introduction

From Social Suffering to Dignity for the World's Poor: Towards Global Justice through Cosmopolitan Recognition Theory

The persistence of poverty around the world evidently remains one of the most insidious and troubling global challenges, with World Bank statistics suggesting during 2013 an estimated 767 million people worldwide living under an internationally designated poverty line of US $1.90 a day. While this apparently dire condition was generally understood in the context of a steady and welcome historical decline in numbers living in 'absolute' poverty over the past 30 years, a recent key World Bank report suggests the COVID-19 pandemic witnessed the largest increase in numbers living in poverty since World War II, with a staggering 71 million more people globally in 2020 suffering this condition than in pre-pandemic times (World Bank, 2022). With a slow recovery predicted, in view of the war in Ukraine and climate conditions affecting global food production, the 11 per cent recent increase in extreme poverty around the world, associated with the pandemic and other factors, evidently entails one of the most challenging situations worldwide, recovery from which is likely to present significant obstacles (World Bank, 2020; World Bank, 2022; Bhala, Basin and Virmani, 2022).

Unsurprisingly, this situation has ignited the attention of normative political theorists, who, confronted with what seems clearly to be one of the most troubling humanitarian problems of current times, offer normative arguments for ethical principles which would respond to the complexity and multidimensionality of poverty worldwide. The task is challenging not least because global poverty involves a large number of deficits and deprivations in different contexts, arising in relation to land, access to essential services, to food, shelter, education and for cultural identity. In response to these issues, philosophers do not usually intervene by advocating for specific policies, although some may do so. The major contribution of philosophers might be thought to lie in arguing for and defending the beneficial, action-guiding values and commitments which would be conducive to improving the life conditions in which the world's poorest, the 'bottom billion' as sometimes called, seem to remain. This book aims to contribute to this dialogue through the philosophical perspective offered by contemporary theories of recognition.

DOI: 10.4324/9781003045038-1

More specifically, this Introduction takes space to outline the broad philosophical challenges raised by the analysis of contemporary global poverty. This discussion is then followed by an overview of the concrete argument developed through the chapters. The first task is especially significant considering the prominence of global poverty on the international agenda, with the United Nations' stated objective of reaching 'Zero Hunger' worldwide by 2030 (United Nations, 2015). Despite the risks of commenting too generally, highly relevant and central to this goal is the resolution to 'free the human race from the tyranny of poverty and want and to heal and secure our planet, [and ensure that] no one will be left behind' (UN, 2015: 1; Weber, 2017). Alongside these goals, the no less challenging task of reducing inequalities between nations has been pledged, and the acknowledgement raised of the equally significant fact that extreme forms of destitution and deprivation are found not only in the major European cities but also in the Global South so frequent in the humanitarian imagination.

Whilst the ambition of these international goals is multifaceted, and has included the laudable aims of hunger eradication, universal education and the need to develop trade and investment practices and labour opportunities (UN, 2015: 7), much existing political critique focuses on dominant implementation strategies relied on by international organisations which pursue the goals of sustainable poverty alleviation and development (Weber, 2017; Carant, 2015; Sano, 2020). Specifically, the central strategy recommended by the United Nations of strengthening the commercial interests and trade practices of poorer nations has been identified as presuming a neoliberal economic framework, without explicitly defending the essential human rights of the poor to water, food and essential services (Weber, 2017). Therefore, while it seems true that the United Nations operates with a background aim of seeking to respect, protect and fulfil international human rights, the means through which they have pursued these goals, especially by aiming to promote economic growth, seems to confirm their strong belief in a direct economic growth-poverty alleviation correlation, despite the loopholes which have been identified in ensuring the dignity of the lives of the very poor (see Shawki, 2018; Gore, 2015; Sengupta, 2018). In reaction to these strategies, the UN and World Bank's 'market episteme' (Weber, 2017) has been strongly scrutinised by philosophers such as Thomas Pogge and Mitu Sengupta, who draw attention to the illicit financial flows and international investment agreements facilitated by global institutions which, they argue, persistently maintain vast proportions of the world in poverty (Pogge and Sengupta, 2015; Schweiger, 2016).

Other political philosophers, meanwhile, voice concerns with the tendency to focus too heavily on international institutions in debates concerning global poverty. Significantly, for political theorist Monique Deveaux, this focus risks being all-encompassing and, therefore, obscuring from view initiatives led and organised by those who are poor and deprived themselves (Deveaux, 2015, 2018, 2021). Put differently, too heavy a focus on the reform of international financial institutions risks deflecting ethical attention from the agency of the very poor to define their fundamental needs (Weber, 2017). Whereas Deveaux, therefore, principally focuses on the role of poor-led movements in narrowing inequality and achieving global justice, this book takes up an allied and connected approach which concentrates on the philosophical justification for the struggles of the very poor through the concept of 'recognition' in contemporary political theory, and which is associated most prominently with writers such as Axel Honneth (1995, 2014), Charles Taylor (1994) and Nancy Fraser (1997). The approach has been extended more recently by continental writers such as Emmanuel Renault (2017) and Jacques Rancière (Honneth and Ranciere, 2016). Broadly stated, I aim to derive from their philosophical arguments resources to defend a critical cosmopolitan recognition-theoretical approach to global poverty, one which acknowledges the equal moral significance of each person and their needs for recognition as a key means to securing their dignity.

0.1 Global Poverty Today, Zero Hunger in the Twenty-First Century and Cosmopolitan Theoretical Responses

Despite, as explained earlier, the significant drawbacks of the implementation strategies recommended by international programmes for sustainable development to achieve rights and justice for the very poor, at the same time the Sustainable Development Goals suggest a conception of poverty around the world today which supports my philosophical turn in this book towards recognition theory. In particular, these agenda-setting goals go well beyond conceiving questions of global poverty purely as a matter of economic deprivation, and openly acknowledge the multidimensionality of this condition (Pomati and Nandy, 2020).[1] While this focus seems realistic and advantageous, acknowledging this complexity also runs the risk of lacking a stable conception of the harms caused by global forms of poverty. This predicament is reflected in the fact that a number of different poverty measures have been proposed, arising from the World Bank to the United Nations, and ranging from a focus on social exclusion to absolute poverty and from participatory to monetary approaches. Each of these approaches is clearly likely to be value-laden, and each is likely to generate different knowledge about poverty and the poor (Schweiger, 2014).

Confronted, then, with conflicting measures and definitions (Cuaresma et al., 2018; Schweiger, 2016), an understandable philosophical reaction is to aim to synthesise the different deprivations of global poverty into a single measure to facilitate inter-personal comparisons worldwide. One prominent synthetic approach, from which this book draws much inspiration, is proposed by Amartya Sen's pioneering 'capabilities' perspective (Sen, 1980, 1985a, 1999, 2004, 1997), in an approach which, in key part due to Sen's own contributions, has significantly impacted international development policy and practice.[2]

To explain, Sen classically viewed poverty not just in terms of income or household expenditure but in terms of the ability to achieve different valuable 'functionings', states of being and doing, the different combinations of which could lead to the meaningful assessment of a person's positive freedom. For Alkire (2011), the capabilities approach is therefore able to recognise that, in some locations worldwide, nutritional disadvantages might matter much less to the overall assessment of poverty than, for instance, school attendance. That is, it is likely that different functionings would be weighed and prioritised differently in different contexts, a significant issue considering the capabilities theorists' concern with the substantive freedoms of people to choose how they wish to function, liberties which constitute their overall capacity to lead a life which they 'have reason to value' (Sen, 1999: 75; Nussbaum, 2011). Therefore, to pursue Alkire's example, on the one hand public reasoning may determine that, in the Indian state of Madhya Pradesh, nutritional deprivations are most significant in measuring and overcoming poverty; and, on the other, in the Congo the question of school attendance may be more relevant. This approach, therefore, considers multiple and overlapping deprivations, such as the fact that malnutrition may be coupled with a lack of work in some contexts; water may have to be fetched from an area of regular violence; or poor services may be coupled with the persistence of very low incomes (Alkire and Foster, 2011: 3–4). As Graf and Schweiger (2014) rightly argue, the attention to the complexity of human lives and consideration of different priorities in terms of human functionings seems to suggest good reasons for responding to global poverty through this approach.

As suggested, in this book I draw much inspiration from the insights of the capabilities approach to support the dignity and agency of the very poor. I also consider, however, Graf and Schweiger's (2016) astute point concerning the limitations of viewing the harms of poverty only as a lack of positive freedom, as does the capabilities approach, rather than also in terms of the experiences of denigration and social suffering which arise from structural inequalities, issues which have been more central to recognition theories. Rather than viewing these approaches as opposed, however, it seems more plausible to conceptualise negative experiences of moral injury and social suffering arising from poverty as 'conversion factors' which may be taken to affect a person's positive freedoms and capabilities to live a life they strongly value (Hvinden and Halvoren, 2018; Chiappero-Martinetti and Salardi, 2008). Therefore, I take the view in this book that there is a close though not always straightforward relationship between the essential agency capabilities of the very poor and significant human needs for 'recognition', the lack of which may be taken to indicate crucial forms of social suffering. I defend a crucial correlation between capabilities and recognition theories, a connection which seems plausible given recognition theory's central commitment to the value of self-realisation, to be outlined below, and which is likely to be consistent with the capabilities theorist's focus on positive freedom. However, while the two theories may be thought mutually consistent, recognition theories offer the advantage of highlighting the political implications of freedom as self-realisation, by suggesting ways in which dignity may be found in active struggles over the definition of basic needs, rather than seeming to presuppose, as might be thought true of the capabilities approach, a potentially de-institutionalised link between goods and freedom (Clark, 2005). To summarise these issues differently, recognition theory extends the insight of the capabilities approach, by focusing on the complexity of the 'conversion factors' involved in undermining the positive freedoms of the poor, such as experiences of social suffering and moral injury; and they highlight, perhaps more keenly than the capabilities approach, the highly political ways in which human needs are defined and claimed through active struggles.

Of course, this last point bears a complex relation to Sen's conception of capabilities. Through his long-standing conception of 'development as freedom', Sen (1983; 1999) has attributed special ethical importance to the value the poor may derive from freedoms which enable them to participate in collective decision making. However, while his perspective therefore clearly values the subjective experiences and voices of the poor, capabilities theories are more generally sceptical than recognition-based approaches as regards subjective mental states. That is, the capabilities approach remains concerned that concentrating on the subjective perceptions of human beings, as reflected in the welfare economists' 'revealed preference' approach, might insufficiently attend to impacts of structures of power and unjust social arrangements (Teschl and Comim, 2005; Khader, 2009). This point is of clear significance to the fraught debates concerning the role of unjust power maintaining people in perpetual cycles of poverty.

While, therefore, Sen's own focus on the need for active participation by the poor in dialogues concerning social choices could be thought to support recognition theorists' focus on subjective experiences of hurt, moral injury and denigration (Clark, 2013; Joshi, 2020), other presentations of the capabilities approach, such as that of Martha Nussbaum (2011, 2016), seem at least on the surface less hospitable to considering these subjective experiences, given their conception of capabilities as a stable list of fundamental entitlements. While their apparent equation of capabilities and constitutional guarantees might provide a sense of certainty in debates concerning global poverty, it seems problematic readily to assume a correlation between (a particular list of) capabilities and human dignity. Doing so may discount the theoretical and practical learning which may arise from the theorist's focus on, for example, subjective experiences of shame, hurt and loss, a focus on which, in turn, promises to reveal a more dynamic conception of how the lives of the very poor may be dignified. Therefore, from the perspective taken in this book, the negative psychological experiences of poverty-related social suffering remain significant worldwide. As Rylko-Bauer and Farmer (2016) suggest, structural violence harms the very poor in ways which are often normalised through everyday experiences and through institutions, resulting in deaths, injuries and the reproduction of violence. Theoretical attempts to protect the dignity of the lives of the very poor would, therefore, seem to do well to go beyond the focus on basic capabilities, recognising that knowledge about the human good which flows from the suffering of the poor probably could not be known in advance by theoretical fiat.

Therefore, while the capabilities approach has rightly had a significant impact on international development initiatives (Sen, 1999: 87), this book aims to take an allied approach by focusing on agency which arises from social suffering. To do so is inevitably ambitious, given the elusiveness of the concept of social suffering both within recognition theory and in social studies more broadly. For instance, research into social suffering has been conducted prominently in the field of medical anthropology, with Kleinman, Das, Lock and Lock (1997) extensively exploring the concept in post-trauma situations following the devastation of war and civil conflict. Despite the 'fuzziness' or intrinsic elusiveness of the concept, these studies suggest that, in fact, the 'ineffability' of social suffering, or the difficulties of explaining the concept through rational, medical discourse, provides a productive focus for analysis and critique of global poverty. The concept suggests forms of pain and violation which cannot completely be expressed in the language of rights or a distributive injustice, not least because the idea seems to stand in an ambiguous position between reason and emotion. Yet this very ambiguity might, I suggest, promise a more subtle and flexible perspective on global poverty even than the capabilities approach. For Kleinman, Das, Lock and Lock, social suffering 'results from what political, economic and institutional power does to people, and reciprocally, from how these forms of power themselves influence responses to [...] social problems' (1997: ix). Already, an avenue seems to be suggested which extends the capabilities approach, through a broad-ranging concept in the normative analysis of poverty's many dimensions.

0.2 The Contribution of Theories of Recognition

Theories of recognition in contemporary political theory are prominently known for their focus on the sense of moral injury, grievance and social suffering experienced by the exploited, excluded and oppressed (Honneth, in Fraser and Honneth, 2003: 129; Taylor, 1994; Fraser, 1997).[3] One question which immediately confronts the application of their insights to worldwide questions of poverty is how far the harms of poverty may genuinely be conceived in terms of these subjective experiences. Writers such as Seglow (2009) have been, for instance, concerned about the limitations of conceptualising the elemental wrongs of grinding poverty as a matter of inadequate self-regard or self-esteem, both central ideas of recognition theory. Another core question is whether recognition theories, associated with the third generation of Frankfurt School thought, may realistically apply beyond particular nation-states. Given that recognition theories have most usually focused on modern capitalism and its formation in richer Western societies (see Corradetti 2013; Anderson, 2011; Wiggerhaus, 1994), genuine dilemmas seem to arise as to whether human needs for mutual recognition may be applied globally.

The first issue, namely whether material oppression or economic hardship may be realistically viewed as a problem of misrecognition, is one which I shall eventually answer positively. Chapter 1 presents what I hope to be a convincing case for reconceiving what often appear pure questions of distributive injustice in terms of the idea of misrecognition. The ongoing humiliation and degradation of people worldwide through poverty may destroy the self-conceptions of the very poor, undermining their sense of value and their own capacity to pursue their own goals (Hutchinson, Abrams and Christian, 2007, cited in Graf and Schweiger, 2014: 263). The intuitive defensibility of this argument is reflected in the writings of one of the major current recognition theorists, Axel Honneth (1995, 2014). As suggested earlier, through particular interpretations of Hegel's early 'Jena' writings as well as his later works, Honneth contests the idea of justice as a matter of Hobbesian agreement of hypothetical warring individuals in a 'state of nature' who bargain over material interests. Rather, for Honneth, pursuing justice consists in achieving mutuality with others, in a way that reflects the dialogical conception of self-formation crucial to Hegel's classic depiction of a 'struggle for recognition' in the *Phenomenology of Spirit* (2008 [1807]), or selfhood formed intersubjectively through dialectical interaction between lord and bondsman. While Hegel's original idea could be utilised in different ways in contemporary political theories (see Sembou, 2003), Honneth takes the idea to model the modern individual's search for self-realisation in his contemporary recognition theory in the following way:

> [E]very human being depends essentially on a context of forms of social interaction governed by normative principles of mutual recognition; and the disappearance of such relations of recognition results in experiences of disrespect and humiliation which cannot fail to have damaging effects on the individual's identity-formation.
>
> (Honneth, in Fraser and Honneth, 2003: 173)

Although recognition theorists such as Charles Taylor (1994) also draw on this same initial Hegelian idea to defend the intersubjective basis of selfhood and identity, the further and more testing question suggested earlier is whether any specific ideals of recognition may be universalised across different nations. Although Honneth (2012) has briefly considered the issue of globalising the politics of recognition as a matter of inter-state relations, and has also voiced significant hopes, which may be viewed as overly sanguine, of the ever-increasing international realisation of human rights as a form of recognition, to date he has not extensively attempted to apply his own substantive recognition theory beyond the nation-state. This is despite the fact that his long-standing foci on social processes of work and labour and on the social pathologies of unemployment and economic marginalisation in the context of changing patterns of capitalism seem immediately relevant to analysing global forms of poverty. These factors, at least initially, suggest the international applicability of his recognition theory, an application which a growing literature has pursued (e.g., Staples, 2012; Burns, 2013; Burns and Thompson 2013). Significantly, too, these interventions seem to mirror attempts to globalise other normative political theories which have been firstly associated with the nation-state. This trend is exemplified by one of the foremost philosophers of the age, John Rawls (1971, 1999), whose later work seeks to globalise his social contract theory, even while resisting a cosmopolitan political agenda as such. It is within this trend of applying theories of justice beyond the state (Pogge and Moellendorf, 2008; Brock and Brighouse, 2005; Brock, 2009) that I attempt this book's cosmopolitan extension of recognition theory.

Under conditions of intensifying globalisation, deepening structural inequalities worldwide as well as the massive increase in world communications, it seems vital to conceptualise the deepest problems of oppression, social invisibility and non-recognition as global problems. What Frankfurt School writers typically refer to as 'social pathologies' or 'societal misdevelopments' (Harris, 2022; Feenberg, 2014) may seem to emerge intuitively as global phenomena, including precarious labour conditions and problems of denigration and disempowerment which continue to affect people even in societies in which the basic needs of most people have been met. This is despite the fact, as Burns and Thompson (2013: 41) suggest, as 'new Hegelians' recognition theorists are usually communitarian rather than cosmopolitan thinkers.

More specifically, this book's aim to globalise recognition theory considers the contributions of a range of contemporary recognition theorists who have suggested crucial conceptual tools with significant insights into the forms of oppression experienced by the world's poor. Two particular interventions define my point of entry and provide the impetus for my line of argument. The first prominent internationalisation of recognition theory in recent years, focusing especially on global wealth disparities between the First and Third World, is raised by Volker Heins (2008, 2012). Heins strongly defends the internationalisation of recognition, especially focusing, as I do in this book, on Axel Honneth's (1995) commitment to the value of self-realisation. For Heins, the significance of human needs for self-realisation should not be viewed as intrinsic only to advanced capitalist states, as they are in fact highly urgent to acknowledge in non-Western developing nation-states without pre-existing, functioning welfare systems. For Heins, recognition theories are more illuminating than other international political theories or more 'technocratic', resource-distributive development policies which focus mainly on commodity reallocation, not least because they acknowledge the structural relationship of disadvantage between economically advanced and developing nations. Despite this broad defence, Heins (2008) raises considerable doubts, as do I in Chapter 1, concerning the transnational application of Honneth's (1995) specific recognitive principles of love, rights and esteem. Taking my cue in Chapter 1 from Heins' concerns, the task of articulating an alternative cosmopolitan recognition theory constitutes the core undertaking of this book.

Additionally, with arguments defending Honneth's modes of recognition, in a series of insightful studies Gottfried Schweiger urges the universal relevance of this theory to debates concerning global poverty. In particular, while it is clear that recognition theorists have usually assumed the advanced capitalist nation-state as the location of mutual recognition, Schweiger contends that their central theoretical claims were always intended to be applied universally in a certain sense. For instance, the human need for self-realisation relates to certain 'general patterns of human behaviour' (Honneth, 1995: 174) which may be regarded as anthropological constants, normatively required of any society worldwide to enable human beings to flourish. For Schweiger, theories of recognition should best be defended by assuming a dialectic between the absolute universal core of recognition attributable to all human beings on the one hand, and on the other the cultural and social ways that norms of recognition are expressed in particular societies (Schweiger, 2012: 80; Petherbridge, 2011). Although, in Chapter 1, I question Schweiger's defence of this universalist potential, or 'surplus validity', arising from Honneth's normative principles of recognition, it nonetheless seems persuasive to follow Schweiger's (2014) claim that the sentiments of moral injury on which recognition theorists focus are likely to be human universals. While it seems inevitable that different societies would need to specify, from the perspective of their own institutions and forms of life, how they respond to these moral injuries and support self-realisation, the need for this universalist response, when thinking of the deepest problems of worldwide poverty, seems compelling. These existing perspectives, then, suggest an initial favourable case for applying the theory to abject forms of poverty worldwide, and to attempt to dignify the world's poor by focusing particularly on their social suffering.

0.3 Chapter-by-Chapter Overview

Given the briefness of the initial overview, I take space in Chapter 1 to provide a fuller justification for conceiving global poverty as a matter of misrecognition. While two of the most prominent recognition theorists, Axel Honneth (1995) and Nancy Fraser (1997), seem to suggest different but analytically persuasive theoretical rationales for potentially viewing questions of material deprivation and poverty in terms of recognition theory, the task of applying their analyses to the harms of global poverty seems to beg many questions. Although it seems reasonable to assume all human beings possess intrinsic needs for recognition, which poverty is likely to undermine, nonetheless locating a universal threshold for these needs is likely to be less than straightforward. On the one hand, Fraser's dual systems analysis risks continually returning to conceive global poverty as a question of redistribution. On the other, Honneth's theory seems afflicted by the problem of specifying a universal threshold for his recognitive principles of love, rights and esteem. For example, specifying a universal or cosmopolitan conception of social esteem risks proving to be impossible across different forms of life, not least owing to the disputed nature of the criterial bases for esteem within different social groups even in advanced capitalist societies. Additionally, even under advanced capitalism, where the openness of the criteria for esteem could seem advantageous, the 'positional' nature of this form of respect renders it likely that people who are severely marginalised from labour market participation, for example, may be wholly deprived of this good.

Therefore, Chapter 1 opens up the challenge of articulating another form of universal recognition theory, one responsive to the deep harms of global poverty. As the first step, Chapter 2 begins to locate some more promising conceptual avenues, such as Honneth's lesser known theories of antecedent recognition and reification (Honneth, 2008, 2008a). As a very minimal substrate of cosmopolitan recognition, antecedent or 'primary' recognition suggests the moral value of minimal responses even to distant others around the world in terms of humane empathy, in such a way that seems transculturally relevant and applicable across different forms of life. Not only does this idea provide a more likely cosmopolitan basis from which to challenge global poverty than seems possible through Honneth's substantive recognition theory, it also seems true, correlatively, that Honneth's comparatively recent post-Marxist presentation of reification as the 'forgetfulness of recognition', the antithesis of primary recognition, promises a deep critique of the tendency towards inaction in the face of poverty by individuals in the affluent world. Applying Honneth's concepts proves additionally useful, I argue, by contesting some other influential moral interventions of global poverty, such as Peter Singer's (2015) endorsement of the effective altruism movement. While Singer's core intuition productively challenges the First-World reification of the global poor in a certain sense, his recommended solution, namely a utilitarian commitment to maximising the global aggregation of utility, risks reinforcing forgetfulness of the humanity of the very poor in curious ways.

As Chapter 2 therefore defends the ethical imperative for citizens of affluent societies personally and politically to oppose the forgetfulness of global poverty, there remain significant questions as to the defence of the full self-realisation of the very poor through this theoretical approach, especially in view of the complexity and multidimensionality of poverty. Chapters 3 and 4 respond by presenting a two-tier cosmopolitan recognition theory in terms of the concepts of, first, the agency and, second, the empowerment of the global poor. While the focus on these values draws significant inspiration from recent debates in development ethics and particularly from the capabilities approach, as outlined previously, for reasons suggested at the outset my defence of recognition-based conceptions of agency and empowerment aim to surpass a pure emphasis on positive freedom in the capabilities approach. The core but elusive concept of social suffering enables recognition theories to understand the way structural constraints impact individual capacities for agency in conditions of dire poverty.

More specifically, Chapter 3 defends a concept of what I label, with acknowledgement of Sen's influential phrase (Sen, 1999: 75), 'reason-to-value' agency. This conception differs from Sen's concept of agency capability, however, not only because it is complexly related to the social suffering on which recognition theorists have prominently focused. Furthermore, where the very poor struggle to 'get by' and to survive their economic constraints, I emphasise this form of agency as a limited but significant gateway for their recognition struggles. By focusing on Emmanuel Renault's (2017) and Iain Wilkinson and Arthur Kleinman's (2016) theories of social suffering, the resulting conception of agency contributes to a cosmopolitan recognition theory by acknowledging some basic but crucial ways that the very poor may often act creatively, assessing their priorities and mitigating their vulnerabilities. Renault (2017) especially focuses on how the very poor may experience their social suffering as invisibility rather than through the overt expression of a grievance, as seemingly suggested by mainstream recognition theories. Of course, a cosmopolitan recognition theory should clearly avoid the tendency to make a virtue out of the non-ideal, and it should not regard agency which arises from suffering as an end-in-itself, not least because these acts often express survival and necessity rather than emancipation. At the same time, these acts may express everyday dignity in important ways; and it does not seem unlikely that they may also contain the basic grounds from which the poor could initiate their struggle to define their needs, even if these actions are grounded in limited forms of trust and common identity. Welfare-based protections seem crucial for protecting these forms as agency, as they promise the gateway to more coordinated recognition struggles of the poor.

Chapter 3 also argues, however, that the sole focus on the agency arising from social suffering would clearly not suffice in a cosmopolitan recognition theory, as it would not alter structural inequalities nor give rise to genuinely emancipatory struggles over 'recognition', if this term is taken to involve the re-definition of needs and moral rights. A recognition-theoretical concept of empowerment also seems vital, because it seems likely that it is only by acting over and above the context of necessity that the poor and the powerless could articulate their conception of their needs, interests and rights in ways that would move them sustainably towards self-realisation. On the basis, then, that cosmopolitan recognition theorists concerned with dire poverty should also be concerned with empowerment, Chapter 4 takes up Jay Drydyk's (2008) related concept of 'durable empowerment'. Reformulating his idea enables me to support the concept of 'inter-sphere durable empowerment', a concept which, I argue, finds considerable support within Charles Taylor's (1994) much debated liberal recognition theory.

While Taylor, like Honneth, does not offer an explicitly cosmopolitan conception of his recognition theory, and although his theory has correctly been more often associated with minority rights and multiculturalism, by drawing on his later conceptions of 'modern social imaginaries' and the idea of strong evaluation in his concrete recognition theory, I pursue the idea that empowerment assists to lift people out of perpetual precarity and cycles of poverty. Specifically, Taylor's theory suggests that the empowered recognition struggles of the poor would ideally involve a psychological dimension, entailing an inward capacity to imagine and conceptualise change. Second, and equally significant, this conception of empowerment would involve a strong 'inter-sphere', or social dimension. This is because, when the poor move towards empowerment, they are likely to do so by utilising their increased power and capacity within one sphere of life, such as in the sphere of labour, potentially to transform and expand their control over other life-spheres too. Finally, though no less significantly, I argue that this recognition-theoretical conception of empowerment would be strongly normative or moral, in that it would involve a capacity to choose and act with collective consciousness or an awareness of group-based historical injustice. Without this consciousness, people might seem empowered even when acting according to preferences formed under domination, a situation which Taylor's recognition theory clearly opposes. Globally, for the very poor, realising all three dimensions of empowerment is likely to be complex. Given the fact that the very poor inevitably belong to different social and minority groups, forming collective consciousness is likely to raise the question of 'solidarity with whom?'. The challenges for the very poor in developing collective consciousness, or 'power-with', is explored in this chapter through a focus on some prominent poverty alleviation initiatives which have been thought to empower women, especially in poorer, emerging economies, namely microcredit programmes.

Chapter 5 takes the analysis of the recognition-based durable empowerment of the very poor further, by focusing on the core subjective, inner-capacity of what some feminist writers have called 'power-within', or the psychological form of empowerment. Here I extend the argument in Chapter 4 which demonstrates that this form of power would be important to enabling those who are poor to depart from poverty traps to enable them to overcome their social suffering in a sustained sense. To be sure, empowerment could not simply be a psychological matter, which may be extraordinarily challenging when one faces structural constraints. Nonetheless, forming an inward capacity to conceptualise a better life or a more just world seems a crucial component in dignifying one's life. This chapter, therefore, further examines the potential tensions between the normative dimension of empowerment, often referred to as power-with, and the psychological component, also so crucial in development ethics in encouraging the capacities of the poor potentially to transform power-structures in different spheres of life, and to raise claims concerning their needs and rights.

The seeming tension between these two dimensions of empowerment is highlighted well by considering French philosopher Jacques Rancière's recent contribution to recognition theory. Rancière is well known in political philosophy, more broadly, for advancing a distinctive, non-identitarian and universalistic idea of the 'equality of speaking subjects' (Rancière, 2011). Also, given his long-standing concerns with the poor and excluded in Western philosophy, it is significant that he has recently conceptualised the recognition struggles of the socially excluded to involve mobilising capacities to reconceptualise a material situation, for example economic hardship, as an injustice rather than as an inevitable feature of reality. It is this capacity which, for Rancière, promises the emancipated claims of those who are poor and powerless for a better world. While I strongly defend some core insights of the Rancièrian conception of recognition, it also seems crucial to consider the structural constraints which may inhibit the poor and powerless from mentally conceptualising the possibilities of a better world, an issue which I explore through an analysis of the disputes arising over the Sardar Sarovar dam project within prominent urbanisation and development programmes in India. This analysis leads me to suggest surpassing Rancière's idea, or at least supplementing it with a specific conception of collective consciousness or 'power-with'. The empowered recognition struggles of poor communities, for instance enabling them to contest dominant conceptions of 'progress' and 'development', would involve a certain form of collective consciousness, namely that their specific communities have often historically suffered exclusion from the means to inscribe their concerns, priorities and needs onto established political agendas.

If these arguments represent, then, persuasive readings of current recognition theory, and if they amount to an innovative cosmopolitan extension of this framework, as I hope, I will have suggested that the combination of the focus on survivalist, reason-to-value agency and on the capacities of the poor for durable empowerment would provide a twin set of universal commitments, which may be action-guiding in terms of dignifying the lives the world's poorest through their recognition struggles. Of course, one potential concern with this argument may be that the main focus on norms and value-commitments under-specifies who, within states and the international community, for example, is obliged to meet the needs of encouraging the very poor around the world in terms of agency and empowerment in the senses defended. This is a complex issue, which speaks to the nature and scope of normative political theory. I comment more extensively on this issue in defence of recognition-based approaches in the Conclusion. For the moment, it is worth reiterating that it is of course clear that normative political philosophers cannot abdicate responsibility for defining moral and political obligations as well as normative values. At the same time, philosophers might more realistically offer arguments for action-guiding principles, rather than deciding definitively for or against particular international development policies, in such a way which would resolve all complex issues of obligation. That is to say, the more modest role of cosmopolitan recognition theorists would be to suggest the values which might meaningfully inspire the struggles of the poor for recognition, and to unfold the meaning of acknowledging the humanity and dignity of the poor and powerless.

By drawing, however, on specific examples where poor communities have mobilised their capacities and struggle for recognition, and in presenting the central reflections and arguments in this book, my hope is to contribute to extending the normative application of recognition theories, which have been overridingly associated for too long with state-centred campaigns within particular nations. The pursuit of agency and empowerment seems to suggest universalisable values which might animate the struggles of the very poor for and over the recognition of their needs, priorities and rights. The argument developed through the chapters explicitly acknowledges the social suffering involved in severe forms of poverty afflicting the world at the moment, suggesting how the claims of the very poor may emanate from this suffering. If, from the outset, recognition theories are fundamentally concerned with self-realisation as a path towards dignity, an essentially contested concept as much philosophical discussion attests,[4] the hope is that the particular conceptions of agency and empowerment developed in this book, from the perspective of both established and newer recognition theories, might provide key conceptual tools from which to universalise the theory in response to one of the most troubling and pressing international predicaments.

Notes

1 Sustainable Development Goal Target 1.2, for instance, is formulated specifically as the aim of 'by 2030 (reducing) at least by half the proportion of men, women and children of all ages living in poverty in all its dimensions, according to national definitions'. Moreover, the Sustainable Development Goals' Multidimensional Poverty Index (MPI) assists to measure progress towards SDG-1, according to a variety of indicators. For an overview of these goals, and, at the time of writing, the recent reports from the United Nations in terms of progress towards poverty alleviation goals, see https://sdgs.un.org/goals/goal1. Last accessed 03.03.23.

2 The literature connecting the capabilities approach to international development policies and practices is extensive and wide-ranging. It would be practically impossible address all of the different debates which have arisen concerning education, literacy programmes, health inequalities, for example, in this book. However, some crucial readings include Thérien (2012), Devin (2020), Stanton (2007) and Quizilbash (1996).

3 As will be explored more specifically in Chapter 1, Honneth's key thought is that 'social suffering and discontentment possess a normative core. It is a matter of the disappointment or violation of normative expectations of society considered justified by those concerned. Thus, such feelings of discontent and suffering, in so far as they are designated "social", coincide with the idea that society is doing

something unjust, something unjustifiable' (Honneth, in Fraser and Honneth, 2003: 129).

4 While the aim of this book is, as the title suggests, to outline values which would support the dignity of the world's poor, it is almost unquestionable that human dignity is a philosophically contested concept, one which, in itself, seems to lack a stable definition in the literature. For controversies over the meaning of human dignity, see Sensen (2011). Additionally, while for this reason I do not define the term 'dignity' conclusively in the book, in some clear ways my argument suggests that, in the context of global forms of poverty, achieving dignity would be a matter of self-determination, agency and resistance to disempowerment. For philosophical accounts which have made similar conceptual connections in the moral critique of poverty, see Hojman and Miranda (2018), Schmidt am-Busch (2015) Brune (2021).

References

Alkire, Sabina and James Foster (2011). 'Counting and Multidimensional Poverty' *Journal of Public Economics* 95/7-8: 467–487.

Anderson, Joel (2011). 'Situating Axel Honneth in the Frankfurt School Tradition', in *Axel Honneth: Critical Essays – With a Reply by Axel Honneth* (London: Brill), pp. 31–57.

Bhala, Surjit, Karan Bhasin, and Arvind Virmani (2022). 'Pandemic, Poverty and Inequality: Evidence from India', IMF Working Paper No. 2022/069, International Monetary Fund, Washington DC. http:ssrun.cmi/abstract=4092620.

Brock, G. (2009). *Global Justice: A Cosmopolitan Account* (Oxford: Oxford University Press).

Brock, G. and H. Brighouse (eds). (2005). *The Political Philosophy of Cosmopolitanism* (Cambridge: Cambridge University Press).

Brune, Jens Peter (2021). 'Human Dignity and Poverty: A Precarious Connection?' in E. Pribytkova and G. Schweiger (eds), *In Search of a Social Minimum: Human Dignity, Poverty and Human Rights* (Cham: Springer).

Burns, Tony (2013). "The Right to Have Rights': Slavery, Freedom and Citizenship in the Thought of Aristotle, Hegel and Arendt' in Gabriel R. Ricci (ed), *Culture and Civilisation Volume 5, Cosmopolitanism and the Global Polity* (New Brunswick: Transaction Publishers), pp. 181–207.

Burns, Tony and Simon Thompson (2013). 'Introduction', in *Global Justice and the Politics of Recognition* (Palgrave MacMillan).

Carant, Jane Briant (2015). 'Unheard Voices: A Critical Discourse Analysis of the Millennium Development Goals' Evolution into the Sustainable Development Goals', *Third World Quarterly* 38/1: 16–41.

Chiappero-Martinetti, E. and P. Salardi (2008). 'Wellbeing Process and Conversion Factors: An Estimation', HDCP-IRC Working Paper Series. Human Development, Capability and Poverty International Research Centre, Working Paper 3/28, pp. 1–30.

Clark, D. A. (2005). 'Sen's Capabilities Approach and the Many Spaces of Human Wellbeing', *Journal of Development Studies* 41/8: 1339–1368.

Clark, David Alexander. (2013). 'Creating Capabilities, Lists and Thresholds: Whose Voices, Intuitions and Value Judgements Count?' *Journal of Human Development and Capabilities* 14/1: 172–184.

Corradetti, Claudio (2013). 'The Frankfurt School and Critical Theory', in *The Internet Encyclopedia of Philosophy*. Available at: http://www.iep.utm.edu/frankfur/. Accessed 12.11.22.

Cuaresma, Jess Crespo, Wolfgang Feugler, Homi Karas, Karim Bekhtiar, Michael Brottager and Martin Hoffer (2018). 'Will the Sustainable Development Goals be Fulfilled? Assessing Present and Future Global Poverty', *Palgrave Communications* 4/29. http://doi.org/10.1057.c41599-018-0083-y. Accessed 1.12.22.

Deveaux, Monique (2015). 'The Global Poor as Agents of Justice', *Journal of Moral Philosophy* 12/2: 125–150

Deveaux, Monique (2018). 'Poor-Led Social Movements and Global Justice', *Political Theory* 46/5: 698–725.

Deveaux, Monique (2021). *Poverty, Solidarity and Poor-Led Social Movements* (Oxford: Oxford University Press).

Drydyk, Jay (2008). 'Durable Empowerment', *Journal of Global Ethics* 4/3 (December): 231–245.

Feenberg, Andrew (2014). *The Philosophy of Praxis: Marx, Lukacs and the Frankfurt School* (London: Verso Books).

Fraser, Nancy (1997). *Justice Interruptus: Critical Reflections on our "Postsocialist" Condition* (New York: Routledge).

Fraser, Nancy and Axel Honneth (2003*). Redistribution or Recognition? A Political-Philosophical* Exchange (London: Verso).

Gore, Charles (2015). 'The Post-2015 Moment: Towards Sustainable Development Goals and a New Development Paradigm', *Journal of International Development* 27: 717–732.

Graf, Gunter and Gottfried Schweiger (2014). 'Poverty and Freedom', *Human Affairs* 24: 258–268.

Harris, Neal (2022). *Critical Theory and Social Pathology: The Frankfurt School Beyond Recognition* (Manchester: Manchester University Press).

Hegel, G.W.F. (2008 [1807]. *Hegel: The Phenomenology of Spirit.* Translated and with an Introduction by Michael Inwood (Oxford: Oxford University Press).

Heins, Volker (2008). 'Realising Honneth: Redistribution, Recognition and Global Justice', *Journal of Global Ethics*: 141–153.

Heins, Volker (2012). 'The Global Politics of Recognition', in S. O'Neill and N. H. Smith (eds), *Recognition Theory as Social Research* (London: Palgrave MacMillan), pp. 213–230.

Hojman, Daniel A. and Miranda Alvaro (2018). 'Agency, Human Dignity and Subjective Wellbeing', *World Development* 101: 1–15.

Honneth, Axel (1995). *The Struggle for Recognition* (Cambridge: MIT Press).

Honneth, Axel (2008). 'Reification: A New Look at an Old Idea', in M. Jay (ed), *Reification: A New Look at an Old Idea* (Oxford: Oxford University Press), pp. 17–96.

Honneth, Axel (2008a). 'Rejoinder', in M. Jay (ed), *Reification: A New Look at an Old Idea* (Oxford: Oxford University Press), pp. 147–160.

Honneth, Axel (2012). 'Recognition between States: On the Moral Substrate of International Relations', in *The I in We: Studies in the Theory of Recognition* (Cambridge: Polity Press), pp. 137–152.

Honneth, Axel (2014). *Freedom's Right: The Social Foundations of Democratic Life* (New York: Columbia University Press).

Honneth, A. and Jacques Ranciere, (2016). Katie Genel and Jean-Phillippe Deranty ed., *Recognition or Disagreement.* (New York: Columbia University Press).

Hvinden, Bjorn and Rune Halvorsen (2018). 'Mediating Agency and Structure in Sociology: What Role for Conversion Factors', *Critical Sociology* 44/6: 865–881.

Joshi, Devin K. (2020). 'The Human Development and Capabilities Approach as a Twenty-First Century Ideology of Globalisation', *Globalisations* 18/5: 781–791.

Khader, Serene (2009). 'Adaptive Preferences and Procedural Autonomy', *Journal of Human Development and Capabilities* 10/2: 169–187.

Kleinman, Arthur, Veena Das, Margaret Lock and Margaret M. Lock (1997). *Social* Suffering (Berkely: University of California Press).

Nussbaum, Martha (2011). *Creating Capabilities: The Human Development Approach* (Cambridge, MA/London: The Belknap Press of Harvard University Press).

Nussbaum, Martha (2016). 'Introduction: Aspiration and the Capabilities List', *Journal of Human Development and Capabilities* 17/3: 301–308.

Petherbridge, Danielle (2011). *Axel Honneth: Critical Essays, with a Reply by Axel Honneth*, 1st edition. Social and Critical Theory series, vol. 12 (Leiden: Brill Academic Publishers).

Pogge, Thomas and D. Moellendorf (eds). (2008). *Global Justice: Seminal Essays. Vol. 1; Global Responsibilities* (London: Paragon Press).

Pogge, Thomas and Mitu Sengupta (2015). 'The Sustainable Development Goals as Drafted: Nice Idea, Poor Execution', *Washington International Law Journal* 24/3: 571–588.

Pomati, Marco and Shailen Nandy (2020). 'Measuring Multi-Dimensional Poverty According to National Definitions: Operationalising Target 1.2 of the Sustainable Development Goals', *Social Indicators Research* 148: 105–126.

Quizilbash, M. (1996). 'Capabilities, Wellbeing and Human Development: A Survey', *Journal of Development Studies* 33/2: 143–162.

Ranciere, Jacques (2011). 'The Thinking of Dissensus: Politics and Aesthetics', in Paul Bauman and Richard Stamp (eds), *Reading Ranciere* (London: Contiuum), pp. 1–17.

Rawls, John (1971). *A Theory of Justice* (Cambridge, MA: Harvard University Press).

Rawls, John (1999). *A Law of Peoples* (Cambridge, MA: Harvard University Press).

Renault, Emmanuel (2017). *Social Suffering*, trans. Maude Dews (London: Rowman and Littlefield).

Rylko-Bauer, Barbara and Paul Farmer (2016), 'Structural Violence, Poverty and Social Suffering', in D. Burton and L.M. Burton (eds), *The Oxford Handbook of the Social Science of Poverty* (Oxford: Oxford University Press), pp. 47–74.

Sano, Hans-Otto (2020). 'How Can a Human-Rights Based Approach Contribute to Poverty Reduction? The Relevance of Human Rights to Sustainable Development Goal One', in M. Kalterborn, M. Krajewski and H. Kuhn (eds), *Sustainable Development Goals and Human Rights* (Dordrecht: Springer), pp. 11–28.

Schmidt am-Busch, H.C. (2015). 'Personal Freedom without Private Property? Hegel, Marx and the Frankfurt School', *International Critical Thought* 5.4: 473–485.

Schweiger, Gottfried (2012). 'Globalizing Recognition: Global Justice and the Dialectic of Recognition', *Public Reason* 4 (1–2): 78–91.

Schweiger, Gottfried (2014). 'Recognition Theory and Global Poverty', *Journal of Global Ethics* 10/3: 267–273.

Schweiger, Gottfried (2016). 'The Sustainable Development Goals: Pitfalls and Challenges, Where We Now Need to Start Making Progress', in H. Gaisbauer, G. Schweiger and C. Sedmark (eds), *Ethical Issues in Poverty Alleviation* (Dordrecht: Springer), pp. 133–148.

Seglow, Jonathan (2009). 'Rights, Contribution, Achievement and the World: Some Reflections on Honneth's Recognitive Ideal', *European Journal of Political* Theory 8/1: 61–75.

Sembou, Evangelia (2003). 'Hegel's Idea of a 'Struggle for Recognition', in *The Phenomenology of Spirit', History of Political Thought* 24/2: 262–281.

Sen, Amartya (1980). 'Equality of What?' in A. Sen (ed), *Choice, Welfare and Measurement* (Oxford: Blackwell), pp. 353–369.

Sen, Amartya (1983). 'Poor, Relatively Speaking', *Oxford Economic Papers* 35/2: 153–169.

Sen, Amartya (1985). *Commodities and Capabilities* (Amsterdam: North-Holland).

Sen, Amartya (1997). *Choice, Welfare and Measurement* (Cambridge, MA: Harvard University Press).

Sen, Amartya (1999). *Development as Freedom* (New York: Anchor Books).

Sen, Amartya (2004). 'Capabilities, Lists and Public Reason: Continuing the Conversation', *Feminist Economics* 10/3: 77–86.

Sengupta, Mitu (2018). 'Transformational Change or Tenuous Wish-List? A Critique of SDG-1: 'End Poverty in All Forms Everywhere'', *Social Alternatives* 37/1: 12–17.

Sensen, Oliver (2011). 'Human Dignity in Historical Perspective: The Contemporary and Traditional Paradigms', *European Journal of Political Theory* 20/1: 71–98.

Shawki, Noha (2018). 'Global Basic Rights, Positive Duties, Extraterritorial Obligations and Mediating Institutions: Do the Sustainable Development Goals Deepen the Institutionalisation of a Global Responsibility to End Poverty?' *Social Alternatives* 37/1: 3–11.

Singer, Peter (2015). *The Most Good You Can Do* (Yale: University of Yale Press).

Stanton, Elizabeth A. (2007). *The Human Development Index: A History*. Working Paper series 127. Political Economy Research Institute. Available at: http://scholarworks.umass.edu/cgi.viewcontentcgi?article=1101&contextperiworkingpapers. Accessed 7.12.22.

Staples, K. (2012). 'Statelessness and the Politics of Misrecognition', *Res Publica* 18/1. Special issue on Theory and Practice *in the Politics of Recognition and Misrecognition*: 93–106.

Taylor, Charles (1994). 'The Politics of Recognition', in A. Gutman (ed), *Multiculturalism: Examining the Politics of Recognition* (Princeton: Princeton University Press), pp. 25–74.

Teschl, M. and Flavio Comim (2005). 'Adaptive Preferences and Capabilities: Some Preliminary Conceptual Explorations', *Review of Social Economy* 63/2: 229–247.

Thérien, Jean-Philippe (2012). 'The United Nations and Human Development: From Ideologies to Global Policies', *Global Policy* 3/1 (February): 1–12.

United Nations (2015). 'Transforming our World: The 2030 Agenda for Sustainable Development'. Available at: http://www.un.org/ga/search/view _doc.asp?symbol =A/RES/70/18Lang=E. Accessed 7.11.22.

Weber, Heloise (2017). 'The Politics of 'Leaving Noone Behind': Contesting the 2030 Sustainable Development Goals Agenda', *Globalizations* 14/3: 399–414.

Wiggerhaus, Rolf (1994). *The Frankfurt School: Its History, Theories and Political Significance* (Cambridge, MA: MIT Press).
Wilkinson, I. and A. Kleinman (2016). *A Passion for Society: How We Think about Human Suffering* (Berkeley, CA: University of California Press).
World Bank (2020). *Poverty and Shared Prosperity 2020: Reversals of Fortune* (Washington, DC: World Bank). http://doi.org/10.1596/978-1-4648-1602-4. Accessed 14.11.22.
World Bank (2022). *Commodity and Markets Outlook: The Impact on the War in Ukraine on Commodity Markets* (Washington, DC: World Bank).

1 Conceptualising the Moral and Political Wrongs of Global Poverty

From Global Redistribution to a Cosmopolitan Theory of Recognition

1.1 Introduction

Closely echoing the observations raised in the Introduction, a significant proportion of the world, 18 million by some estimates, die daily from poverty-related causes. It would be difficult to overstate the need for global attention to this issue (Pogge, 2005, citing UNICEF, 2005). In response to this dire predicament, political philosophers writing from the perspective of liberal theories of global justice have mostly offered normative responses focused on resource-redistribution. They have concentrated on severe material deprivations which, despite the progress made both by the Millennium and Sustainable Development Goals, many people in the world today continue to encounter as regards basic material resources such as food, income, clothing, shelter and medical care.[1] While mindful of the risk of overgeneralising their responses, liberal theories typically concentrate on the underfulfilment of core social rights (Pogge, 2016; Kahn, 2016). However, a pure resource-redistributive response may seem increasingly at odds with a more complex portrait of poverty emerging from a 'human development' perspective. As also suggested in the Introduction, Sen's (1990, 1999, 2002) prominent capabilities approach has expressed dissatisfaction with traditional economists' metrics for evaluating deprivation. Rather than focusing purely on the issue of redistribution, the capabilities approach, as also outlined previously, seeks to analyse the condition in terms of the multifaceted suffering poverty often entails (Gaisbauer, Schweiger and Sedmark, 2016: 3).

However, taking account also of the range of questions which arise surrounding the normative grounding of the capabilities approach (see Deneulin, 2002), such as the ideal conception of human life or human nature or the good life which the theory recommends, or which structural constraints the approach considers to undermine its central conception of capabilities as positive freedoms, this first substantive chapter analyses the rationale for turning attention to theories of recognition instead in a normative response to global poverty. Does the approach suggest theoretically innovative grounds for bypassing an approach based purely on resource-distribution? Tackling this core question enables the foundation for the perspective I aim

DOI: 10.4324/9781003045038-2

to develop, namely, as suggested earlier in the Introduction, a cosmopolitan recognition theory which views global poverty as a failure of intersubjective standards of positive regard, dignity and esteem for humanity of all in the world. In brief, I aim to argue that recognition-based approaches provide distinctive theoretical support for the material human needs of the very poor, whilst also suggesting a persuasive intersubjective basis to morally support the basic capacities of the world's poorest billions to resist the connected non-material harms of poverty.[2]

With this broad aim in mind, it should also be noticed that one immediate concern with relying on theories of recognition to tackle global poverty may be that, without assuming a hypothetical agreement between rich and poor in terms of a global social contract often presumed by liberal cosmopolitan theories, it will inevitably be challenging to defend the rights of such a vast constituency as all those who experience global poverty. Although some prominent liberal cosmopolitan writers defend their views by appealing to a social contract metaphor, presuming human beings largely to pursue the same interests for mutual advantage worldwide, a cosmopolitan recognition theory would turn away from this approach. It would do so on account of a reluctance to view questions of global justice purely as a matter of maximising self-interest. Rather, for recognition theorists, human beings are assumed to be connected on the basis of the shared features of humanity, such as our mutual dependency on relationships of positive regard from others. Again, as outlined in the Introduction, derived from the idea of mutuality in Hegel's famous master-slave dialectic, which is well known for defending the intersubjective basis of personhood, recognition theories view the acknowledgement of others' humanity as a condition for realising one's own.[3] From this perspective, intersubjective recognition is understood as a vital human need (Taylor, 1994: 58, citing Hegel 2008 [1807]).

In response to this seemingly ambitious claim, however, one immediate critical reaction may be that its moral entailments may not, understandably, appear self-evident, especially as regards a predicament as wide and multifaceted as global poverty. In this chapter, I therefore aim for a preliminary defence of a recognition-based view of global poverty, primarily by considering the insights and drawbacks of Axel Honneth's (1995; Honneth, in Fraser and Honneth, 2003) influential theory. I focus in particular on its contrast with more familiar liberal, contractarian approaches. Although Honneth's critical recognition-theoretical approach to questions of economic disadvantage seems preferable, I nonetheless identify some challenges connected with his substantive moral theory of recognition in this debate. Yet, in spite of these drawbacks, the capacity of his theory to translate questions of material deprivation into problems of misrecognition paves the path which I take in this book towards an approach to dignify the world's poor through recognition theory.

The chapter is structured as follows. Section 1.2 addresses Thomas Pogge's agenda-setting approach to global distributive justice. His major perspective on the causal responsibility of the affluent nations emanates from his liberal cosmopolitan focus on resources and institutions. In identifying some difficulties with his approach, Section 1.3 introduces recognition-based theories to ground an alternative normative approach to global poverty. This task is undertaken by tackling the defining debate between Honneth and critical theorist Nancy Fraser, asking whether global poverty may best be viewed in terms of redistribution or recognition. Having defended the potential of Honneth's approach over Fraser's in relation to a cosmopolitan recognition theory relevant to global poverty, Section 1.5 considers Honneth's three substantive moral principles of recognition from a global justice perspective. Although I suggest caution as regards the potential to universalise Honneth's substantive recognitive principles of love, rights and esteem, the general defence of his theoretical insights grounds the path taken in this book towards a cosmopolitan recognition theory responsive to global poverty as an acute problem confronting the contemporary world.

1.2 The Liberal Cosmopolitan Agenda: Resource-Redistribution and the Political Theory of Global Justice

Emanating from the defining perspective of John Rawls (1971) in relation to equality in liberal-democratic nations, the project of globalising economic redistribution through social rights to alleviate world poverty has often appeared to liberals as a plausible development of Rawlsian social contract theory. Writers taking up this perspective include Luis Cabrera (2004), Charles Beitz (2005), Darrell Moellendorf (2018) and, most prominently, Thomas Pogge (2002, 2005, 2016). Proposing economic and political agendas for global justice, they defend not only resource-redistribution on the basis of key social and economic rights under the Universal Declaration of Human Rights, but also mechanisms for global governance. While the debates within liberal cosmopolitanism have been internally complex and ongoing, their moral core may be emphasised by highlighting their dominant view of global poverty as an economic issue, and as a predicament which calls for material redistribution and a defence of universal social rights. As most liberal approaches typically take their cue from Pogge's defining agenda for global redistribution, I take space at this early point to outline his core defence of this redistributive approach, in order to later emphasise the rationale for responding, alternatively, in terms of a cosmopolitan recognition theory.

Pogge's project to globalise the implications of Rawls' difference principle, an approach which requires redistribution to the least well off within particular nations, has, as suggested, defined much of the debate within liberal cosmopolitanism (Jaggar, 2010).[4] In particular, Pogge's ambitious call for global redistribution seemed to transform debates about how citizens of affluent countries should respond to profound poverty persisting alongside the increasing affluence of elites. This agenda seemed radical due to liberalism's often-cited agnosticism as regards structural inequalities within society, and the broader tendency in the popular imagination of affluent states to view global injustice as a 'cosmic misfortune' rather than a matter of human agency (Jaggar, 2010: 2). Confronted with widespread disbelief in the developed world that extreme poverty had any implications for the moral obligations of ordinary people, Pogge's outraged reaction to a condition which, he insists, causes one third of all human deaths per year (Pogge, 2005) has proved extremely galvanising. In particular, he takes the abdication of moral responsibility by liberal elites to be deepened by persistent beliefs concerning 'explanatory nationalism', or the idea that severe poverty in the Global South should be viewed purely as an outcome of the corruption of leaders and other local, contextual factors. Whilst conceding local factors play a role, for Pogge they are largely side-effects of the policies of international institutions, which interact with national institutions to create a global order which systematically disadvantages poor people (Jaggar, 2010: 2; Pogge, 2005).

The ambitious normative conclusions which Pogge draws from Article 25 of the Universal Declaration of Human Rights, namely a right to an adequate standard of living including health and wellbeing globally, relate, he argues, to the 'respect-protect-fulfil' triad central to the activities of international agencies. Reflecting on this triad, Pogge attributes to the affluent, whom he takes morally to legitimate if not support these institutions if they fail to campaign against them, the responsibility to avoid depriving, to protect from deprivation and to aid the deprived. While he does not rule out the possibility that the affluent also have positive moral duties to assist, for Pogge it would be more prudent and psychologically convincing to rely on a less ambitious negative duty. Even asserting the duties of the affluent to refrain from harming the global poor would have, he claims, significant implications for alleviating world poverty (2016: 21). Therefore, for Pogge, it is not unreasonable to expect the compliance of ordinary people with negative duties to resist collaborating, in his words, 'in the design or imposition of social institutions which foreseeably and avoidably cause human rights to be unfulfilled' (2016: 27).[5]

Much of the scholarly attention to Pogge's globalisation of the Rawlsian social contract theory understandably pivots on the reasonableness of assuming the compliance of ordinary people with the outcomes generated by international institutional policies (Chandhoke, 2010; Satz, 2005). For Pogge, at least, morally problematic collusion could be assumed if people acquiesce to institutional policies which may be reasonably thought to bring about worldwide poverty. Although he usually resists the further suggestion that citizens of affluent states directly violate the economic rights of the poor, a global social contract may be implied in which the affluent are existentially and practically linked with the global poor through the institutions which mutually shape their lives (Pogge, 2016: 28).[6]

While the aspiration to globalise Rawls' domestic theory of the social contract seems laudable, attributing to the comparatively affluent even an indirect causal role in upholding global poverty has seemed highly controversial to many. To clarify, Pogge's cosmopolitanism depends on the idea that a person in the affluent world has duties to all humanity due to a common interdependence on international institutions, a position which suggests widespread collective responsibility for the effects of these institutions where they bear negative impacts for vast segments of the world's population. Taking his cue from Rawls' recognition that issues of justice and injustice are initially matters of institutional design (1971: 3), ordinary people are responsible, he argues, to the extent that they implicitly uphold an unjust institutional system (2016: 33). For Pogge, international institutions such as the World Trade Organization, the World Bank and the International Monetary Fund form a global order which foreseeably and avoidably denies the social rights of the 'bottom billion' of the world (Pogge, 2016: 33).[7] As he states, 'taken together, these supranational factors generate a massive headwind against the poor' (2016: 37).

While to many these claims will hold an almost unquestionable rhetorical appeal, some have also raised concerns about their de-personalised and over-institutionalised nature. Whilst not contesting the focus on monetary redistribution through social rights, Kok-Chor Tan (2010), for instance, draws attention to examples of extreme poverty worldwide which have a wider range of causes and origins than the focus on international financial institutions would suggest. For Tan, this causal pluralism suggests that the normative case against global poverty should rest on a connection between human beings as a matter of shared humanity rather than on their connection through international institutions. Neera Chandhoke (2010: 75) similarly contends that, when one considers the effects of poverty on, for example, infant mortality in a poor country such as Mali, it becomes clear that a host of factors contribute to this problem, such as lack of national resources, the failure of the government to establish maternity clinics as well as the impacts of development policies. None of these factors is uniquely reducible to the effects of the global institutional order in the linear sense adequate to establish causal responsibility. For Chandhoke, it is not only that it would be more convincing to view these factors in terms of the effects of a colonial history, the legacy of which significantly shapes many nations' current economies. Connectedly, the risk created by contractarian approaches such as Pogge's is of presenting a somewhat reductive rhetoric of 'the rich' and 'the poor', or of 'us' and 'them', which fails to identify shared human interests in such a way as to deconstruct the opposition between donors and recipients of aid or between developed and underdeveloped nations. This focus, she contends, casts 'the global poor' as the 'consumers of acts, whether these are acts of harm or duty, performed by the West' (Chandhoke, 2010: 80).[8]

In fairness to Pogge, however, the focus on international financial institutions forms part of a wider causal story of the factors which are taken to contribute to global poverty (Pogge, 2002); and it may not be ultimately mistaken to view these factors as complexly connected. Moreover, if a global social contract could be inferred, it would then not seem unreasonable to assume those who bear the most moral responsibility for global poverty to be citizens and governments of wealthy and powerful nations, as the latter at least undoubtedly play key roles in upholding the policies of this global order (Jaggar, 2010: 4). However, the need to supplant Pogge's perspective with a more strongly intersubjective, recognition-based approach is revealed first by considering Pogge's more detailed defence of his position according to a 'causal contribution principle' (Pogge, 2007; Patten, 2005). This principle identifies three causes of global poverty which establish the obligations of the affluent as regards global poverty but which, despite Pogge's explicit claims, seem to point to issues of intersubjective regard between populations of the world rather than questions of maldistribution through international financial institutions alone. Without discounting the role of institutions, then, Pogge's own causal narrative seems to point away from conceiving global poverty exclusively as harm to material interests calling for redistribution.

More specifically, of the three causal factors Pogge identifies to ground the claim regarding the affluent's violation of negative duties towards the world's poor, only the first factor appears explicitly to refer to international financial institutions. At this stage, Pogge explicitly refers to the loan conditionalities extended to poor countries by organisations such as the World Bank which limit a borrowing government's abilities to make policy decisions, eroding control over national development strategies and consequently maintaining the world's poor below the United Nations' dollar-a-day baseline (Pogge, 2005: 12).[9] While alternative voices insist the poverty reduction policies of institutions such as the World Bank have in fact succeeded in reducing world poverty,[10] Pogge not only disputes these benefits, but further argues, in the second strand of his causal principle, that the global poor have not been compensated for exclusion from the economic proceeds of the resources in which their countries are often naturally rich (2007a: 12). For Pogge, through policies such as International Borrowing Privileges implemented by the World Bank, leaders of poor nations may transfer ownership or dispose of national resources, even if these disposals may not work to the benefit of their citizens.[11]

While seeming persuasive as a moral critique of institutional policies, it is unclear, however, that these factors alone would suffice to justify Pogge's strong global contractarian claim. What might be seen to be the deeper issue is not that particular policies have particular effects at a moment in time, so much as that the underlying decision-making structure and relations of inequality worldwide seem likely to perpetuate these effects into the future. Significantly, Pogge is aware of the ongoing under-representation of the nations of the Global South in core international institutions (Pogge, 2016; Vestergaard, 2013). Logically, this under-representation may seem not only to call for cash transfers to the global fund which Pogge recommends institutionally as the content of the negative duties of the affluent, but rather as more expansive forms of global cooperation between North and South which would promote the agency and empowerment of peoples of economically dominated countries. Additionally, conscious that his theoretical defence of a global social contract would be likely to involve an appeal to a stronger premise concerning unjustified global inequality, Pogge supplements his causal narrative with reference to a 'common and violent history' which occurred globally between the affluent and impoverished nations, which, he argues, has produced the current global disparity of wealth (Pogge, 2005: 37; 2002: 203).[12] Contesting the controversial view that standards of living in Africa and Europe would be approximately the same if Africa had never been colonised, for Pogge it seems clear that the history of imperialism and colonial expansion produced the current power-relations in the world order (Pogge, 2002: 203; Von Kreigstein, 2010). For Pogge, even if a different interpretation of history were proposed which seemed to justify the current radical inequality in the world, the Lockean argument would remain, suggesting that the current situation is justified only if, hypothetically, the unequal distribution is one to which all participants could rationally be taken to consent (Pogge, 2005). From Pogge's perspective, it would seem irrational in any hypothetical state of nature to consent to being denied what Locke takes as the limit on untrammelled capitalist accumulation, namely the proviso that one be left 'enough and as good' for subsistence. For Pogge, the exclusion of millions of people from the proceeds of the world's natural resources without retaining essential resources for living could not be plausibly assumed as a distribution to which a rational person could consent.

However, it seems reasonable to suggest that Pogge's reasoning as regards the idea of rational agreement within a fictional state of nature is not itself a cause of global poverty, but rather evokes an independent moral argument which arises from his use of social contract theory. If this is so, it seems Pogge's actual attribution of causal responsibility to affluent countries for global poverty, which from his perspective grounds the negative duties of the affluent nations, would rest quite strongly on his historical argument concerning the injustices of slavery and colonisation. Yet, as Chandhoke suggests, the historical claim is likely to be such a far-reaching idea that neither the reform of institutions nor redistribution of material resources alone would suffice to rectify the resulting inequalities. For Chandhoke (2010), this historical narrative of imperial expansion has resulted not only in distributive inequalities but perceptions between wealthier and poorer nations which engender problematic conceptions of 'the global poor' and their level of 'development' (Dogra, 2013). In this context, over and above global redistribution, normative political theorists might, for example, ethically favour postcolonial modes of development. At least, if Pogge's causal narrative depends on the historical argument, there seems to be substantial doubt not only concerning the use of cash transfers alone to resolve global poverty, but even, potentially, as to the legitimacy of the original global social contract (Mills, 2010). One reason for this is that Pogge's expansive historical claim seems to raise wider ethical questions, such as whether monetary reparations are the most apt response to histories of slavery and imperialism (Collste, 2014), whether reparation necessitates apologies or other symbolic measures, as well as the roles of redistribution and recognition in reacting to this historical narrative of inequality. Given the breadth of these issues, there seem reasons for cosmopolitan theories to transcend an exclusive focus on redistributive duties implied by a global social contract alone (Lu, 2011; Noxolo, 2012; Ypi, Goodin and Barry, 2009).

Put differently, the ambiguities in Pogge's liberal cosmopolitanism suggest a strong case to search for a more expansive intersubjective theory to ground a normative response to global poverty, one which would be conscious of problems of domination marring a global social contract. The legacies of historical injuries are more likely to be experienced by the extremely poor not only as a lack of material goods, although these issues are crucial, but also as raising wider questions of the dignity and esteem owed between people on the basis of their common humanity.[13] As Tomon (2018) argues, through an analysis of the capabilities approach, despite the clear advantages of setting internationally designated poverty lines in monetary terms, the ability to participate in society as a fully accepted member is also intrinsic to wellbeing, an issue which continually complicates efforts to conceptualise poverty in terms only of access to material goods, or even the rights corresponding to those goods. If inter-societal, interpersonal and global relations play a key role in perpetuating norms which evaluate certain people as unequal or as excluded, an intersubjective theory would go beyond a pure focus on material interests at the root of poverty, and insist instead that poverty involves a dynamic interaction between one's own self-conception and capacities and the reactions and responsiveness of others.

Echoing these observations is Ruth Lister's (2015) concern that much current poverty research, which is reflected by the focus on material interests in Pogge's globalised social contract, tends to over-emphasise providing statistics in terms of income and purchasing power. This focus can appear paradoxical, as many poor people attest to a feeling of invisibility or the sensation that 'they do not count'. Considering, equally, Sen's (2005) argument that standards of living are best evaluated not in terms of the possession of goods but rather how well human beings are able to convert resources into a valued life, these critical reflections on Pogge's liberal contractarian response already suggest reasons to turn towards a cosmopolitan recognition theory which would respond to the structural injustices involved in global poverty. Typically referring to Hegel's master-slave dialectic in defining the intersubjective basis of human self-consciousness, modern recognition theories (Taylor, 1994; Honneth, 1995; Fraser and Honneth, 2003) suggest that the dignity and esteem of others, even potentially of distant others, are vital for affirming one's own. These initial theoretical assumptions, then, guide my aim to defend an alternative cosmopolitanism to that raised by Pogge's influential critique of global poverty.

Because one of the core insights of this approach is the view that one's own self-regard must involve dignifying others' lives,[14] a cosmopolitan recognition theory promises to respond to Pogge's moral insights through a keener focus on problems of domination and exclusion. As Burns and Thompson (2013: 17) suggest, recognition theories are as much concerned with 'voice' and representation as with material redistribution. These theories, therefore, promise opportunities to consider legacies of historical injury such as colonialism by shifting normative attention to a dialogue through which cultural distinctiveness and indigenous knowledges may be respected (O'Neill and Walsh, 2014: 309). With these advantages in mind, there seems at least an initial case for pursuing a theory of global justice beyond the state in recognitive, rather than purely redistributive, terms.

1.3 Redistribution or Recognition? Global Poverty Beyond the Causal Contribution Principle

Outside the arena of liberal cosmopolitanism, a significant debate arose some 20 years ago between critical theorists Nancy Fraser and Axel Honneth concerning the normative scope of the concepts of redistribution or recognition (Fraser and Honneth, 2003). This debate seems crucial to consider, despite its state-based character, as it clarifies in an initial sense the prospects for framing the deep economic oppression involved in global poverty as a problem of misrecognition. While Fraser suggests an ethically sensitive and flexible dual focus on cultural and market-based inequalities, Honneth's recognition-theoretical approach more purposively synthesises the harms involved in poverty into a single theory which translates experiences of material oppression in late capitalist societies into disappointed social expectations for esteem, dignity and respect. As I shall argue, it is Honneth's theory rather than Fraser's which suggests a framework sufficiently flexible to mount a critique of historical structural inequalities which lead to modern poverty, without assuming problematic analytical distinctions between material and symbolic forms of oppression around the world.

To consider Fraser's account first, then, following her long-standing defence of a multilayered approach to problems of injustice in modern societies (see Fraser, 2000, 2007), Fraser influentially proposes a 'dual-systems' theory to counteract the overriding significance liberal societies seem to attribute to struggles over symbolic or recognitive injustices in a 'post-socialist' era, a time in which faith in traditional class-based movements has waned. For Fraser, a theory which attends to both market inequalities and status disadvantages is indispensable for interventions into complex current problems of domination (Fraser and Honneth, 2003: 35). Responding to a wide range of current inequalities involves attending to both market-based inequality and the affirmative or transformative struggles over social status waged by identity-focused groups. This dual focus would resist the tendency of identity-related struggles over recognition in advanced economies such as the USA to take centre stage (2003: 110), to a point of undermining socialist struggles on the basis of waged labour. For Fraser, most subaltern groups are two-dimensional or 'bivalent', in the sense that their disadvantages are likely to have both cultural and market-based aspects. Locating normative solutions to their disadvantage depends on careful attention to the zone, arena or sphere in which a particular instance of injustice is manifested (2003: 105). Accordingly, some solutions will involve recognition, in the sense of enhancing social status, and others will more clearly necessitate redistribution or the economic restructuring of the wider society.

While Fraser's core objective in this debate was not to raise issues concerning global justice, her perspective assists an understanding of global forms of poverty by clarifying that, while poverty is surely characterised by chronic denials of material needs, probably necessitating redistribution, it may also involve a lack status or dignity in the symbolic order of society. For Fraser, the fact that culture and the economy are analytically distinct but empirically interpenetrating spheres is perhaps most clearly exemplified by her presentation of gender as a 'bivalent' basis of oppression, which involves both status and economic disadvantages (Fraser, in Fraser and Honneth, 2003: 65). When campaigns for the comparable worth of women's and men's labour are considered, for instance, economic interventions would be more practically effective if they occur alongside, and in fact they would often only make sense in the context of, efforts to alter gender coded patterns of cultural value attributed to different forms of work. This example leads Fraser to suggest that, while the economic structure and status order of society differ analytically, they frequently interpenetrate at the level of subjective experiences and in terms of the required normative solutions. Analogously, the disadvantages confronting the very poor might only genuinely be tackled by attending to both forms of disadvantage, in such a way that ensures what Fraser refers to as 'participatory parity' (Fraser, 1997: 38), or the overall capacity of people to participate in their societies on equal terms.

More recently, moreover, Fraser (2010) extends her analysis by outlining a third category, namely political representation. Specifically, for Fraser this additional perspective will often be crucial to determine the forum, level or 'scale' in which particular justice-claims should be evaluated. That is to say, without considering the issue of political representation alongside recognition and redistribution, normative solutions risk mistaking whether, for example, a national or international framework provides the legitimate arena for considering specific campaigns for justice (Fraser, 2010: 711). While the additional perspective of political representation seems in many ways vital, for the moment at least I sidestep what Fraser identifies as the 'problem of the frame' in order to concentrate on some difficulties already besetting her perspectival dualist account.

When one further examines Fraser's distinction between culture and the market, the question may be how one might plausibly separate these categories analytically, unless they are taken to be in a sense ontologically divergent too. In other words, if these spheres generate inequalities which are conceptually separate in the sense of being irreducible to one another, even though they may be intertwined from a subjective perspective, there seems theoretical scope to claim that, objectively, some groups experience an economic rather than a cultural or 'recognitive' injustice. Armstrong and Thompson (2009: 14) therefore seem right to comment that Fraser apparently maintains a belief in the ontological distinction between culture and the economy, which inevitably complicates her assertion that most groups experience both, or 'bivalent', disadvantages. At least, it appears difficult to see how the idea of an analytical divergence may be understood, unless some disadvantaged groups are assumed, such as in the case of traditional struggles over waged labour, to be primarily involved in redistributive struggles. However, if it is theoretically possible to conceive groups such as poor unionised workers as primarily struggling over maldistribution rather than misrecognition, then there would be scope to suggest that struggles against global poverty relate to, and primarily pursue, a redistributive agenda. Yet the difficulties with such a potential return to a redistributive solution are expressed well by Majid Yar (2001). He argues that, while Fraser's analytical distinction suffices from a pure social-scientific perspective, it is less intuitive to mobilise this distinction in relation to any normative claims regarding justice. This is because justice-claims in general are intrinsically 'recognitional' in the sense that most of the terms such as 'exploitation' and 'deprivation', which Fraser (1997) seems to associate with the politics of redistribution, also refer to intersubjective relations which make a 'moral claim upon others' (Yar, 2011: 295). This point would not be theoretically apparent from the perspective of Fraser's dual-systems theory.

Therefore, given the risk that Fraser's theory may play down the non-material, intersubjective aspects of poverty-related suffering, as raised earlier in the previous section's analysis of Pogge's liberalism, I shall argue that critical theorist Axel Honneth's rejoinder seems more intuitive. From the perspective of his early, defining left Hegelianism in *The Struggle for Recognition* (1995) to later works exploring late-modern social freedom in *Freedom's Right* (2014), Honneth's contribution does not question Fraser's resistance to the liberal tendency to prioritise identity-based struggles. Unsurprisingly, given his early starting point in reactions to classical Marxism,[15] he insists that, in view of a growing underclass even in advanced economies and the intense wealth of elites under unrestrained capitalism (Honneth, in Fraser and Honneth, 2003: 112), the compelling issue is not whether to opt for redistribution over recognition as a normative goal. The real, underlying philosophical question concerns the normative language which best represents the demands of the exploited or the underclass of traditional socialist thought. For Honneth, recognitive frameworks respond more vitally, by linking, in his words, the 'social causes of widespread feelings of injustice and the normative objectives of emancipatory movements' (2003: 113).

For Honneth, when considering vast economic disparities in modern societies, one needs to avoid forming what he calls a 'theoretically unbridgeable chasm' between symbolic and material aspects of social reality (2003: 114). At the root of ethical resistance to serious economic deprivation, he argues, lies an injustice which is experienced as a social injury to one's legitimate claims for recognition. In this sense, both distributive inequalities and struggles over cultural identity should be understood in terms of institutional disparities in conferring respect (2003: 114). Honneth's proposed revaluation of maldistribution as misrecognition seems to respond to the subjective impacts of poverty in recent research (Samuel et al. 2018; Jo, 2013), analyses which have been taken by McCrudden (2013) and Lister (2015) in the British context as crucial to a more empowering discourse on poverty. Moreover, while Honneth has to date not fully engaged global justice issues,[16] his starting point in recognition theory suggests how intersubjective standards of regard between people in the world may fail due to a range of historical injustices which produce structural inequalities. As Iris Young (2006) contends from the perspective of her allied 'social connection' model of global justice, while global structural inequalities obviously raise complicated historical questions of causal responsibility, it is the complexity of these causes which should encourage the search for a different basis of global justice. That is, the complexity of causality should lead the theorist to focus instead on forward-looking justice. In a similar vein, for recognition theorists such as Honneth, it is the intersubjective basis of personhood rather than the question of blame or causation which would ground a normative response to global poverty.

These points appear to clarify why Honneth responds to Fraser by suggesting that, across a wide range of disadvantaged groups in modernity, the sources of human beings' self-regard depend on intersubjective recognition.[17] Following his central claims in *The Struggle for Recognition*,[18] for Honneth the need for recognition is a 'quasi-transcendental interest of the human race' (Honneth, in Fraser and Honneth, 2003: 174). Extreme poverty may thus be bound up with gross deficiencies of material need, but the injustice it expresses is a matter of human relations rather than tangible goods as such. That said, as suggested previously, Honneth accepts Fraser's concerns regarding too heavy a focus on identity-based movements, such as those surrounding gender and multiculturalism. While these movements are undoubtedly politically significant, as they 'increasingly resist the disrespect and marginalization rooted in an institutionalized value-structure which is constitutively tailored to the idealized characteristics of the white, male, heterosexual citizen' (2003: 118), many contemporary recognition claims cannot be reduced to struggles over identity, as normally conceived. Rather, they arise in varied circumstances where people react to a violation of legitimate expectations of respect, for instance where poverty is 'feminized', a condition which typically affects single mothers with limited job qualifications, or in the case of the long-term unemployed, who often experience social isolation and the depressing experience of finding their skills outmoded in a changing labour market (2003: 119). For Honneth, these experiences tend to draw people into exhaustive, embittered activities and desperate attempts to maintain the integrity of the psyche (2003: 120). Moreover, they are comparatively hidden politically, especially as they diverge from the standard conception of new social movements as focused on culture, ethnicity or sexuality. The grievances expressed in these contemporary struggles may broadly relate to identity, but they are as much related to material oppression as to questions of culture, normally conceived.

Moreover, in a further move which seems promising for a recognition-based response to global poverty, Honneth resists Fraser's proposal to separate movements for equal treatment before the law, such as in the form of social rights, and struggles over identity or status (Fraser, in Fraser and Honneth, 2003: 123). Honneth disputes this distinction on the basis that the recognition of African-Americans after slavery and the development of feminism unsettle any clear distinction between identity-based and material struggles (Honneth, in Fraser and Honneth, 2003: 123). In view of the wide scope, then, of recognitive struggles, which may be both material and cultural, what is needed is not a dual-systems theory, but 'an improved insight into the motivational sources of social discontent and resistance' (2003: 125).

Honneth further deepens his conception of material oppression as a question of misrecognition by referring to the fact that poor-led movements in European history were motivated by the idea that 'their ways of life and achievements [...] were not recognized by the rest of society' (2003: 131). For Honneth, historically it was when the poor were able to align their struggles with colonised groups or women's protest movements that they were able to gain insight into their condition. In a sense, this point raises a crucial issue concerning the nature of empowerment in a cosmopolitan recognition theory, to which I shall return in Chapters 4 and 5. For now, however, the important insight seems to lie in Honneth's idea that struggles over material distribution do not simply concern distributive outcomes as such. This is because, according to Honneth, capitalism is at the outset not a distributive system so much as a system of normative principles governing distribution, a point which suggests that oppositions to material oppression are, from the very beginning, symbolic struggles or struggles over recognition (2003: 137).

While it would be impossible to reprise all the details of the rich and complex debate raised by Honneth and Fraser in the space available in this chapter, the broad comparison presented between their positions suggests crucial insights on both sides regarding the symbolic and representational aspects of poverty. Honneth's perspective, however, appears more compelling from the perspective of the concerns raised previously with liberal contractarianism, in the sense of seeming to avoid the potential reduction of the normative remedy for material inequality to purely redistributive solutions, a possibility which seemed at risk by Fraser's perspectival dualist account.

Rather, Honneth's framework appears to offer the tools for responding to poverty worldwide without reducing the issues into institutionally-derived harms to material interests, and by suggesting instead that material and identity-related conflicts both relate to unmet expectations for dignity and respect.

1.4 Global Poverty and Cosmopolitan Recognition Theory: Love, Rights and Esteem

While the recognitive framework above appears to hold significant advantages, these background observations do not in themselves suggest which needs, capacities or goods may be regarded as universal transnationally applicable, the lack of which would define poverty as a universally harmful form of misrecognition. Given persistent background controversies over whether the universalisation of particular needs are liable to unjustly override the capabilities of the very poor to choose their mode of living (Maslow, 1943; Tay and Diner, 2011; Rudra, 2009; Reader, 2006), the focus on an overarching human need for 'recognition' may seem frustratingly ambiguous. Therefore, even if the premise that the desire for recognition as a vital human need is accepted, the challenge seems to be to suggest what is concretely entailed by the claim that extreme poverty denotes misrecognition. On the one hand, it seems reasonable to suggest that a society which ensures human recognition would secure all citizens a relational form of autonomy or what Honneth more usually refers to as 'self-realisation' (Honneth, 1995: chapter 1). However, globalising or universalising this idea raises difficult questions concerning the means of achieving this goal l. I therefore close this chapter by arguing that, while Honneth's theory proves useful in the move towards a theory of global justice, his recommended recognitive principles of love, rights and esteem (1995: chapter 5) prove especially difficult to universalise globally and cross-culturally as the necessary pathways towards protecting the basic agency of the very poor around the world.

While this will ultimately be my conclusion, the advantages of the recognition-based approach are nevertheless worth reinforcing before moving towards a critique. Schweiger (2014) rightly argues that the cosmopolitan focus on the norm of self-realisation, if achievable, would be preferable to the liberal preoccupation with resources. Rather than assume a transparent understanding of the needs of the poor, the concept seems to suggest the means through which the poor would define their own aspirations. Heins (2008) echoes this point by suggesting, as explained in the Introduction, that the premises of recognition theory seem preferable to 'technocratic' redistributive approaches to global justice on grounds of being 'ethically individualistic, victim-sensitive and universal'. Moreover, in debates concerning global poverty, Schweiger (2014: 270) further warns against the conceiving of individuals simply as atoms pursuing their interests in a Hobbesian contract (Honneth, 1995: 168), Instead, he rightly values the turn in recognition theory towards the subjective experiences of the poor and their rights to feel respected. It seems best, as Schweiger astutely argues, to avoid the deontological liberal emphasis on rights and duties in a social contract, and to opt instead for a teleological approach with mutual recognition as a shared goal (2014: 267).

Despite these significant advantages, there are likely to be substantial drawbacks with attempting to apply Honneth's substantive principles or modes of recognition from a universalistic or cosmopolitan perspective. As raised in the Introduction, Thompson (2013) and Heins (2010); 2012 rightly raise concerns that Honneth's substantive theory inevitably presumes the 'thick' cultural values of a nation-state. Focusing on Honneth's first recognitive principle, namely love and care (Honneth, 1995: 35–39), keenly illustrates this point. Understood as a principle of strong affective attachment between significant others (Thompson, 2013: 91), Honneth refers closely to the writings of developmental psychologists such as David Winnicott and the psychoanalytical theory of Jessica Benjamin to present a detailed account of love and care as intrinsic to the healthy development of the person's capacities for individuation and autonomy (1995: 39). Applied from a cosmopolitan perspective, this conception of the individuating function of love and care may justify the protection of bodily integrity owed to all human beings. A violation of this principle could be inferred in contexts of severe poverty, just as, for example, the principle may be thought violated in acts of mass rape, genocide and ethnic cleansing. This application of the principle of love and care may seem defensible because, whereas on the surface Honneth construes the goods of love and care to be realised in the intimate sphere only, ultimately its formative role has many implications for a person's self-conception as a rights-bearer in the public sphere (1995: 39).

The potential cosmopolitan interpretation of the principle of care, however, brings many complexities. It seems particularly challenging to suggest which forms of reciprocity should be owed to people worldwide, in such a way that would neither paternalistically override, nor become complexly embroiled in, contextual, cultural or national norms (Robinson, 2016; Nguyen Minh et al, 2017). Additionally, while it seems reasonable to suggest that every person, irrespective of their geographical location in the world, requires at least a minimal amount of love and care to appreciate their own value as persons,[19] it is difficult to count on the psychological, or even the social and political, ability of people in the developed, comparatively affluent world, for example, to know how to care for the distant needy. While some feminists have strongly defended the globalisation of the care principle (Held, 2006), with writers such as Tronto taking the principle to connote 'the ongoing and permanent status of all humans [...] as vulnerable' (2011: 96), nonetheless this normative idea usually suggests a contextual principle referring to the 'concrete' rather than the 'general' other.

On the positive side, then, if recognition theorists were to globalise the care principle, doing so might entail ensuring that cultural relations of support exist across different societies, enabling people to develop the self-confidence to resist social domination and to sustain affective attachments to their broader society. Poverty-related social suffering may undermine the capacities of the poor and excluded to extend and receive recognition, potentially rendering their agency self-defeating or paradoxical (Yar, 2001, Samuel et al. 2018).[20] However, just as the normative implications of this principle do not always seem self-evident even within the advanced capitalist societies presumed by Honneth's discussion in *The Struggle for Recognition*, they are likely to become increasingly diffuse and potentially prone to paternalistic interpretations when viewed globally. Additionally, while it seems relevant in some immediate and obvious ways to focus on human vulnerabilities and needs for care as regards such a wide and deep problem as global poverty, it also seems fair to suggest the focus on suffering and vulnerability would most likely need to be balanced with attention to the creative agency and rationality of the very poor.

These are complex issues to which I shall return in later chapters. For now, I turn to Honneth's second normative principle, namely recognition as rights or political respect (1995: 113). At first glance, this principle seems the most readily universalisable of Honneth's substantive modes of recognition. In *The Struggle for Recognition*, Honneth seems intrinsically to connect rights-claims and dignity, or in his terms the value of self-respect (1995: 114). As Jonathan Seglow (2009) suggests, for Honneth rights-recognition, most acutely exemplified by the struggles of African-Americans for civil rights in the USA, is a mode of recognition which is always articulated progressively and incrementally worldwide. Every society expresses an unfinished journey in terms of the vulnerable or disempowered groups who have mounted moral claims to these rights (Honneth, 1995: 114; Seglow, 2009: 63). Furthermore, Seglow characterises the value Honneth attributes to rights as both substantive and 'recursive', in the sense that right-holding refers not just to the possession of a good secured by right, such as welfare benefits in the case of social rights, but also to the dignity which right-holders gain and may potentially exercise in relation to others by the fact of having these rights (2009: 64).

Therefore, while the universalist dimensions of rights-recognition seem clear at first glance, on further analysis the historically progressive campaigns for rights which Honneth seems especially to associate with dignity or self-respect appear difficult to view at a fully international or cosmopolitan level. While it seems clear that international frameworks, such as the World Social Forum, campaign for the social rights of the poor, Seglow rightly observes that it is still more probable that the actual activity of struggling for rights is likely to occur more frequently within nation-states. Honneth's moral interest in this form of recognition does not seem to lie in the passive receipt of rights or prerogatives simply bestowed by an external agency, such as through international agencies, so much as in the dignity of an active campaign which expresses the person's rational autonomy.[21] Therefore, a cosmopolitan recognition theory would not discount the role of the international human rights regime in enhancing the dignity and social rights of the poor but would view the recursive value of rights as most likely realised in local, rather than cosmopolitan, contexts. As Seglow further observes, because international human rights are often secured by aid agencies, donors and other institutions of which the recipients of these rights are not directly members, the idea of those who are very poor 'claiming' rights against their interaction partners universally or internationally seems in many cases seems rather tenuous (2009: 68). Thus, whilst Schweiger's (2015) idea of a dialectic between the cosmopolitan and universal and the local or national in realising the norms of human recognition seems in many ways compelling, paradoxically rights-recognition may in some contexts be problematic to universalise due to the fact that, for Honneth, the dignity of rights-claiming occurs in the context of an active struggle (Friedmann, 1996).

Finally, the mode of recognition in Honneth's substantive theory which seems most problematic to universalise in the case of global poverty is likely to be the third principle, namely social esteem. The intuitive idea that all human beings should enjoy self-esteem seems inevitably to lead to the idea that the source of self-esteem is likely to be complexly connected with what Rawls (1971) calls 'the social bases of self-respect', and, therefore, the absence of humiliation and degradation within particular societies. However, almost self-evident problems seem to arise with regard to universalising this idea. Understood as the non-tangible reward people receive for their contribution to shared goals (Honneth, 1995: 123), the principle of social esteem appears even more clearly dependent than love and rights on the values of particular nations, cultures and forms of life. For Honneth, liberal societies distribute social esteem according to complex criteria, including desert, productivity and social contribution; and even within particular societies, groups and communities are likely to defend their own criterial bases for esteem, on account of which they feel united by shared values and objectives which enable them to show one another solidarity and, potentially, assert resistance against the larger society (Honneth, 1995: 127). These complexities are deepened by the fact that, for Honneth, while the distribution of esteem in market democracies is often indirectly related to income, it is possible that economically underprivileged groups might experience low social esteem according to income-based criteria but potentially high esteem according to other bases. Honneth's general definition of social esteem as 'the social standing of subjects [...] measured in terms of what they can accomplish for society within their particular forms of self-realization' (1995: 125) therefore seems particularly complex from the perspective of a cosmopolitan recognition theory. Even within particular states, it seems true people in different contexts are esteemed '*qua* certain kind of person' (Laitinen, 2002: 463). These esteem indicators do not follow the norm of universal dignity but rather appeal to 'intersubjectively shared value horizon' (Honneth, 1995: 121), which are liable to be highly disputed, contestable and vague.[22]

For Honneth, this complexity arises from the fact that, with the collapse of traditionally hierarchical societies in the West, most modern states are 'value pluralist' (1995: 125). As Heins (2008: 148) suggests, this shifting value pluralism renders esteem especially complex to globalise, as there seems to be no meta-standard for esteem or any readily available global 'esteem-dispositive'. The most reasonable universalisation of Honneth's esteem principle may be thought to involve resisting and opposing the comprehensive dis-esteem of poor or subaltern groups, in so far as comprehensive dis-esteem may be thought to lead to social exclusion. However, to guard only against very extreme forms of comprehensive dis-esteem may seem insufficient in the context of global poverty. Building the social esteem of the poor and socially excluded to enable them to depart from cycles of deprivation seems to call for attention to the values and priorities within particular forms of life (Page and Czuba, 1999).[23] Yet the project of building social esteem of all marginalised and excluded people in turn encounters the difficulty that esteem is a positional value, which by definition cannot be equally distributed (Jutten, 2017). While Laitinin (2010) seems correct to suggest the need, at least, to protect the excluded and marginalised from 'stigmatising disesteem', it seems inherent to the positional nature of esteem that in competitive market societies some people would be dis-esteemed in this sense. At least, there would be a need to ensure a universal threshold at which human beings are taken to experience adequate social esteem, a task which, for the reasons discussed, seems fraught with difficulties.

At the same time, Honneth still seems to regard social esteem as a universal need, a point which explains why, as he suggests, most social groups struggle to control the 'means of symbolic force' (1995: 127), or the values and characteristics they believe to be worthy or defining. As regards these contests over the criterial bases for social esteem, Thompson's suggested interpretation that all should 'have equal chances to enjoy esteem' (2006: 77) seems promising from the perspective of a cosmopolitan theory. However, eventually the idea of equal opportunities for esteem itself appears to pivot back towards the reality of disputes over the criterial bases of this value, disputes which also imply an epistemic problem of knowing when a person's overall social esteem has been raised. While Honneth seems to believe that, in any given society, esteem is vital because it produces solidarity and therefore social cohesion, it is difficult to see how capitalist societies could be interpreted to contain a meaningful threshold for social esteem for all, since almost by definition, these types of social organization distribute social esteem unequally, at least if esteem is related to economic achievement (Jutten, 2017: 21; Seglow, 2009). Taken together, these challenges suggest that even understanding the nature of the social esteem needed for empowering people against the vulnerability of poverty would be a highly contextual and cultural issue.

Illustrating the issues in competitive market societies, Jutten (2017) suggests that, in advanced capitalist states, very poor workers who make considerable sacrifices for their children might adhere to their own conception of esteem by defining their values in opposition to those of the upper-middle classes. Self-sacrifice, thrift and reliability may be valued, for example, in contrast with the goods of entrepreneurship, faith in the future and self-determination. Moreover, it seems likely that criteria for esteem may be gender-specific, a point exemplified by Jutten's references to men in Boston in the USA who at times define their own group's sense of social esteem in contrast to the attributes they confer on single mothers claiming welfare benefits. These examples illustrate that, even more deeply than love and rights, esteem might relate to cultural and contextual modes of empowerment which cannot be easily globalised. Therefore, while avoiding stigmatising dis-esteem in the lives of the poor and powerless worldwide seems vital, if doing so would involve empowering them to resist the domination which downgrades their conception of a worthwhile life, controversies over the criterial bases of social esteem seem to beset a cosmopolitan recognition theory. These considerations suggest the need to search for further concepts and approaches in order to globalise recognition theory to meet the aim of dignifying the world's poor.

1.5 Conclusion

With the difficulties of globalising the principles of love, rights and esteem in mind, how should a cosmopolitan recognition theory move forward? This chapter has aimed for a preliminary defence of a cosmopolitan recognition theory in the context of ongoing and dire forms of worldwide poverty. Despite the progress made under the aegis of Millennium and Sustainable Development Goals, the number of deaths brought about by this condition continues at intolerable levels. Taking my cue from the core debate over approaches to global poverty inspired by Rawls in terms of a social contract, I argued that it makes sense to conceptualise the continually extreme levels of worldwide poverty not so much in terms of a global social contract but rather as a deficit of intersubjective recognition. After defending the value of a turn towards concepts of recognition and misrecognition in normative political theory, there nonetheless seemed significant problems with globalising the principles of Honneth's substantive recognition theory. In so far as a cosmopolitan recognition theory would entail affirming others' dignity as a condition of one's own subjectivity, the major challenges involved in globalising Honneth's theory fully seem associated with dilemmas concerning the criterial bases for social esteem across societies and life-forms.

Acknowledging these difficulties involves searching, I suggest, for different conceptual and normative resources in recognition theory, which has, over time, developed in a number of directions beyond Honneth and Fraser's defining dialogue. Therefore, in the next chapter, I turn to some lesser discussed areas of Honneth's recognition theory, namely his concepts of reification and antecedent recognition (Honneth, 2008). Through these concepts, I present an elemental case for challenging the lack of personal and political will in the comparatively affluent world to attend to the dire problems of global poverty. The form of cosmopolitan recognition theory for which I aim concentrates not on the externally imposed duty to others from the perspective of a global social contract, but rather on the conditions of our own subjectivity and self-regard as human beings.

Notes

1 Closely following the empirical observations concerning global poverty in the Introduction, it is worth further noting that in 2015, 10 per cent of the world's population lived on less than US $1.90 a day, compared with 11 per cent in 2013. This figure represents a decrease from nearly 36 per cent in 1990. (see Gabriel, 2017). Despite these advances, as the Introduction also outlined, the COVID-19 pandemic has produced one of the of most significant setbacks in the fight against global poverty since World War II. Key additional sources confirming this predicament include Sumner (2020) and Barbier and Burgess (2020).

2 As equally suggested in the Introduction, this book is guided by the idea that political theories based on capabilities and recognition are not opposed. However, conscious of the concerns with conceptualising the harms of poverty simply as a lack of positive freedom, my suggestion is that recognition theories go beyond the capabilities approach by highlighting further 'conversion factors', including the social suffering of the very poor, which affect positive freedom and self-realisation.

3 Although this book does not extensively discuss the Hegelian origins of recognition theory, one of Hegel's defining insights, especially relevant to later recognition theories, is that only in accepting the consciousness and intentionality of others may we also grasp our own selves, which is to say our actions and utterances, as intentional, purposive selves. This thought is explained by Hegel's *Phenomenology of Spirit* (2008 [1807]), where the interpersonal encounter logically culminates in a struggle over life and death. These arguments were later developed by Kojève (1980). Hegel's idea is itself derived from Fichte who claims that subjects become conscious of their own autonomy by being challenged, or 'called upon', by the actions of another subject (see Fichte, 2005).

4 One of Pogge's most favoured solutions to global poverty takes the form of his 'global resources dividend', which demands a transfer from the affluent nations of a percentage of net profits from natural resources into a global fund which would could be used directly to assist the global poor (Pogge, 2007b).

5 There is now a very large debate in the critical literature dealing with Pogge's approach which specifically raises the question of whether his arguments justify positive duties rather than purely negative duties not to harm the global poor. While I do not engage this area of debate in this chapter, as I believe the recognition-based concern with Pogge's approach is a different one, as regards the nature of Pogge's relationship to positive duties of assistance see, for example, Gilabert (2005) and Reitberger (2008).

6 This point relates to Pogge's early argument that Rawls' social contract theory should be globalised, an argument which Rawls himself resists (Pogge, 1988).

7 As one example of the supranational rules mediated by competition, Pogge argues that the World Trade Organization Treaty, while mandating open and competitive global markets, contains no uniform labour standards to protect workers from abusive and stressful labour conditions. This lack of labour protec-

tion inevitably draws poor countries into a vicious 'race to the bottom' where, competing for foreign investment, they must outbid one another by offering ever more exploitable workforces (Pogge, 2016: 34).

8 Significantly, Chandhoke deepens her point by asking: 'Do those of us who live in India have any kind of duty towards the poor in other countries? And if we do not, do we lack the status as moral beings who count?' (2010: 80). This point draws attention to the complexity of poverty in the current world, which would be problematic to conceive in terms of an opposition between the wealthy North and an impoverished South.

9 As Pogge further contends, 'poverty avoidance would [...] be better served if the poor countries did not have to pay for what market access they get by collecting billions in economic rents to be paid to rich country corporations for use of their "intellectual property"' (2005: 12).

10 From some commentators, it is not that institutions such as the World Bank fail to take poverty seriously. On the contrary, while they are serious about this task, the issue may be, however, that employ a particular understanding of poverty alleviation as a matter of alignment with the 'rules' of the global market. For some, this situation means that World Bank policies are at once committed to poverty alleviation and the 'proletarianisation' of the global poor (Cammack, 2002, 2004). Similarly, the World Trade Organization protects market freedoms by increasing aggregate wealth, which, theoretically at least, is understood to enhance the ability of all states to protect economic and social rights and therefore alleviate poverty. However, again this conception of poverty alleviation appears to depend on a particular background acceptance of the rules of the global market.

11 Pogge's more specific claim in this context is that 'the global poor get to share the burdens resulting from the degradation of our natural environment, whilst having to watch helplessly as the affluent distribute the planet's abundant natural wealth amongst themselves – the global elite do this, whilst the poorest fifth of humankind are just about as badly off as human beings could be whilst still being alive' (2007a: 12).

12 Pogge's response to alternative readings of the history of imperialism is that, even if such readings were plausible, the reality is that here and now actual populations of poorer countries are 'deeply shaped and scarred by their country's involuntary encounter with European invaders' (Pogge, 2005: 12).

13 In connection with the impoverishment of former colonised nations, moreover, it is worth remarking that the postcolonial, psychological dimensions of poverty-related oppression are evocatively and famously discussed by Frantz Fanon in *The Wretched of the Earth* (London: Grove Atlantic, 2007 [1961]). Fanon's psychological account of misrecognition of formerly colonised peoples is the subject of a wide debate, including in Hussain Abdihahi Bulhan, *Frantz Fanon and the Psychology of Oppression* (New York: Springer Science and Business Media, 2004). While I do not concentrate specifically on these postcolonial conceptions of recognition theory in this book, I do so in Mookherjee (2023, forthcoming).

14 The phrasing used draws inspiration in part from Toni Morrison's collection, *The Sources of Self-Regard* (Random House, 2020).

15 For an exploration of the relationship between Honneth's thought and classical Marxism, see Deranty (2013).

16 This is with the exception of Honneth's comparatively early (and optimistic) discussion in Honneth (1997).

17 In this sense, Honneth's turn away from conceptualising recognition claims as principally those waged over cultural identity, or 'identity' in any strong sense, strongly contrasts with Charles Taylor's recognition theory, to which I turn in detail in Chapter 4.

18 Hegel wrote that '[recognition] is absolutely the double process of both self-consciousnesses [...] Action from one side only would be useless, because what is to happen can only be brought about by means of both'. As a result, 'these self-consciousnesses recognize themselves as mutually recognizing one another' (2008 [1807]: 231).

19 Honneth's claim in this context draws complexly on object-relations theory, amongst other approaches. As he argues: 'love relationships are to be understood here as referring to primary relationships in so far as they are based on the model of friendships [...] and are constituted by strong emotional attachments among a small number of people' (1995: 95).

20 I return to some of these complexities of the agency of people who attempt to survive poverty in Chapter 3.

21 In fact, Honneth's language in these passages reveals the strength of the connections that he draws between universal respect and rights. At times, as Thompson points out, he even seems to equate respect with 'legal recognition' (1995: 94, 173), suggesting that to respect others is to recognise them as legal persons (1995: 94, 173; Thompson, 2006: 49).

22 In this context, Thompson explains that 'one society may value individuality over family loyalty. Or one society may be more committed to tradition rather than to innovation. It follows that the qualities in virtue of which esteem is due may vary from time to time and place to place' (2006: 75). This point seems especially important in terms of the prospects of universalising a particular threshold for esteem.

23 The term empowerment is contested, of course, as is the concept of basic agency. Page and Czuba (1999) rightly characterise empowerment as a multi-dimensional process which enables people to gain control over their lives. I present a recognition-theoretical concept of empowerment in Chapter 4.

References

Armstrong, Chris and Simon Thompson (2009). 'Parity of Participation and the Politics of States', *European Journal of Political Theory* 8/1: 109–122.

Barbier, Edward and Joanne Burgess (2020). 'Sustainability and Development after Covid-19', *World Development* 135: 1–4.

Beitz, Charles (2005). 'Cosmopolitanism and Global Justice', in *Current Debates on Global Justice* 9/1–2: 11–27.

Cabrera, Luis (2004). *The Political Theory of Global Justice: A Cosmopolitan Case for the World State* (London: Routledge).

Cammack, Paul (2002). 'Attacking the Poor', *New Left Review* 13: 125–134.

Cammack, Paul (2004). 'What the World Bank Means by Poverty Reduction, and Why it Matters', *New Political Economy* 9/2: 189–211.

Chandhoke, Neera (2010). 'How Much is Enough, Mr Thomas, How Much will Ever be Enough?' in A. Jaggar (ed), *Thomas Pogge and his Critics* (London: Polity Press), pp. 11–27.

Collste, Goran (2014). *Global Rectificatory Justice* (Dordrecht: Springer).

Deneulin, Severine (2002). 'Perfectionism, Liberalism and Paternalism in Sen's and Nussbaum's Capabilities Approach', *Review of Political Economy* 14/4: 497–518.

Deranty, Jean-Philippe (2013). 'Marx, Honneth and the Goals of Contemporary Critical Theory', *Ethical Theory and Moral Practice* 16: 745–758.

Dogra, Nandita (2013). *Representations of Global Poverty: Aid, Development and International NGOs* (London: Bloomsbury Publishing).

Fichte, Johann Gottlieb (2005). *Fichte: The System of Ethics* (Cambridge: Cambridge University Press).

Fraser, Nancy (1997). 'From Redistribution to Recognition?', in *Justice Interruptus: Rethinking Key Concepts of a Postsocialist Age* (London: Routledge), pp. 11–39.

Fraser, Nancy (2000). 'Why Overcoming Prejudice is Not Enough: A Rejoinder to Richard Rorty', *Critical Horizons* 1/1 (February): 22–28.

Fraser, N. and Honneth, A. (2003). *Redistribution or Recognition? A Political-Philosophical Exchange* (London: Verso).

Fraser, Nancy (2007). 'Feminist Politics in the Age of Recognition: A Two-Dimensional Approach to Gender Justice', *Studies in Social Justice* 1/1 (Winter): 23–35.

Fraser, Nancy (2010). 'Injustice at Intersecting Scales: On 'Social Exclusion' and 'The Global Poor'', *European Journal of Social Theory* 13/3: 363–371.

Friedman, J. (1996). 'Rethinking Poverty: Empowerment and Citizens' Rights', *International Social Science Journal* 48/148: 161–172.

Gabriel, Iason (2017). 'Effective Altruism and its Critics', *Journal of Applied Philosophy* 34/4: 457–473.

Gaisbauer, Helmut P., Gottfried Schweiger and Clemens Sedmak (eds) (2016). *Ethical Issues in Poverty Alleviation* (Dordrecht: Springer).

Gilabert, Pablo (2005). 'The Duty to Eradicate Global Poverty: Positive or Negative?' *Ethical Theory and Moral Practice* 7: 537–550.

Hegel, G. W. F. (2008 [1807]). *The Phenomenology of Spirit* (Oxford: Oxford University Press).

Heins, Volker (2008). 'Realizing Honneth: Redistribution, Recognition and Global Justice', *Journal of Global Ethics* 4/2: 141–153.

Heins, Volker (2010). 'Of Persons and Peoples: Internationalizing the Critical Theory of Recognition', *Contemporary Political Theory May* 9/2: 149–170.

Heins, Volker (2012). 'The Global Politics of Recognition', in S. O'Neill and N. S. Smith (eds), *Recognition Theory as Social Research* (London: Palgrave MacMillan Press), pp. 213–230.

Held, Virginia (2006). *The Ethics of Care: Personal, Political and Global* (Oxford: Oxford University Press on Demand).

Honneth, A. (1995). *The Struggle for Recognition: The Moral Grammar of Social Conflicts* (Cambridge, MA: MIT Press).

Honneth, Axel (1997). 'Is Universalism a Moral Trap?', in James Bohman and Mattias Lutz-Bachman (eds), *Perpetual Peace: Essays on Kant's Cosmopolitan Ideal* (Cambridge: Cambridge University Press), pp. 155–179.

Honneth, Axel (2008). 'Reification and Recognition: A New Look at an Old Idea', in M. Jay (ed), *Reification: A New Look at an Old Idea* (Oxford: Oxford University Press), pp. 16–94.

Jaggar, Alison (2010). '"How Much is Enough, Mr Thomas? How Much will Ever Be Enough?" in A. Jaggar (ed), *Thomas Pogge and his Critics* (London: Polity), pp. 66–83.

Jo, Y. (2013). 'Psycho-Social Dimensions of Poverty: When Poverty Becomes Shameful', *Critical Social Policy* 33/3: 514–531.

Jutten, Timo (2017). 'Dignity, Esteem and Social Contribution: A Recognition-Theoretical View', *Journal of Political Philosophy* 25/3: 259–280.

Kahn, Elisabeth (2016). 'Poverty, Inequality and Obligations to Take Political Action', in Gaisbauer, Schweiger and Sedmak (eds), *Ethical Issues in Poverty Alleviation: Studies in Global Justice*. Dordrecht: Springer, pp. 209–227.

Kojève, Alexandre (1980). *Introduction to the Reading of Hegel* (Ithaca: Cornell University Press).

Laitinen, Arto (2002). 'Interpersonal Recognition: A Response to Value or a Precondition of Personhood?' *Inquiry* 45/4: 463–478.

Laitinen, Arto (2010). 'On the Scope of 'Recognition': The Role of Adequate Regard and Mutuality', in Hans-Christoph Schmidt am Busch and Christopher Zurn (eds) *The Philosophy of Recognition: Historical and Contemporary Perspectives* (London: Rowman and Littlefield pp. 319–342.)

Lister, Ruth (2015). '"To Count for Nothing": Poverty Behind the Statistics', *Journal of the British Academy* 3: 139–165.

Lu, Catherine (2011). 'Colonialism and Structural Injustice: Historic Responsibility and Contemporary Redress', *Journal of Political Philosophy* 19/3 (Special Issue: Politics, Philosophy and Society), September: 261–281.

Maslow, A. H. (1943). 'A Theory of Human Motivation', *Psychological Review* 50: 370–396.

McCrudden, C. (2013). 'In Pursuit of Human Dignity: An Introduction to Current Debates', Understanding Human Dignity, Proceedings of the British Academy/ Oxford University Press. University of Michigan Public Law Research Paper, no. 309.

Mills, Charles W. (2010). 'Realizing (Through Racialising) Pogge', in A. Jaggar (ed), *Thomas Pogge and his Critics* (Oxford: Oxford University Press), pp. 151–174.

Moellendorf, Daniel (2018). *Cosmopolitan Justice* (New York: Routledge).

Mookherjee, Monica (2023). 'Recognition and Poverty', in C. Sedmak and G. Schweiger (eds), *The Routledge Handbook of the Philosophy of Poverty* (London: Routledge), forthcoming.

Morrison, Toni (2020). *The Sources of Self-Regard: Selected Essays, Speeches and Meditations* (New York: Vintage Press).

Nguyen Minh, T. A., Roberta Zavoretti and Joan Tronto (2017). 'Beyond the Global Care Chain Boundaries: Institutions and the Ethics of Care', *Ethics and Social Welfare* 11/3: 199–122.

Noxolo, P., P. Rashoram and C. Madge (2012). 'Unsettling Responsibility: Postcolonial Interventions', *Transactions of the Institute for British Geographers* (July) 37/2: 418–429.

O'Neill, Shane and C. Walsh (2014). 'Recognition and Redistribution in Theories of Justice Beyond the State', in T. Burns and S. Thompson (eds), *Global Justice and the Politics of Recognition* (London: Polity Press), pp. 128–142.

Page, Nanette and Cheryl I. Czuba (1999). 'Empowerment: What is it?', *Journal of Extension* 37/5: 1–5.

Patten, Alan (2005). 'Should We Stop Thinking about Poverty in Terms of Helping the Poor?', *Ethics and International Affairs* 19/1 (March): 19–27.

Pogge, Thomas (2002). *World Poverty and Human Rights*, 1st edition (Cambridge: Cambridge University Press.

Pogge, Thomas (2005). 'Real World Justice', *The Journal of Ethics* 9: 29–53.

Pogge, Thomas (2007). *Freedom from Poverty as a Human Right: Who Owes What to the Global Poor?* (Oxford: Oxford University Press and UNESCO).

Pogge, Thomas (2007a). 'Introduction', in T. Pogge (ed), *Freedom from Poverty as a Human Right: Who Owes What to the Global Poor?* (London: UNESCO Publishing), pp. 1–11.

Pogge, Thomas (2007b). 'Eradicating Systemic Poverty: Brief for a Global Resources Dividend', *Sur Revista Internacional de Direitos Humanos* 4/6; originally published as Thomas Pogge (2001), in *Journal of Human Development* 2/1: 59–77.

Pogge, Thomas (2016). 'Are We Violating the Human Rights of the Global Poor?', in Gaisbauer, Schweiger and Sedmak (eds), *Ethical Issues in Poverty Alleviation: Studies in Global Justice*, vol. 14 (Springer), pp. 17–42.

Rawls, John (1971). *A Theory of Justice* (Cambridge, MA: Harvard University Press).

Reader, S. (2006). 'Does a Basic Needs Approach Need Capabilities?' *Journal of Political Philosophy* 14/3: 337–350.

Reitberger, Morgan (2008). 'Poverty, Negative Duties and the Global Institutional Order', *Philosophy and Economics* 7/4: 379–402.

Robinson, Fiona (2016). 'Paternalistic Care and Transformative Recognition in International Politics', in Patrick Hayden and Kate Schick (eds), *Recognition and Global Politics: Critical Encounters between State and World* (Manchester: Manchester University Press), pp. 159–174.

Rudra, N. (2009). 'Why International Organizations Should Bring Basic Needs Back In', *International Studies Perspectives* 10: 129–150.

Samuel, Kim, Sabina Alkire, Diego Zavaleta, China Mills and John Hammock (2018). 'Social Isolation and its Relationship to Multidimensional Poverty', *Oxford Development Studies* 46/1: 83–97.

Satz, Deborah (2005). 'What Do We Owe to the Global Poor?', *Ethics and International Affairs* 19/1: 47–54.

Schweiger, Gottfried (2014). 'Recognition Theory and Global Poverty', *Journal of Global Ethics* 10/4: 267–273.

Schweiger, Gottfried (2015). 'Recognition and Poverty', *eidos* 22: 148–168.

Seglow, Jonathan (2009). 'Rights, Contribution, Achievement and the World', *European Journal of Political Theory* 8/1: 61–75.

Sen, Amartya (1990). 'Development as Capability Expansion', in J. DeFilipis and S. Saegert (eds), *The Community Development Reader* (London: Routledge), pp. 319–328.

Sen, Amartya (1999). *Development as Freedom* (New York: Anchor Books).

Sen, Amartya (2002). *Rationality and Freedom* (Cambridge, MA: Harvard University Press).

Sen, A. (2005). 'Human Rights and Capabilities', *Journal of Human Development* 6/2: 152–166.

Sumner, Andrew (2020). 'Estimates of the Impact of Covid-19 on Global Poverty', WIDER Working Paper, no. 20201/43. Available at: https://www.econstor.eu/handle/10419/229267. Accessed 10.12.22.

Tan, Kok-Chor (2010). 'Rights, Harm and Institutions', in A. Jaggar (ed), *Thomas Poage and his Critics* (London: Polity Press), pp. 46–65.

Tay, L. and E. Diner (2011). 'Needs and Subjective Wellbeing around the World', *Journal of Personality and Social Psychology* 101/2: 354–365.

Taylor, Charles (1994 'The Politics of Recognition', in A. Gutmann (ed), *Multiculturalism: Examining the Politics of Recognition* (Princeton: Princeton University Press), pp.25-73.

Thompson, Simon (2006). *The Political Theory of Recognition: A Critical Introduction* (London: Polity Press).

Thompson, Simon and Majid Yar (eds) (2011). *The Politics of Misrecognition* (London: Ashgate Publishing).

Thompson, S. (2013). 'Recognition Beyond the State', in T. Burns and S. Thompson (eds), *Global Justice and the Politics of Recognition* (London: Palgrave MacMillan), pp. 88–107.

Tomon, Graciela (2018). 'Communities and Capabilities', *Journal of Human Development and Capabilities* 19/2: 121–125.

Tronto, Jean (2011). 'Democratic Feminist Ethics of Care and Global Care Workers: Citizenship and Responsibility', in Rhianne Mason and Fiona Robinson (eds), *Feminist Ethics and Social Policy: Towards a New Global Political Economy of Care* (Chicago: University of Chicago Press), pp. 162–177.

UNICEF (United Nations Children's Fund), (2005). *The State of the World's Children* (New York: UNICEF).

Vestergaard, Jakob (2013). 'Protecting Power – How Western States Retain their Dominance in the World Bank', *World Development* 46: 153–164.

Von Kreigstein, Hasko (2010). 'A Bad Argument for a Good Case: Pogge on Poverty and Negative Duties', *Sago: Rivista de Estudiantes de Filosofia* 20: 57–68.

Yar, Majid (2001). 'Beyond Nancy Fraser's Perspectival Dualism', *Economy and Society* 30/1: 288–308.

Young, Iris Marion (2006). 'Responsibility and Global Justice: A Social Connection Model', *Social Philosophy and Policy* 23/1: 102–130.

Ypi, Lea, Robert E. Goodin and Christian Barry (2009). 'Associative Duties, Global Justice and the Colonies', *Philosophy and Public Affairs* 37/2: 103–105.

2 Cosmopolitanism and Distant Others

Reification and the Forgetfulness of Global Poverty in Recent Recognition Theory[1]

2.1 Introduction

The previous chapter raised the initial case for believing that a normative critique of global poverty would be more strongly pursued from a recognition-based perspective than through more familiar resource-distributive frameworks. The concepts and insights of recognition theorists such as Fraser and Honneth seemed more useful than approaches in liberal cosmopolitan justice in view of their focus on the human aspects of poverty. This was so, on account of the possibility of invoking their approaches to emphasise the subjective experiences of the poor, and owing to their focus on structural constraints which lead to entrenched poverty-related suffering. However, in view of the concerns raised previously as regards the globalisation of Honneth's substantive principles of recognition, the current chapter turns to examine the role of some lesser studied concepts in Honneth's corpus to locate the starting point for a response to global poverty through cosmopolitan recognition theory. Specifically, I draw from conceptually prior but frequently overlooked ideas in Honneth's writings to critique the tendency of citizens in affluent states to discount their moral capacity to contribute by alleviating the social suffering caused by worldwide poverty. This layer of Honneth's theory offers insights into why some existing philosophical approaches, especially utilitarian perspectives, may prove ultimately paradoxical in their defence of the dignity of the global poor.

More specifically, this chapter turns to Honneth's discussion of the concept of 'antecedent recognition' and its opposing concept, namely the idea of 'reification' (Honneth, 2008). The inaction of the comparatively affluent, which may be understood frequently as a consequence of their sense of emotional distance or 'overload' when confronted with knowledge of the realities of serious worldwide poverty, seems to reflect Honneth's (2008) conception of reification as a form of 'person-identification failure'. I argue that the moral critique of reification further implies a moral obligation to attempt 'de-reify' the global poor by questioning the legitimacy of anti-poverty strategies which concentrate on purely statistical analyses. Additionally, it suggests the need to scrutinise some influential approaches

DOI: 10.4324/9781003045038-3

to global poverty alleviation, such as Peter Singer's commitment to the 'effective altruism' movement, which makes a strong case for motivating the comparatively affluent in the world to contribute maximally to philanthropic causes. While Singer's approach seems to react critically to the reification of the global poor by encouraging the emotional connection of the affluent with those who are less fortunate materially, there is nonetheless a strong need to surpass Singer's utilitarianism to fully recognise the complex sufferings and agency associated with global poverty on the basis of a cosmopolitan recognition theory.

My discussion is organised in the following way. Section 2.2 argues that a cosmopolitan recognition theory which best addresses global poverty would begin by focusing on the frequent closure of the moral imagination in the affluent world, observing how inaction is often justified in ways which appear opposed to minimal human empathy. I pursue this line of argument by unfolding Honneth's distinctive concepts of reification and antecedent recognition. This discussion leads to a justification, in Section 2.3, of a cosmopolitan bond and a shareable conception of human nature to ground obligations to de-reify the global poor, which in turn provides the impetus to challenge inaction in the face of global poverty from the perspective of recognition theory. While Section 2.4 interprets the frequent inaction in relation to global poverty in the affluent world as a form of what Honneth evocatively labels the 'forgetfulness of recognition' (Honneth, 2008: 52), and more specifically what I further interpret as a 'deep fictive' form of forgetfulness, Section 2.5 finally turns towards Peter Singer's (2015) endorsement of the effective altruism movement. Analysing Singer's theory from the perspective of Honneth's concept of reification leads to the conclusion that a cosmopolitan recognition theory should go further than Singer's utilitarian approach to overcome such forgetfulness, and to provide a basis for securing the dignity and agency of the world's poor.

2.2 A Deeper Recognition Theory: Antecedent Recognition and Reification

Despite the problems identified in the previous chapter with universalising his substantive modes of recognition, Honneth's wider writings in fact suggest a more potent pathway for a moral critique of the harms of global poverty. In particular, Honneth's less frequently discussed concepts of antecedent recognition and reification (Honneth, 2008, 2008a) suggest how a failure to appreciate the human standpoint of the extremely poor is often normalised in the affluent world in such a way that contradicts a minimal conception of human empathy. Considering the large structural injustices underlying global poverty, and the magnitude of the problem from the perspective of ordinary citizens in the developed world, it is worth beginning with this layer of Honneth's recognition theory to locate a moral challenge to attitudes frequently found in affluent nations towards global poverty.

That is, Honneth's concepts serve to highlight how the interests, agency and suffering of the global poor are often discounted in the affluent world. Whilst the concept of agency is one which is notoriously problematic to define, I rely on a conception which consists at least in the psychological, material and normative conditions to act and live above the realm of pure physical survival (Cudd, 2014).[2] As extreme poverty is likely to undermine agency in this sense, it seems useful to view modern forms of reification, especially as understood through Honneth's theory, as undermining the capacities of the comparatively affluent to view the global poor fully as agents in these terms. Briefly, then, the focus on Honneth's concept of reification seems to promise a starting point for a cosmopolitan critique of global poverty which, I suggest, provides a useful gateway for an approach based on recognition theory.

As a preliminary caveat, however, it is worth emphasising the importance of not overstating the issues, and seeming to suggest that the comparatively affluent always fail to respond to dire poverty worldwide. It is also wise not to be oblivious to the significance of different possible reasons for inaction in relation to global causes in the affluent world. Where people do not react to wide-ranging global economic problems, many factors are clearly in play, including the fact that some prioritise local over global causes and that, at times of serious economic constraints, even comparatively affluent people suffer their own significant hardships (Van Heerde and Hudson, 2010). Therefore, it would be unreasonable in many situations to take inaction in relation to global causes as a matter of intentional blindness. Nonetheless, as an indication of the scope of inaction when confronted with the facts of widespread poverty, comparatively recent OECD figures related to the USA suggest an average donation per person of one-thousandth of an annual income (Gabriel, 2016: n.1). If such minimal action may be viewed as an ethical problem, and if this situation could be understood to misrecognise the human interests of the very poor, it is worth considering whether the idea of reification provides a productive basis from which to formulate a duty to oppose, in Honneth's evocative phrase, 'the forgetfulness of recognition' (2008: 52).

This deeper layer of Honneth's recognition theory may be introduced by explaining that, underneath his substantive moral concepts of love, rights and esteem lies a more basic concept of what he refers to as primary or 'antecedent' recognition (Honneth, 2008). For Honneth, this form of affective acknowledgement constitutes the precondition of the norms of human interaction in his substantive theory. Although in one sense it seems true that Honneth's tendency to label all of these concepts equally as 'recognition' produces some confusion, by antecedent recognition he seems to have in mind a bare acknowledgement one is dealing with people rather than with objects or with things. As a number of Honneth's interpreters suggest, the concept is intended to be neutral between different conceptions of the person and ethical conceptions of the good life (Hull, 2013; Butler, 2008). This conceptually minimal idea suggests a basic responsiveness to the world arising merely from the 'spontaneous, non-rational recognition of others as human beings' (Honneth, 2008: 52). Drawing on Cavell's social theory, developmental psychologists such as Winnicott and Dewey's and Heidegger's philosophical defences of a sense of involved care for the world, Honneth defends a form of engaged responsiveness to others in the world, one which would constitute the natural starting point for all human relations (2008: 37–39). It is in this sense that, for Honneth, 'recognition precedes cognition' (2008: 56).

The potential cosmopolitan critique of global poverty suggested by this concept may be best understood by examining its counterpart, which Honneth presents in terms of a reconceived version of the Marxist concept of reification. Although Honneth first discussed this concept in an essay concerning the historical invisibility of African-Americans (Honneth, 2001), his later essay (2008) is dedicated to more generally unfolding the concept of reification as a denial or suppression of primary recognition in different social forms. This later essay seems more compelling for this chapter's purposes, as here Honneth depicts how the breakdown of the basic or even visceral human responsiveness involved in primary recognition may bear extreme results, such as in the mass-scale loss of empathy exemplified in the mid-twentieth-century's Holocaust (2008: 75). With this example, Honneth suggests the potentially extreme effects of not responding to others with a sense of shared humanity. To conceive reification from the perspective of recognition theory seems highly distinctive, and, as I shall suggest, insightful for a normative response to global poverty. While the idea of reification itself famously derives from Marxism, classically described by Georg Lukács (1967 [1923]) as the alteration of the experience of the members of a capitalist society in such a way that naturalises an understanding of their environment, and which produces an illusion of 'thing-likeness' in reality, Honneth's conception differs from Lukács' concept as well as from the related concept of objectification, as I aim to explain.

Hull (2013) rightly suggests the distinctiveness of Honneth's conception of reification by emphasising how it connotes an autonomous social process which differs from the seemingly analogous idea of objectification. In reification, intentional human actions tend to appear to human beings as natural or static outcomes of universal laws, producing a mentality which leads people to apprehend the social world around them as a simple immutable and unchangeable fact (Gunderson, 2020). As Hull explains, this mentality is produced through a certain illusion, according to which states of affairs are naturalised whereas in reality they may be humanly created or have dimensions of human agency. This analysis reflects Honneth's definition of reification as a suppression of a person's primary responsiveness to others and the world. As he explains, by reification '*I thereby mean to indicate the process by which we lose the consciousness of the degree to which we owe our knowledge and cognition of other persons to an antecedent stance of empathetic engagement and recognition*' (2008: 56, my emphasis).

Although reification may appear similar to the related and more familiar idea of objectification, the two concepts do not seem to be synonymous. Martha Nussbaum's (1995) conception of reification as a sub-category of objectification helps to highlight the distinction. For Nussbaum, objectification is often characterised by, inter alia, the following features: Fungibility, instrumentality, denial of autonomy and subjectivity, and inertia. From this perspective, reification would amount to a form of objectification on grounds that the former concept expresses both instrumentalisation and denial of subjectivity. Hull (2013: 60–61), however, correctly counter-argues that Nussbaum's analysis seems only to hold by relying on a Kantian moral framework, from which perspective both reification and objectification are assumed to involve deliberateness or intentionality. Yet, neither Honneth nor Lukács take reification to involve intentional, self-responsible acts, whereas, in contrast, objectification may be more frequently assumed to be intentional. Thus, reification would not deny others' subjectivity, such as the personhood of subaltern groups or the very poor, in the same way that sexual objectification may deny women's subjectivity. In the latter concept the objectifier may be assumed to be at least partially conscious of the meaning of their act. For instance, in the context of the objectification involved in slavery (Nussbaum, 1995: 261), the slaveholder seems to pretend, despite being aware that reality is otherwise, to treat the slave as a mere means to his ends.[3] In contrast, for Honneth reification would not involve this form of intentional, cognitive pretence. He does, however, wish to present reification as an ethical problem, and, as I shall argue, a particular ethical problem as regards global poverty could be inferred from his concept.

For now, while concepts of reification and objectification may both be taken to entail a kind of illusory or false conception of other human beings, the key difference seems to lie in the weaker degree of cognitive responsibility in reification. The causal explanation Honneth provides for reification, however, is rendered more complex on account of his divergence from Lukács' earlier formulation of the concept in terms of the Marxist notion of capitalist exchange. In *History and Class Consciousness*, Lukács argued that the error involved in reification arises through a transformation of a person's immediate experience. Honneth substantially agrees with this idea, and with Lukács' further conception of reification as a process involving, in his words, 'a relation between people takes on the character of a thing; [...] and thus acquires a "phantom objectivity"; an autonomy that seems so strictly rational and all-embracing as to conceal every trace of its fundamental nature: the relation between people' (1967 [1923], cited in Hull, 2013: 51; see also Mussell, 2013). However, despite this consensus, Honneth disagrees with Lukács' key causal claim that reification singularly occurs under capitalist exchange systems. For Honneth, this explanation would vastly under-describe contemporary instances of reification (2008: 53). The causal neutrality or openness of Honneth's conception leads him to characterise the phenomenon simply as a form of 'person-identification failure', according to which, for whatever reasons, a person fails to realise the entity with whom they are dealing is a human being. As reification suppresses an evident truth, it involves a certain form of forgetting, the causal explanation for which may not be always be purely economic. As Honneth expresses the point, in all contexts of reification, 'a person unlearns something he or she previously and intuitively mastered' (2008: 79).

Briefly, then, Honneth departs from Lukács' emphasis on the proletariat's prime role in reification on grounds that racism and sexism may also lead to forms of reification which cannot be explained in purely economic terms.[4] For Honneth, the amnesia or lack of attentiveness involved in reification may in some instances arise from patriarchy or more broadly from modernity's calculating, rational commitment to abstract personhood and its drive to quantify social problems, a standpoint which, following Adorno, risks intensifying under conditions of rapid modernisation (see also Giddens, 1994). However, whether reification is local or global, for Honneth the detached spectatorship it involves is always, in his evocative phrase, 'the forgetfulness of recognition' (2008: 52). This idea evokes Adorno's assertion, himself indebted to Lukács, that 'all reification is a forgetting' (Adorno and Benjamin, 1999: 321).

Honneth's avoidance of a Marxist narrative renders his concept open to a potential cosmopolitan application. According to this view, no comprehensive conception of the good life or of personhood lies at the root of the primary form of affective involvement with the world which reification denies. Yet this minimal substrate of human acknowledgement may be forgotten, as suggested so acutely by the twentieth-century rise of fascism (2008: 78). Of course, one first question arising from Honneth's idea would be whether it would be unrealistic to extend the implications of reification globally. Furthermore, if Honneth's idea is that antecedent recognition means that one's primary sense of involvement with the world cannot truly be lost, in that people are best understood only transiently to 'unlearn' something of which they remain conscious in a deeper sense, the ethical implications of the concept for a response to global poverty may seem too ambiguous.

As a preliminary response to these questions, for Honneth at least, it seems clear the concept of reification has significant ethical implications. While it would oversimplify the concept to suggest all human beings may be so equally and fully affected that they fail to feel any responsibility in the face of global poverty, it does not seem unreasonable to suggest that under conditions such as intense globalisation, many in affluent societies do predominantly experience global poverty as a distant, irremediable problem (Fox, 2016). Honneth's concept of reification may assist to explain why, despite the speed and frequency of global communications, the comparatively affluent in the global North might regard the problem as a distant issue, evoking sentiments of resignation, compassion fatigue and world weariness, the reified stance that '*things are the way they are*' (Gunderson, 2020: 18, my emphasis). It may explain why, despite the progress apparently made in recent years in affluent nations in encouraging interest in development aid and philanthropy through campaigns such as Live8 and Make Poverty History (see Van Heerde and Hudson, 2010; Silvio, 2013),[5] there seem to remain, as suggested earlier, widespread tendencies in the developed world to remain psychologically and practically disengaged. If this interpretation seems plausible, I next further examine the possible 'reification illusions' (Gunderson, 2020) involved in late-modern perceptions of global poverty, before returning to the specific form of forgetfulness which Honneth's theory may seem to imply in relation to the reactions of the comparatively affluent to extreme poverty in the modern world.

2.3 Cosmopolitan Recognition Theory and Reification Illusion in Global Poverty

As suggested earlier, Honneth seems to conceive primary recognition as culturally neutral, almost a bare datum of human thought (Varga, 2010), devoid of assumptions concerning the good life. That is, the concept seems to suggest a basic condition of individuation, the psychological ability to distinguish oneself from another as a distinct mental and physical entity and to perceive the need to comprehend another's standpoint (2008: 18), a capacity which is suppressed by reification. In contrast with Lukács' idea that reification constitutes an ontological mistake or a 'distorted stance' in relation to reality (see Lukacs, 1967 [1923]: 80; Honneth, 2008: 25-26), for Honneth the denial of primary recognition through reification undermines a minimal, transcultural conception of morality (2008: 78). It is this moral critique of the denial of human empathy which, I now suggest, promises to ground a cosmopolitan critique of the reification illusions created by at least some international policies in relation to global poverty.

In one sense, it seems true the implications of asserting this moral violation would not seem very clear or determinate. Although, for Honneth, the psychologically numbing effects of modern bureaucratic rationality may be morally problematic, at times he also concedes that adopting a rationalist perspective is not only crucial but inevitable (2008: 72). That said, in the context of the late-modern drive towards rationality, progress and economic development, Honneth's concept suggests the sheer challenges the comparatively affluent would confront in conceiving the distant victims of global poverty in holistic, human terms (Gabriel, 2016: 15). This sense of moral and psychological distance renders it more likely to discount one's own capacity to intervene to contest global structural inequalities, on grounds that the problem is too massive, too endemic to corrupt societies or otherwise too entrenched for individual action to assist. These views, which could be more or less sincerely held, may also be fuelled by the proliferation of media images of famine, natural disaster and malnutrition (Boltanski, 1999). To the extent that they lead to psychological overload or even a 'crisis of pity', it seems an endemic effect of modernity, depicted also by Adorno and Horkheimer

(2002), to shield oneself from the fact that the huge structural inequalities dividing the world's rich and poor are not enduring facts about human existence. In this vein, it is relevant to consider Parton and Kirk's (2011) recent report exploring new modes of public engagement in global poverty initiatives. They suggest that, despite recent media attention to campaigns such as Make Poverty History, public engagement with the structural issues underlying global poverty in the United Kingdom, for example, remains low. As reflected also in Pogge's reactions to popular attitudes to global poverty in Chapter 1, their findings suggest continuously widespread tendencies to regard global poverty as internal to states, brought about by factors such as famine, civil conflict, natural disasters and poor governance, as well as extensive concerns about the 'Live Aid Legacy' and its seeming presumption of symbolically colonialist relationships between donors and recipients of aid.

However, if the reaction to this widespread attitude of reluctance to donate to international causes is to be seen in part as the outcome of the reification of global relations and of global poverty in particular, another of the risks in the comparatively affluent world may be an over-ready acceptance of international policies which frame the global poor as statistics or as a 'problem' to be resolved. In other words, reification may often encourage the comparatively affluent to accept what Gunderson calls the tendency of reification to 'enframe' other human beings, in this case those who experience poverty, by too readily acquiescing to policies which seem to conceive those who should be regarded as ends (for instance, people and humanity) as means, and means (such as technology) as ends. According to Gunderson (2020: 4), the enframing tendency of reification tends to result in 'possibility blindness', or narrowed perceptions concerning the opportunities for social and political change. This is so, even though it may be difficult to discern which of the individual's reactions express reification as such. For example, a rational awareness of the limits of personal philanthropy may be justifiable, and it may not be inconsistent with campaigning for international financial institutions or national governments to commit more seriously to development aid. Therefore, the complexity of the effects of reification seems crucial to consider. Additionally, against the tendency towards disengagement from global problems, it is clear some individuals in the affluent world do actively support poverty alleviation measures, and that some existing movements seem explicitly to avoid reifying the global poor. For example, Monique Deveaux has recently focused on land reclamation movements by the property-less in Brazil as campaigns which significantly challenge the apparently Western ideas of social and economic rights grounded in capitalist property relations (Deveaux, 2015, 2021; Chari, 2010). Similarly, the poor mobilisation organisations in Bangladesh, Nijera Kori, and the slum and pavement dweller movement in India to which Deveaux draws attention, also seem to challenge the reductive view of poverty alleviation as only a matter of statistics or the proportions of people lifted above particular purchasing thresholds. Support for these movements in the affluent world might be thought reasonably to counter the 'enframing' tendencies of reification in Honneth's sense.

At the same time, given the core role which international institutions play in tackling global poverty, it seems reasonable to suggest that resisting reification might also involve, in part, critical evaluation of international institutional policies, such as those of United Nations and the World Bank. In this context, it is significant that some have viewed the Millennium Development Goals' policies of setting targets to reduce the numbers of people in absolute poverty, which pre-dated the current strategies under the Sustainable Development Goals, as especially problematic for their focus on reducing the number of people suffering under the World Bank's poverty line. Whilst from many perspectives these objectives were practically indispensable, concerns were raised that setting targets in relation to such a complex human problem as poverty risks underestimating its human face, in such a way which almost inevitably 'simplifies, reifies and abstracts' (Fukuda-Parr et al., 2014: 4). Equally, conceptualising poverty alleviation as a matter of increasing purchasing power could be considered to turn attention away from the structural causes of global poverty. Although they seem advantageous in the sense of rendering poverty reduction measurable, taken alone at least or as the main focus for poverty alleviation, these strategies may be considered to weaken the public perception of the need to campaign for global structural change (Caney, 2015). If, therefore, as Sen (1990) has long held, tackling extreme deprivation involves considering the various human capabilities at stake,[6] a perspective which attempts to counter reification would question approaches based on target-setting. At least, individuals in the comparatively affluent world would realistically devote critical thought to the sufficiency of these policies. As Iris Young (2010) argues, ordinary people in affluent states have both the capacity for and means to knowledge. Despite reification, people are capable of gaining knowledge of the structural injustices which produce and sustain global poverty.[7] Whether or not they use this capacity to support policies, such as greater partnership between emerging and advanced economies to encourage the agency and empowerment of the poor (Saith, 2005; Guther, 2010),[8] Honneth's moral critique of reification seems to suggest opposing initiatives or pathways which obscure the human face of the suffering involved in extreme poverty (Fukuda-Parr, 2014; Latour, 1987; Merry, 2011; Porter, 1994), and which also, perhaps crucially, deepen the comparatively affluent's de-sensitisation to human suffering, as one of the most pervasive outcomes of reification (Morgan, 2014).

The discussion so far of the possible effects of reification on First-World reactions to poverty alleviation strategies does, however, beg certain questions. One might ask, for instance, whether everyone should be equally viewed as a victim of reification, and whether the 'de-reification' of distant others is ever wholly achievable. While I shall discuss this issue more deeply in the following section, for now at least it seems fair to say it could follow from Honneth's conceptions of primary recognition and reification that an ethical obligation to act with empathy and solidarity has been failed when rational people, through the institutions they participate in or support, do not undertake critically to scrutinise their own perception of their obligations towards distant others.[9] The stakes involved in failing to do so are emphasised by Hayden's compelling observation that nearly half of the world's population lives on less than a dollar a day, a daily destruction of dignity which has caused unprecedented suffering. As a possible effect of reification, for Hayden it is the modern emphasis on instrumental and bureaucratic rationality which only too often divests people of a sense of moral responsibility in modernity (2007: 28).

2.4 The Challenges of Departing from the Reification Illusion: Fictive Forgetfulness and Global Poverty

The question of who should be taken to be affected by reification, whether rich and poor alike, seems connected with a further question which arises from Honneth's concepts, and which would have further implications for how the ideas of primary recognition, reification and de-reification may be understood from a cosmopolitan perspective. In particular, the concern may be that the idea of primary recognition may seem too minimal to enable human understanding between people who potentially hold vastly different world-views. On this account, in view of deep global structural inequalities, it would be psychologically impossible for comparatively affluent individuals in the First-World to identify with the problems and hardships of distant individuals even minimally, and hence to overcome the reifying tendencies of their reactions. In response to this problem, I contend that this sense of human connection would become psychologically plausible if the form of 'forgetfulness' often involved in the affluent First-World's reification of global poverty is construed as metaphorical, or as a 'deep fictive', rather than a literal form of forgetfulness. Therefore, in response to the objection that de-reification would be implausibly demanding in a current world of extreme inequalities of wealth, it is worth emphasising the distinction between the literal and metaphorical senses in which the term 'forgetfulness of recognition' may be understood in Honneth's conception of reification.

This point may be supported by noticing first that Honneth's discussion of the forms of forgetfulness involved in reification is wide-ranging, and that it potentially suggests different forms and degrees to which this forgetting might occur. Explicitly, he wishes to suggest reification would be extreme, occurring at the 'zero point of sociality' (Honneth, 2008a: 157), and exemplified by the limit-case of the Holocaust. On the other hand, however, Honneth's discussion of reification in fact seems most potent and realistic when he also indicates the banal and quotidian nature of acts of reification, especially in the form of self-reification in the context of a job interview or of Internet dating; and where he refers to three dimensions of reification, namely the reification of others, of objects and of nature (2008:

78). In the case of self-reification, when one partially reifies oneself for the purpose of securing a job, what or how one forgets seems distinct than in the extreme cases in which one seems literally to forget the humanity of others. Honneth's association of reification with everyday habits of thought, rather than necessarily with a one-time drastic human rights violation such as genocide seems truest to contemporary forms of reification. To invoke Adorno's similar conception, reification seems to work through the modern meta-processes of rationalisation, industrialisation and secularisation, according to which morality is only too frequently reduced either to rule-following or to a form of cold calculation, which produces the instrumentalisation of indifference to, or detachment from, one's own full humanity or that of others. For Adorno, what seems crucial is the pervasive banality or even the necessity of this form of thought in modernity, as 'without such coldness one could not live' (Adorno, 1998 [1967]: 274). While, at times, Honneth seems officially to wish to avoid calling the banal instances true reification, in the sense that it is more difficult to suggest why they are morally concerning, at times he concedes these everyday acts of could express reification (Honneth, 2008: 78), a point which again seems to suggest different forms of forgetfulness involved in different relationships of reification.

In summary, then, Honneth explicitly refers to the genuine possibility of extreme forms of forgetfulness involved in reification, where one literally forgets or loses the sense that those one is dealing with are human beings. Somewhat paradoxically, for Honneth these literal examples of reification may often be best highlighted through fictional works:

> Perhaps the activity of war as we experience it in novels and films can serve as a better example. In these contexts we often see or read how the purpose of annihilation becomes so much a purpose in itself that even in the perceptions of those not involved (e.g. women and children), all attentiveness for human qualities is lost. In the end, all members of the group presumed to be the enemy come to be perceived as life-less, thing-like objects [...] In this case, every trace of existential resonance seems to have vanished so completely that we cannot even label it emotional indifference, but only "reification".
>
> (2008a: 156)

However, the fact that these examples are drawn from film and cinema should not detract from how, literally, primary recognition of others' humanity seems to be forgotten in these cases. In contrast, Honneth also describes more seemingly innocuous instances of reification in the real world, such as in the case of a tennis player who partially objectifies her opponent for the sake of winning a championship. In this example, it seems more problematic to suggest the person has truly lost the sense of her opponent as a human being (2008a: 155). The forgetfulness does not seem to be a real obliteration of consciousness of others as human beings; and it may, for this reason, be better regarded as a 'fictive' or hypothetical form of forgetfulness or as temporary instrumentalisation. In reaction to the strong, literal conception of forgetfulness, some critics such as Sayers (2009) and Lear (2008) rightly object that conceiving reification as an extreme atrophy of empathy seems exceptional, an idea which could only apply in the case of some extremely dramatic, direct rights violations. Yet, if one instead weakens the concept to include ordinary habits of instrumentalising or calculating thought, the concept might then include many instances of everyday ideological misrecognition. While these forms of conduct may be in different ways unfair or unjust, the concern would be that 'fictive' or hypothetical forms of forgetfulness, exemplified by the tennis player, would not suggest the morally problematic forgetfulness which would explain Honneth's real concerns about reification.

Given that neither literal nor transiently banal conceptions of forgetfulness seem perfectly to describe the morally problematic form of detachment from human problems involved in First-World reactions to global poverty suggested earlier, then, it seems useful to extend Honneth's theory to suggest there may also exist a third form of forgetfulness, what may be called a 'deep fictive form', which would be morally problematic in the relevant sense. This form of forgetfulness would fall between the literal case, the cinematic depiction of wartime killing, and the seemingly innocuous reifications involved in the tennis championship. What seems to occur in the First-World evasiveness as regards global poverty is neither a complete obliteration of consciousness of the fact people suffer from hunger and malnutrition or a purposive act of partially instrumentalising others. There is, typically, no denial or even ignorance of the suffering. Instead, more typically, the 'forgetfulness' seems to involve fictionalising this suffering as unrelated to one's own form of life or to wider global structures of oppression. Put differently, in what could be labelled 'deep fictive forgetfulness' one does not literally create a thing-like enemy of the poor nor disregard their rights to life. However, one forgets the complexity of their rights and their subjectivity and the structural relations which bind one's subjectivity to theirs. Deep fictive forgetfulness, then, seems to constitute a moral problem, because whereas one does not lose the sense of others as fellow humans, one tells oneself a simplifying story which hides the complexity of other lives and one's relations to those lives. The result would be a denial of what Varga and Gallagher (2012) call, in relation to Honneth's concept of primary recognition, 'affective proximity'. This ethical proximity seems necessary for people to be open to extending what Honneth calls 'existential sympathy' to particular others (2008a: 152).[10] Deep fictive forgetfulness still appears distinct from the more intentional concept of objectification, as considered previously. While both deep fictive reification and objectification would involve a form of partially conscious, or at least not unconscious, pretence, again, as in all concepts of reification, the degree of responsibility would still be weaker in the conception suggested here.

If this interpretation of Honneth's theory seems plausible, then it seems the concepts of reification and antecedent recognition may be useful concepts to ethically challenge those who are reluctant to intervene in global causes, specifically on questions of global poverty. Of course, even then, the central question might be which values a global recognition theory would concretely endorse to remember the humanity and dignity of the global poor. While a critique of reification alone does not in itself determine a full cosmopolitan recognition theory, it seems significant that, whilst officially seeming to present reification as a matter of literal forgetfulness (2008a: 157), Honneth eventually concedes reification often does form 'part and parcel of some more intensified forms of human conduct', even occurring when people do minimally acknowledge others' personhood (2008a: 157). It is significant, therefore, that Morgan (2014) and Jutten (2010) both correctly challenge the idea that reification in Honneth's sense would involve people completely losing their sense of the reality of others as human beings. If it could be seen as a matter, as I have suggested, of deep fictive forgetfulness, it seems unlikely that, absent the most extreme conditions, people completely lose this awareness. This point seems reflected in Iris Young's (2006) assertion that, when a person in an economically advanced state purchases a pair of shoes, they are usually aware that their action presupposes a chain of actions, including the work undertaken in sweatshops in the global South. In fact, and ultimately, the form of the 'forgetfulness of recognition' suggested in this section seems to support Honneth's objection to Lukács' conception of reification for its overly 'totalizing ramifications', or its inability to suggest how ordinary human beings could ever break free of the illusion of reification (Honneth, 2008: 54).[11] For Lukács, reification seems to cause people comprehensively to lose their capacity for empathy, an outcome which Honneth finds implausible. As he ultimately concedes, despite appearances, reification should not be assumed to connote an absolute loss of awareness of others' humanity, most deeply because 'it cannot be true that our consciousness is dispossessed of this fact of recognition' (2008a: 152).

2.5 Deep Fictive Forgetfulness and Effective Altruism: The Paradoxes of Peter Singer's Solution to World Poverty

The implications of the conception of reification developed above may still seem ambiguous; and it is, of course, the challenge undertaken in the book to articulate the full cosmopolitan recognition theory which might follow from these arguments. For now, however, the remainder of this chapter pauses to consider the potential paradoxes of one of the most prominent recent moral theories in responding to global poverty from the perspective of the concept of reification suggested above. Peter Singer's much-debated commitment to the effective altruism movement (2016 [1972], 2010, 2015) seems to hold both advantages and drawbacks in overcoming the forgetfulness of global poverty. Examining the difficulties with his normative solutions in turn assists in highlighting the key normative values on which a cosmopolitan recognition theory might especially concentrate, and which form the objective of my arguments in later chapters.

First and most famously articulated in response to the Bangladeshi famine in 1972, Singer's utilitarian approach identifies the potential of the comparatively affluent to envisage a moral connection with distant others, and to acknowledge a shared capacity for human suffering. For Singer, human beings are ethically obliged to act on this minimal acknowledgement irrespective of geographical boundaries (2016 [1972]: 15). The fact that the comparatively affluent often discount these connections and fail to donate to the greatest extent possible to alleviate world hunger represents a significant ethical problem, one which, in turn, motivates Singer's plea for the comparatively affluent to react to what appears to be willful blindness towards the moral claims of the destitute around the world. Obviously, the fact that Singer himself does not rely on concepts of 'reification' or 'misrecognition' is understandable, given the development of his utilitarianism quite separately from traditions of Frankfurt School thought. Moreover, as regards the philosophical foundations of his approach, Singer's early defence of his position appeared noticeably free from any extended justification even of his own utilitarian perspective. Rather, Singer's major objective appeared to be to assert the argument's intuitive and commonsensical appeal, suggesting those who disagree with his presumption of equal human interests 'need read no further' (2016 [1972]: 4).

Despite Singer's early reticence to justify his utilitarian arguments for maximum donation to world hunger, it nonetheless seems reasonable to assume his implicit reliance on earlier utilitarian philosophers such as Bentham (1970 [1879] and Sidgwick (2019 [1874]), who based their ethical theories on the significance of each person's capacity to experience pleasure and pain. While Singer's initial assumption of the priority of these essential capacities seems useful to challenge what I have depicted as the modern reifications of global poverty, the line of argument risks not fully acknowledging the potential conflicts which may arise over conceptions of pleasure and pain worldwide. In fact, the risk is that Singer's impartialism may even, curiously, sidestep first-person subjective experiences of suffering in such a way that may not adequately de-reify relations with the global poor, at least from the perspective of this chapter's interpretation of Honneth's idea of reification.

Before pursuing this critique, however, it seems crucial first to concede the value of Singer's first premise, and how it may broadly oppose reification. As Singer states in connection with his much-debated 'Comparable Moral Significance' principle,[12] the facts of geographical distance, or the argument that if others gave to a similar extent, one's own obligations towards global poverty would lessen (2016 [1972]: 28), seem to be arbitrary considerations raised by comparatively affluent individuals to rationalise inaction when confronted with serious poverty worldwide. For Singer, while it is undoubtedly demanding, the comparatively affluent ought to extend their moral imagination to view the interests of distant others as equal to their own; hence, they should act immediately and positively in the interests of those who suffer from lack of resources such as food and shelter. By distancing his theory from causal explanations for global poverty or world hunger, such as in Pogge's approach, Singer takes the primary responsiveness to global suffering as both psychologically possible and morally compelling. The egalitarianism of Singer's utilitarian premise seems to reflect Honneth's idea of antecedent recognition, or at least, Honneth's moral critique of reification seems theoretically consistent with, and even implied in, Singer's starting point. It seems likely that a de-reifying cosmopolitan perspective should avoid controversial debates concerning causal responsibility, that it should assume the universal relevance of worldwide suffering, and it should normatively recommend reacting to assist, irrespective of national boundaries.

However, on examination, a number of paradoxes seem to arise with Singer's theory from the perspective of de-reifying responses to global poverty. The key controversies include Singer's presentation of the ethical solution to urgent questions of famine and world hunger in the form of his later commitment to the effective altruism movement (Singer, 2015; MacAskill, 2014; Gabriel 2017). These solutions might even risk reinforcing the reification of global poverty in some troubling and unintended ways. If we consider, for instance, Singer's early urgent plea for monetary donation in relation to emergency rescue first, while it seems intuitively correct to suggest that emergency donations and cash transfers may be the most compelling ways of realising human needs in situations such as the Bangladeshi famine, inevitably even in emergency rescue situations, questions arise as to causality, as well as to the practical effectiveness of assistance in contexts where the political causes of famine may be various. Following Sen, for instance, Kahn rightly observes that the causes of famine should not be naturalised but rather should be seen, as Sen has famously suggested, as 'entitlement failure' (Sen, 1990a; Kahn, 2016), a term which draws attention to the social and political causes of maldistribution and the need to respond to those causes rather than focusing only on redistribution.

Of course, on the one hand, Singer's perspective appears to de-reify the global poor by urging immediate remedial action by the comparatively affluent. However, in reality, often the logistics of short-term rescue will involve considering the longer-term effects of development assistance. This is not to dilute the significance of the emergency, or to argue that donations in the context of emergencies risk diverting resources away from general development assistance (Rubenstein, 2007). Rather, as Rubenstein explains, the risk is that distinguishing between (a particular conception of) emergency and development aid risks deflecting attention from a proper evaluation of what may be occurring in an emergency. The distinction might obscure the fact that different emergencies involve different degrees of responsibility and different structural causes. If this point is true, Singer's apparently uncontroversial de-reifying premise seems to become entangled with his later move towards a commitment to effective altruism, as I aim to show, which is likely not wholly to de-reify the relations of the comparatively affluent with the very poor around the world.

While it would be impossible to provide an exhaustive account of the effective altruism movement within the space available, it is at least worth mentioning that Singer's defence of this movement has, since his earlier theoretical response to food security emergencies, involved softening his initial and very demanding position which urged for donation by the comparatively affluent to the point of marginal utility (2016 [1972]: 29). In his more recent writing, in particular *The Most Good You Can Do* (2015), Singer characterises the defence of effective altruism as an ethically pluralist lifestyle choice, defensible on utilitarian grounds but potentially also through other theories, so long as one prioritises not only maximally effective donations to causes such as global poverty, but that one also considers for oneself which career path would enable one to act most beneficially in the world, without, as Singer previously expressed the point, 'sacrificing something of comparable moral significance' (4 2016 [1972]: 15). From the perspective of reification, one key question surrounds Singer's ethical justification even for more limited duties of beneficence of the global poor; and another concerns the de-reifying value of an individual's attempts to quantify their most beneficent contribution to poverty relief.

Taking the issue of philosophical justification for effective altruism first, then, Singer grounds his more recent position by suggesting that, while his argument does not strongly presuppose a utilitarian framework, a minimal commitment to altruism assumes the personal, first-person good to involve a certain commitment to the wellbeing of others too (2015: 92). The altruistic position additionally requires the individual to sacrifice something of significance to meet the wellbeing of others, even if this sacrifice need not reach the point of marginal utility (2015: 93). For Singer, following Hume, the idea is that people usually, above all, pursue self-esteem and that achieving self-esteem involves other-regarding action (2015: 100). This is so, even though effective altruism should not be synonymous with the 'warm glow' people often experience through purely occasional charity giving or further other-regarding actions.

While this argument appears initially logical, Kahn (2016) seems correct to observe that the argument in *The Most Good* might in fact implicitly rely on Singer's previous utilitarianism, in such a way which would not necessarily bolster and support a cosmopolitan theory which aims to challenge the affluent's forgetfulness or reifications of global poverty. Singer seems to take the commitment to altruism not only to entail that one should do good to some extent, but that one should do so to the maximal extent, attempting to make the good 'the most good', on grounds 'one cannot have self-esteem while ignoring the interests of others, whose wellbeing [one] recognizes as *being equally significant*' (2015: 102, my emphasis). For Singer, this ethical impartialism commits one to maximising one's capacities to 'make the world a better place', including through poverty alleviation. However, it seems important to suggest that altruism and empathy on one side, and the commitment to maximising aggregate utility on the other, are not synonymous. The latter is likely to rely on a utilitarian commitment which is potentially controversial from the point of view of opposing the reification of the global poor. While appearing mainly to appeal to common-sense intuitions, the commitment to maximisation seems to risk making extensive assumptions as regards human interests which may be problematic and controversial in relation to poverty around the world, in the sense of taking the interests of the poor to be homogenous and transparently understood.

This critical perspective seems confirmed by the fact that, in *The Most Good*, Singer reiterates his long-standing idea that one is most likely to make an effective difference to the world if one donates to global rather than to local poverty relief, in so far as the donation is likely to benefit resource-poor households in developing countries more extensively than in comparatively poor households in economically advanced states (2015: 95). However, it seems clear that there may be numerous logistical and epistemological obstacles in evaluating which wellbeing benefits are achieved by which interventions, using the equivalent resource donation or cash transfer. Therefore, one issue might be that calculating 'the most good' obviously involves many complex variables, even if one focuses on purely resource-based poverty relief. Singer is not unaware of these complexities, and he refers to the complex choices which may have to be made in particular situations, for instance whether to donate US $100,000 to preventing blindness or on feeding the starving (2015: 129). He also does not discount the need to know more about the lives of people in poverty and their values to determine true cost-effectiveness in particular cases (Singer, 2015). While the strategies of effective altruism may be understandable and even laudable in a world of unmet human needs, it seems paradoxical in some ways that Singer refers mainly to the methods for assessing cost-effectiveness adopted by the World Health Organization and the charitable organisation GiveWell (see Singer, 2015: 152). While following these officially acceptable methodologies may be justifiable on grounds of their dependability, and while, in the real world, there are obviously difficult questions as to whether participatory dialogue over human needs would sufficiently resolve these questions in a reasonable time frame, the question might remain whether the focus on quantification might involve assumptions of impartiality as regards human interests which may not fully tackle the 'forgetfulness of recognition' involved in reification, where this forgetfulness refers to a blindness to the actual standpoints and subjectivity of the very poor around the world.

In one sense, of course, it seems almost inevitable that practitioners must at times make all-things-considered evaluations of the effectiveness of particular interventions. However, from the perspective of the concept of reification raised in this chapter, it would be crucial not to discount what Schweiger (2016) refers to as the need for 'thick' and 'small' knowledge in the global justice debate. In a perspective which will be examined further in Chapter 3, Schweiger argues that 'thinking small' and 'thick descriptions' will often be needed, as these avenues have a value which cannot necessarily be factored into aggregate utilitarian calculations, but which enable people living in poverty sufficient room to express themselves and to have their views heard. According to Schweiger, when it comes to balancing a commitment to impartial human rights and attending to the lived experiences of the poor, 'it is not a question of either/or, but a question of different knowledge bases. "Windows into reality" are needed, otherwise many injustices will simply go unnoticed, unheard and ultimately will not be criticized, constituting an epistemic injustice' (2016: 104). For Schweiger, epistemic injustices towards the global poor should be considered, because poverty victims do not only experience material disadvantages but often also lack the social power to voice their own conception of value and reasons for living.

Effective altruists might of course counter-argue that their approach is not theoretically inconsistent with hearing the voices of the poor, but only that the cost-benefit analysis would have to consider the timescales and probabilities involved in discovering the subjective experiences and perspectives. However, given that it is difficult to see how effective altruists would be able to weigh diverse perspectives of suffering people on a common scale, ultimately the effective altruism movement might, despite its laudable aims, reproduce some of the same reification of global poverty as the international policies considered earlier. Singer seems aware of the challenge that, beyond measurable anti-poverty objectives such as ensuring food security, the analysis of the cost-effectiveness of programmes in relation to health, school enrolment and investment in small businesses in developing countries would be difficult to quantify, owing to the timescale needed to even know the probable benefits to wellbeing in a particular context (2015: 158). From the perspective of effective altruism, if the likelihood of discovering certain knowledge concerning a subjective standpoint of the poor is low, there may be strong reasons to opt against support for indigenous initiatives such as those, as mentioned earlier, raised by Deveaux (2021). As Berkely (2018) explains, ultimately it is also the issue of probabilities which would most likely make campaigning for global structural change a less attractive option for the effective altruist, as the realistic chances of quantifying the beneficial consequences would not be sufficiently clear.

Overall, then, despite the positive consequences of Singer's initial theory, it is effective altruism's commitment to maximising aggregate utility which may, in the nature of the approach, risk oversimplifying and potentially reifying global poverty. The focus on maximisation may inadvertently homogenise the suffering caused by poverty worldwide, as without doing so, its maximising analysis would be difficult to undertake. From the perspective of reification, the problem is not, as Srinivasan (2015) argues, that the utilitarian perspective of the 'impartial spectator' tends to divest an ethical theory of what makes it ethical, namely one's own perspective, but rather that the perspective must inevitably equalise one's own interests with others'. In doing so, it runs the risk of homogenising human interests and standpoints. In this context, Kahn (2016) and Young (2001) also suggest that the maximising impulses of utilitarianism may be problematic. They may even inadvertently reinforce what I have called the 'deep fictive forgetfulness' of global poverty. It seems crucial not to underestimate the complexity of the subjectivity of the poor as human beings, and the way in which their specific social suffering may inform their agency and their reasons for living. Therefore, in contrast with utilitarianism, a cosmopolitan recognition theory would engage the question of global justice by attending to the subjective experiences of the very poor in the midst of structural inequalities. At least, an approach which truly attempts to overcome problems of reification would need to engage experiences of disrespect, moral injury and social suffering in a way which would work to transform collective understandings of justice.

These points seem reflected in what Rubenstein (2016) views as the depoliticising effects of effective altruism. While the movement urges primary recognition of the humanity of distant others in a basic way, the movement's focus on what the individual should do and how they should live may have the effect of playing down the global structural relations which are likely, from the perspective of postcolonial development ethicists for example, to sustain global poverty, and which would therefore call for collective rather than individualist responses. The connected critique from the perspective of reification suggests two possibly more productive avenues for cosmopolitan recognition theory to pursue, namely the focus on the forms of agency which would emerge from the social suffering of the very poor, along with a normative defence on their empowerment in the context of structural constraints.

2.6 Conclusion

Following my critique of Honneth's substantive moral theory in Chapter 1, this chapter aimed to locate a starting point for presenting a full cosmopolitan response to the challenges of global poverty from the perspective of lesser-known concepts within Honneth's recognition theory. By focusing on the cosmopolitan potential of Honneth's concepts of reification and primary recognition, and after presenting this concept as a highly relevant moral critique of tendencies of the comparatively affluent not to respond to urgent questions of global poverty, I offered a particular interpretation of Honneth's post-Marxist concept of reification as the 'forgetfulness of recognition'. In so far as First-World inaction in the face of severe poverty seemed best interpreted as involving a fictive or metaphorical conception of forgetfulness, I argued Singer's utilitarian commitment to the effective altruism movement led to paradoxes in terms of undoing this form of reification, as there seems a need to attend to the complexity of the subjectivity of others' lives and suffering in such a way that would probably elude utilitarian calculations.

While one pessimistic response would be to suggest that, in view of the depth of problems raised by global poverty, it would be implausible to count on human abilities to fully address reification of modernity, nonetheless some avenues may be suggested through Deveaux's (2021) recent conceptualisation of the global poor as agents of justice. Connectedly, as reification could be taken to affect both rich and poor nations alike, it seems likely the task of addressing reification might be undertaken by encouraging partnerships which support the agency and empowerment of the very poor. In any event, and ultimately, the task of de-reifying human relations by attending to the full complexity of the lives of distant others seems crucial in terms of the cosmopolitan recognition theory to be developed in the chapters to come.

Notes

1 Key parts of this chapter draw from my earlier article, Mookherjee (2020), even though the later sections depart from and offer an alternative analysis than in my earlier exploration of this area of Honneth's thought.

2 Cudd (2014) correctly draws attention in debates concerning poverty to different forms and levels of agency. For example, they may include a conception of 'bare' agency which is involved in survival, as well as 'normative agency', defined as the capacity to act, think and decide with a view of a conception of the good life or plan of life. While, as Cudd suggests, this second idea does not obviously amount to liberal autonomy, it is nonetheless more complex than the agency which prolongs physical survival. In Chapter 3, I develop a conception of 'reason-to-value' agency of the very poor, which substantially combines Cudd's two concepts.

3 This reference to Nussbaum's concept of objectification to some extent oversimplifies her own analysis, and of the idea which a highly contested concept in the philosophical literature. For an overview of different philosophical approaches to the concept, see Papadeki (2010).

4 More specifically, Honneth's main concern is that 'Lukács in no way sought to gain knowledge of the ideological convictions that could cause entire groups of people to appear depersonalised and thus as mere things. He was so singularly focused on the effects of capitalist commodity exchange on the behaviour of social actors that he was incapable of taking note of any other social sources of reification' (Honneth, 2008: 78).

5 At the same time, the contrasting claim that public awareness, engagement and commitment to development issues have increased as a result of these international poverty-awareness campaigns would itself be difficult to demonstrate conclusively. It seems to raise difficult questions concerning how personal commitments translate into political commitment or will, or how far they affect national development policies, and whether this is usually so for altruistic or self-interested reasons. Van Heerde and Hudson (2010) provide an interesting and nuanced discussion of these issues in relation to the former Department for International Development (DFID)'s policies for the public awareness of poverty in the United Kingdom.

6 The key target of the first Millennium Development Goal was to halve extreme poverty and hunger rates by the end of 2015. The goal regarding extreme hunger was largely met by 2010, although this outcome included significant regional variations. While South Asia succeeded in meeting this target, this was not true for Sub-Saharan Africa, for instance. Moreover, the first MDG defined extreme poverty through three indicators: (1) the percentage of people living on less than US $1.25 a day; (2) the number of people who live beneath the minimum income level deemed necessary to meet basic needs; and (3) the share of national food consumption by the 20 per cent of the poorest population. It is likely these definitions do, almost inevitably, underestimate the complexity of the basic needs of people living in poverty, especially in terms of the heavy focus in this approach on income or purchasing power (see Fukuda-Parr, 2014).

7 Critical questions already seem to arise at this stage as regards who should take the lead in resisting reification in relation to global poverty. For example, is it imperative that the poor and powerless resist? Or is it the responsibility of elites to demonstrate solidarity with the very poor? Lea Ypi's (2011) discussion of the cosmopolitan avant-garde provides one extremely interesting intervention into this issue.

8 One central issue in evaluating the success of the MDGs was their focused goal of reducing 'by half the *proportion* of people who suffer from hunger' omitted from the picture the absolute number of people living in poverty (Guther, 2010).

9 In fact, within liberal cultures with an established culture of human rights, this intuition may not seem philosophically problematic. In his discussion of moral cosmopolitanism, for example, Linklater (2007) alludes to Rorty's (1989) idea that, embedded in liberal cultures is the idea that 'cruelty is the worst thing we do'.

10 Explicitly, Honneth argues that this form of 'existential sympathy' is antecedent recognition, rather than any particular benevolent reaction to the other, perhaps in terms of humanitarian assistance or campaigns for the social rights of the very poor (Honneth, 2008a: 152). While it does, then, seem clear that Honneth intends the implications of his concepts of antecedent recognition and reification to be very open and arguably ambiguous, it seems to me this openness is an advantage, in that it may have significant implications for a cosmopolitan recognition-theoretical response to poverty.

11 More specifically, Honneth expresses the point in the following way: 'Yet because Lukacs is also compelled to assert that this stance of empathetic engagement can never be lost – since, after all, it lies at the base of all social relations – his conception of society here comes up against its limit. If everything within a society is reified just because it urges the adoption of an objectifying attitude, then human sociality must have vanished completely. All these regrettable consequences result from Lukacs's conceptual strategy of reducing objectification to reification' (2008: 55).

12 This principle demands that, if a person is able to contribute to tackling life-threatening harm to others without sacrificing 'something of comparable moral significance', one ought morally to do so (Singer, 2016 [1972]). A very wide literature clearly exists debating Singer's perspective, only some of which arguments, obviously, I am able to tackle within my argument in this chapter.

References

Adorno, Theodor (1998). 'Education after Auschwitz', in *Critical Models: Interventions and Catchwords* (New York: Columbia University Press), pp. 191–204.

Adorno, Theodor W. and Walter Benjamin (1999). *The Complete Correspondence, 1929–1940* (Malden, MA: Polity Press).

Adorno, T. W. and M. Horkheimer (2002). *Dialectic of Enlightenment: Philosophical Fragments*, trans. E. Jephcott, ed. Schmidt Noerr G. (Stanford, CA: Stanford University Press).

Bentham, Jeremy (1970 [1789]), 'On the Principle of Utility', in J. Burns and H.L.A. Hart (eds), *The Collected Works of Jeremy Bentham: An Introduction to the Principles of Morals and Legislation* (Oxford: Clarendon Press), pp. 1–5.

Berkely, Brian (2018). 'The Institutional Critique of Effective Altruism', *Utilitas* 30/2: 143–171.

Boltanski, Luc (1999). *Distant Suffering: Morality, Media and Suffering* (Cambridge: Cambridge University Press).

Butler, Judith (2008). 'Taking Another's View: Ambivalent Implications', in M. Jay (ed), *Reification: An Old Look at a New Idea* (Oxford: Oxford University Press), pp. 97–119.

Caney, Simon (2015). 'Responding to Global Injustice: On the Right of Resistance', *Social Philosophy and Policy* 32/1: 51–73.

Chari, Amrita (2010). 'Towards a Political Critique of Reification: Lukacs, Honneth and the Aims of Critical Theory', *Philosophy and Social Criticism* 36/5: 587–606.

Cudd, Ann (2014). 'Agency and Intervention: How (Not) to Fight Global Poverty', in Diana Teitjens Meyers (ed), *Poverty, Agency and Human Rights* (Oxford: Oxford University Press), pp. 197–222.

Deveaux, Monique (2015). 'The Global Poor as Agents of Justice', *Journal of Moral Philosophy* 12/2: 125–150.

Deveaux, Monique (2021). *Poverty, Solidarity and Poor-Led Social Movements* (Oxford: Oxford University Press).

Fox, Laura (2016). 'Hardship in the Headlines: Global Poverty and Neocolonialism in the Western News Media', *Artigos*16/29: 191–200.

Fukuda-Parr, Saikko (2014). 'Global Goals as a Policy Tool: Intended and Unintended Consequences', *Journal of Human Development and Capabilities* 15/2–3: 118–131.

Gabriel, Iason (2016). 'Explaining Inaction in the Face of Extreme Poverty', Working Paper for the Study of Social Justice (Working Paper Series SJ036, Oxford University – February), pp. 2–28.

Gabriel, Iason (2017). 'Effective Altruism and its Critics', *Journal of Applied Philosophy* 34: 457–473.

Giddens, Anthony (1994). *The Consequences of Modernity* (Cambridge: Polity Press).

Gunderson, Ryan (2020). 'Things are the Way they Are: A Typology of Reification', *Sociological Perspectives* 64/1: 1–20.

Guther, Tamar (2010). 'When "Doing Good" Does Not: The IMF and the Millennium Development Goals', in D. Avant, M. Finnemore and S. Sell (eds), *Who Governs the Globe* (Cambridge: Cambridge University Press), pp. 262–296.

Honneth, Axel (2001). 'Invisibility: On the Epistemology of "Recognition"', *Proceedings of the Aristotelian Society* 75/Supplement: 111–126.

Honneth, Axel (2007). 'Recognition as Ideology', in David Owen and Bert van der Brink (eds), *Recognition and Power: Axel Honneth and the Tradition of Critical Social Theory* (Cambridge: CUP), pp. 323–347.

Honneth, Axel (2008). 'Reification and Recognition: A New Look at an Old Idea', in Martin Jay (ed), *Reification: A New Look at an Old Idea* (Oxford: Oxford University Press), pp. 17–98.

Honneth, Axel (2008a). 'Rejoinder', in Martin Jay (ed), *Reification: A New Look at An Old Idea* (Oxford: Oxford University Press) (Oxford: Oxford University Press), pp. 147–160.

Hull, George (2013). 'Reification and Social Criticism', *Philosophical Papers* 42/1: 49–77.

Jutten, Timo (2010). 'What is Reification? A Critique of Axel Honneth', *Inquiry* 53/3: 235–256.

Kahn, Elisabeth (2016). 'Poverty, Injustice and Obligations to Take Political Action', in Helmut Gainsbauer, Gottfried Schweiger and Clemens Sedmak (eds), *Ethical Issues in Poverty Alleviation* (Dordrecht: Springer), pp. 209–224.

Latour, Bruno (1987). *Science in Action: How to Follow Scientists and Engineers through Society* (Cambridge, MA: Harvard University Press).

Lear, Jonathan (2008). 'The Slippery Middle', in M. Jay (ed), *Reification: A New Look at a New Idea* (Oxford: Oxford University Press), pp. 131–146.

Linklater, Andrew (2007). 'Distant Suffering and Cosmopolitan Obligations', *International Politics* 44: 19–36.

Lukács, Georg (1967 [1923]). 'Reification and the Consciousness of the Proletariat', in *History of Class Consciousness* (London: Merlin).

MacAskill, William (2014). 'Replaceability, Career Choice and Making a Difference', *Ethical Theory and Moral Practice* 17: 269–283.

Merry, S. E. (2011). 'Measuring the World: Indicators, Human Rights and Global Governance', *Current Anthropology* 52/53: 83–95.

Mookherjee, Monica (2020). 'On Axel Honneth's Cosmopolitanism: The 'Forgetfulness' of Global Poverty as a Form of Reification', *Social Theory and Practice* (October) 46/4: 785–811.

Morgan, Alasdair (2014). ''The Living Entity': Reification and Forgetting', *European Journal of Social Theory* 17/4: 377–388.

Mussell, Simon (2013). '"Pervaded by a Chill": The Dialectic of Coldness in Adorno's Social Theory', *Thesis Eleven* 117/1: 55–67.

Nussbaum, Martha (1995). 'Objectification', *Philosophy and Public Affairs* 24/4: 249–291.

Papadeki, L. (2010). 'What is Objectification?' *Journal of Moral Philosophy* 7/11: 16–36.

Parton, Andrew and Marin Kirk (2011). 'Finding Frames: New Ways to Engage the Public on Global Poverty'. Available at: Finding_Frames_New_ways_to_engage_the_UK_public_in_global_poverty_Bond_2011.pdf (kaidara.org). Accessed 18.7.22.

Porter, T. M. (1994). 'Making Things Quantifiable', *Science in Context* 7/3: 389–407.

Rorty, Richard (1989). *Contingency, Irony and Solidarity* (Cambridge: Cambridge University Press).

Rubenstein, Jennifer (2007). 'Distribution and Emergency', *The Journal of Political Philosophy* 15/3: 296–320.

Rubenstein, Jennifer (2016). 'The Lessons of Effective Altruism', *Ethics and International Affairs* 30/4: 511–526.

Sayers, Sean (2009). Review of A. Honneth, *Reification: A New Look at an Old Idea*', *Mind* 118: 476–479.
Saith, Ashwani (2005). 'Poverty Lines versus the Poor: Method versus Meaning', *Economic and Political Weekly* 40/3: 4601–4610.
Schweiger, Gottfried (2016). 'Epistemic Injustice and Powerlessness in the Context of Global Justice: An Argument from 'Thick' and 'Small' Knowledge', *Wagadu* 15: 104–125.
Sidgwick, Henry (2019 [1874]). *The Methods of Ethics* (London: The Good Polity).
Silvio, Dominic Hakim (2013). 'The Impact of Transnational Aid Campaigns on Public Opinion and Foreign Aid Policy: A Critical Analysis of Make Poverty History (MPH) in Canada', *International Journal of Interdisciplinary Social Sciences Annual Review* 7: 1–12.
Singer, Peter (2010). *The Life You Can Save: How to Play your Part in Ending World Poverty* (London: Pan MacMillan Press).
Singer, Peter (2015). *The Most Good You Can Do: How Effective Altruism is Changing Views about Living Ethically* (London: Text Publishing).
Singer, Peter (2016 [1972). 'Famine, Affluence and Morality', reprinted in P. Singer, *Famine, Affluence and Morality* (Oxford: Oxford University Press), pp. 1–33.
Sen, Amartya (1990). 'Development as Capabilities Expansion', in J. DeFilipis and S. Saegert (eds), *The Community Development Reader* (London: Routledge), pp. 319–328.
Sen, Amartya (1990a). *Poverty and Famines: An Essay on Entitlement and Deprivation* (Oxford: Oxford University Press).
Singer, Peter (2015). *The Most Good You Can Do: How Effective Altruism is Changing Ideas about Living Ethically* (New Haven: Yale University Press).
Srinivasan, A. (2015). 'Stop the Robot Apocalypse', *London Review of Books* 37/18 (24th September): 3–6.
Van Heerde, J. and David Hudson (2010). '"The Righteous Considereth the Case of the Global Poor": Public Attitudes towards Poverty in Developing Countries', *Political Studies* 58: 389–409.
Varga, Samogy (2010). 'Critical *Theory* and the Two-Level Account of Recognition', *Critical Horizons* 11/1: 23–38.
Varga, Samogy and Shaun Gallagher (2012). 'Critical Social Philosophy, Honneth and the Role of Primary Intersubjectivity', *European Journal of Social Theory* 15/2: 243–260.
Young, Iris Marion (2001). 'Equality between Whom? Social Groups and Judgements of Injustice', *Journal of Political Philosophy* 9/1: 1–18.
Young, Iris Marion (2006). 'Responsibility and Global Justice: A Social Connection Model', *Social Philosophy and Policy* 23/1: 102–130.
Young, Iris (2010). *Responsibility for Justice* (Oxford: Oxford University Press).
Ypi, L. (2011). *Global Justice and Avant Garde Political Theory* (Oxford: Oxford University Press).

3 Defining the First Tier of a Recognition-Based Response to Global Poverty

Social Suffering, Survivalist Agency and Humanitarian Concern for the World's Poor[1]

3.1 Introduction

How, therefore, might a cosmopolitan recognition theory respond to serious problems of material deprivation which affect billions of people worldwide? The arguments in the previous chapters have suggested a starting point for a recognition-based response to global poverty, with Chapter 2 defending the idea that Honneth's concepts of reification and antecedent recognition shed crucial light on the ethical problems presented by material oppression in the world. These concepts, I suggested, responded to what has often seemed to be a profound reluctance in the affluent world to respond meaningfully to the dire situation of worldwide poverty.

While this conceptual approach appeared to emphasise a broad starting point in recognition theory, the outcome of my analysis of Peter Singer's response to global poverty in Chapter 2, to recall again, suggested two normative foci for a full response from the perspective of recognition theory. Specifically, I suggested that this approach would first aim for a deeper explanation of how people are harmed by global forms of poverty, beyond the sole issue of lacking material resources. Second, and connectedly, this cosmopolitan approach would concentrate on questions of agency, social suffering and empowerment rather than the impartial human interests suggested by Singer in defence of a utilitarian humanitarian ethos towards the world's poor. Therefore, the first substantive layer of a cosmopolitan recognition theory in relation to global poverty would concentrate on how poverty affects the elemental dignity and agency of many around the world, rather than focusing purely on the question of possessing material resources.

Following my previous arguments, then, the present chapter turns towards the conception of agency which would enable the very poor to survive and subsist. I begin with the intuition that truly acknowledging the claims of the very poor entails recognising that even the most elemental harms of poverty are likely to bear complex implications for people in terms of their capacities to negotiate structural constraints. Supporting

DOI: 10.4324/9781003045038-4

these capacities would highlight practices of human development sufficient to encourage welfare distribution and social rights beyond a pure focus on resources, which would, in turn, support people in mitigating the different vulnerabilities which they experience in sustaining a decent life (Lagon and Kaminski, 2017; Eade, 2010). The complexity of the concept which this chapter defines as 'reason-to-value' agency takes its cue from, but extends the implications of, the insights of the capabilities approach. As suggested previously, this approach has productively aimed to focus human development not only on chronic denials of material needs but also on the political and psychological dimensions of the condition of poverty (Sen, 1990; Deveaux, 2018; Gaisbauer et al., 2016).

Concentrating, then, on the efforts of people around the world to survive extreme poverty, the allusive concept of social suffering provides a key first focus for a cosmopolitan recognition theory. This focus may not seem unexpected in view of the fact that recognition theorists very often begin their analyses by focusing on lived experiences of disrespect and degradation. Whilst Honneth's theory once again suggests a useful point of departure, owing to its core focus on these first-person experiences, this chapter turns away from Honneth's own conception of social suffering to focus instead on the contributions of continental social theorist Emmanuel Renault (2011; 2017) and the Anglophone perspectives of Iain Wilkinson and Arthur Kleinman et al. (2016). Taken together, their insights into the concept of social suffering provide a crucial perspective on the deep objectives of Frankfurt School thought, namely liberation and emancipation, which seem to have particular resonance as regards global poverty.

More specifically, the turn towards the concept of social suffering seems especially apt because, where social structures become pathological, entrenching social and economic inequalities, a cosmopolitan recognition theory would need to scrutinise these forms of oppression, and, in particular, the forms of agency which might emanate from suffering when people struggle to survive the injustices which which Pierre Bourdieu (Bourdieu and Accardo, 1999: 225) has called an 'inequality over rights to the future'. In particular, my discussion will suggest the symbiosis of social suffering and the possibility of a culturally plural or culturally open form of agency. While this form of agency is likely to be relevant to the eventual emergence of the recognition struggles of the poor, it does not count on the emergence of collective movements or recognition struggles in the fullest sense. Put differently, although this form of agency does not presume the unity or coordinated interests needed for full recognition struggles, it considers the ways in which, even in the course of their suffering, people retain the capacity to think, act and decide innovatively according to their conception of the good and reasons for living. This is so, despite the risk that these strategies for survival are likely to amount only to the 'weapons of the weak' (Scott, 1990), which may reinforce or fail to address the deeper social structures maintaining people in cycles of poverty. Despite these limitations, cosmopolitan recognition theory would acknowledge the various ways in which people seek dignity through creative strategising. The concept of reason-to-value agency normatively implies the need to consider protecting these dynamic forms of agency. The important task is not to reify or to accept social suffering as inevitable, but rather to acknowledge that many do exercise dignity and agency in the context of considerable social and economic constraints.

The chapter is structured as follows. Section 3.2 turns to Honneth's focus on social suffering, in particular the relationship which he draws between first-person experiences of social suffering and a consciousness of injustice. The ambiguities in Honneth's conception lead to the chapter's major focus, namely Renault's alternative conception of social suffering, which questions the semantic link presumed by Honneth between suffering and the impetus for resistance against injustice, but which, nevertheless, suggests the potential for creative action despite one's structural constraints. While this conception of social suffering seems to relate to the 'psychosocial' or 'welfare subject' in advanced European states, Section 3.4 develops the global reach of the concept of social suffering by focusing on Wilkinson and Kleinman's (2016) complementary approach. Wilkinson and Kleinman crucially highlight the global humanitarian impulses of the social scientific focus on suffering, implying the need to uncover the 'epistemic' standpoints of the very poor and to unveil non-dominant modes of human development, for example. Section 3.5, finally, highlights the significance of focusing on the symbiosis of suffering and innovative forms of agency in a cosmopolitan recognition theory. Theoretically, despite the limitations of the concept for fully tackling worldwide forms of poverty, the focus on what I call 'reason-to-value' agency implies commitments not only to social rights to protect these forms of agency but also a focus on practices of human development geared towards securing real capacities to mitigate one's vulnerabilities and to live according to one's own idea of the good.

3.2 Honneth and the Question of Material Deprivation: Misrecognition as Moral Injury and a Sense of Injustice

The chapters of this book have so far suggested that Honneth's substantive recognition theory brings both advantages and disadvantages for a normative response to global poverty. On the one hand, his theory contains valuable resources to challenge inequalities of wealth in modern societies. For example, his strong twofold critique of economic inequalities, by referring to deficits in social rights and in the distribution of esteem, seems insightful. However, owing especially to the challenges involved in fully universalising the criteria for esteem in societies globally with their own forms of life, it seemed Honneth's three modes of recognition prove to be problematic avenues for a full cosmopolitan theory. In addition to his focus on reification, however, Honneth contributes a further crucial insight through his key focus on experiences of grievance and moral injury as the psycho-social origin of struggles for recognition (1995: 135–138). This focus on moral injury and distress, which follows from what the person perceives as a disappointed expectation for respect, seems highly relevant for the first substantive layer of a recognition-based response to global poverty.

Honneth justifies his focus on social suffering by insisting that it is these experiences which appear to explain and justify the emergence of struggles against injustice. As he insists, the grievances experienced by the marginalised and oppressed are unlikely to be meaningless or random. Whilst it is conceivable that people may feel aggrieved for obscure reasons, it seems more likely to assume that these sentiments arise from genuine perceptions of withheld respect, in such a way which is likely to be, as Honneth suggests, semantically related to the normative principles of their societies (1995: 136). Of course, the ambiguity arising is whether these moral grievances should be understood from a first-person or objective perspective. The question seems vital, as the diversity of negative sentiments worldwide in response to different forms of inequality could presumably not all be taken as the legitimate starting points for a challenge to global poverty.

The point proves ambiguous through much of Honneth's writings, an ambiguity which seems to be revealed by his statement in *The Struggle for Recognition* that 'the experience of the withdrawal of social recognition – of degradation and disrespect – must be at the centre of a meaningful concept of socially caused suffering and injustice' (1995: 132). It seems unclear from this statement whether the concept depends on the sufferer's own perception, and whether, if so, the sufferer should always be assumed to perceive a link between their experience of disrespect and injustice in the normative order of society. More specifically, the challenge confronting a cosmopolitan recognition theory seems to be that, if Honneth were taken purely to intend to refer to first-person perspectives, it seems genuinely difficult to see how all of these feelings of grievance would ground anti-poverty struggles worldwide. Conversely, it also does not seem unlikely that chronic inter-generational poverty could suppress an individual's consciousness of their condition as a collective injustice. While Honneth's focus on subjective grievances may seem to avoid the pitfalls, as discussed in Chapter 1, of an overly objective conception of misrecognition as damaged social status (Fraser, in Fraser and Honneth, 2003), it seems empirically doubtful that the poor and powerless will always be able to construct a meaningful link between their private experiences and a broader perception of their situation as a collective injustice. For reasons to be explored, it would not be self-evident they would view their situation as 'impersonal aspirations of a social movement' (Honneth, 1995: 163). Bader (2007) therefore seems right to counter-argue that the poor and powerless may be, to a certain degree, psychically incapacitated by their poverty. If this point is true, it suggests the self-conscious emergence of what Honneth calls a 'semantic bridge' between suffering and the perception of injustice would become problematic to assume.

The possibility that Honneth means to refer to first-person perceptions of social suffering seems borne out by his focus on what he takes to be the motivational impulses behind the historical movement towards recognition of social rights in industrialising European states. He interprets the campaigns of the working-classes for labour rights as self-aware movements by the economically disadvantaged. The normative principle of equal rights was 'there from the start as a guiding idea' (1995: 115), he argues, arising from collective perceptions of a justified social grievance. This interpretation does not seem implausible, in that it seems difficult to see how a variety of social movements historically, including labour rights and campaigns for women's suffrage, would have arisen without first-person feelings of discontent. Honneth's argument, therefore, that people are 'incapable of reacting in emotionally neutral ways' to perceptions of injustice (1995: 138) seems apt for a cosmopolitan recognition theory, not least as it appears to resonate with the recent focus in poverty studies on the active struggles of the poor. For example, it seems reasonable to assume the emergence of the land reclamation movements in Brazil of which Deveaux (2021) recently writes originated from subjective awareness of a collective injustice. This perspective would, moreover, suggest the productive view of the poor as agents in their own right, rather than as passive victims of injustice.

However, to return to the point raised previously, it also seems empirically questionable to presuppose the very poor necessarily do form this clear perception of injustice. Rather, many may conceptualise their situation as a question of personal responsibility, which may undermine the prospects of forming a mentality or spirit of resistance (Thompson, 2006: 166). Additionally, given the multidimensionality of poverty raised previously, which may arise as regards health deprivations or deficits in literacy or essential educational resources, it seems especially difficult to count on personal sentiments to lead the very poor to organise collectively. While, as Chapter 2 discussed, Deveaux's examples suggest that collective action and concrete recognition struggles do emerge, in many cases there is likely to be a long and complex route from the experience of distress to the formation of collective resistance. In fact, Honneth himself suggests caveats which imply his awareness of this point, in such a way which suggests that perhaps his real focus is not so much on social suffering as on the idea of struggle.[2] On this basis, Amy Allen (2010) concludes that Honneth's apparent central preoccupation with the concept of struggling for recognition risks leading his theory away from recognising fully that some forms of domination work to prevent the emergence of coordinated social movements.

Given the ambiguities of the role of social suffering in Honneth's theory, it is worth taking a cosmopolitan analysis towards a different version of the concept, one which depends less on Honneth's assumption of a probable linear connection between suffering and the emergence of a social movement against injustice (Pilapil, 2011). In other words, it seems worth examining further the role of social suffering, especially as Honneth's own objective over time has been to question 'ideological' forms of recognition which risk leading the oppressed to ready compliance with the status quo. In particular, in his discussion of the concept of ideological recognition, Honneth refers to the frequent tendency of women especially to be identified with emotional labour to a point of obscuring the forms of suffering this ideological identification might entail (Honneth, 2007; Worsdale, 2017). Connectedly, the alternative conception of social suffering I pursue in this chapter will begin from an awareness of the risks of representing the poor as 'merely poor', an ideological representation which may in a practical sense presume too much compliance and lack of agency (Worsdale, 2017). I aim to suggest that poverty-related suffering may lead to creative forms of agency, even if it does not cognitively disclose the existence of injustice to the sufferer. As Iris Young (2007) similarly argues, drawing on the concept of ideological recognition, it seems clear that only too often suffering may not lead the oppressed to a cognitive understanding of their situation as unjust.

Briefly, therefore, Honneth's thought seems again to provide a key starting point for a cosmopolitan recognition theory, albeit one which seems ambiguous in some ways from the perspective of analysing the harms of global poverty. For cosmopolitan recognition theorists, Honneth's theory proves vital to the world-disclosive potential of starting from the lived experiences of the oppressed. In contrast, however, with Honneth's seeming assumption that suffering will lead to cognitive disclosure of injustice, and thus to the possibility of a unified and purposive recognition struggle with others, I turn to forms of social suffering which cannot always be named as such from a first-person perspective. Although, as I hope to show, they do not always undermine agency, these forms of suffering risk leaving the very poor without the unity necessary for the emergence of a coordinated recognition struggle, and at times with only the most paradoxical strategies of resistance.

3.3 Renault and the Invisibility of Social Suffering: Reorienting the Normative Critique of Poverty as Misrecognition

In order to unfold this more complex conception of social suffering, Emmanuel Renault's theory proves vital. Drawing from theoretical perspectives ranging from French sociologists of work such as Dejours to the much-discussed writings of Bourdieu, Renault focuses on the factors preventing many disadvantaged groups from articulating their experience of injustice with the social unity necessary to form a coordinated campaign for the recognition of a shared injustice (Renault, 2005, 2007a, 2017). Two interlocking features of Renault's conception of social suffering offer a cosmopolitan recognition theory a crucial preliminary focus, namely the subjective unnameability of the experience as suffering and, connectedly, the absence of a collective 'language of pain' uniting diverse people in materially similar situations.

Renault's writings over time have gone substantially beyond the dominant Hegelian focus of recognition theory, even though he clearly locates his theory within this field (Renault, 2007, 2007a). Along with his frequent collaborator Jean-Philippe Deranty, Renault has largely endorsed the key Frankfurt School premises in viewing the moral injuries of real people as the starting point for justice rather than focusing on issues of rights and goods alone (Renault and Deranty, 2007). Specifically, Renault and Deranty take issue with what may be viewed as the surprisingly de-politicising effects of Honneth's tendency to characterise misrecognition as the failure of the conditions of one-to-one or interpersonal respect and esteem. By contesting the idea that feelings of moral injury arise from a society's failure to meet a person's pre-political desire for respect, Renault productively shifts attention to political and economic arrangements which produce forms of suffering which cannot be meaningfully understood in such an institutionally unmediated way (Renault and Deranty, 2007: 98). While Honneth's concept of ideological recognition does of course seem intrinsically concerned with the role of institutions, Renault purposefully shifts attention to forms of social suffering which arise in modern societies in ways which are always from the outset formed by material conditions and institutional structures, and which imply suffering which is likely to have a silencing effect. In contrast, also, with the conception of 'the least well-off' in society as conceived by liberal individualist, Rawlsian justice, Renault takes social suffering as at least partially defined by its incapacity to name itself (Renault, 2010), a point which complicates the link between the experience of suffering and the desire to struggle for the recognition of a shared, oppressed identity.

More specifically, by referring to the social distress depicted by Bourdieu (Renault, 2007: chapter 6; Bourdieu and Accardo, 1999), Renault refers to the diverse experiences found in hesitant and muted responses to social and economic life in advanced European industrialised societies, reactions which often lead to silent compliance with one's situation (see also Peters, 2012), or a 'destiny of inert violence', to invoke Bourdieu's phrase (Bourdieu and Accardo, 1999: 64). For Renault, the focus on social suffering is crucial because 'there is an imperative within critical theory ... to take up the struggle against invisibilization of social suffering within its own discourse' (2009: 164). At the same time, for Renault, it is also theoretically significant that social suffering has proved so elusive to define. More frequently, for example, Bourdieu opts to use the term *misère* (misery; poverty) rather than *souffrance* (suffering), even though one of his major works, *The Weight of the World*, seem centrally concerned with social suffering. For Renault, it is significant that more broadly, across a wide range of studies, also including Dejours' *Souffrances en France* (1998), the concept of social suffering remains under-specified, a *terme sans concept*, or a term without a definition (2007a: 330).

In aiming to explore the concept more explicitly, Renault's first dimension of social suffering overlaps with some Anglophone conceptions which focus on lived experiences of pain, damage, injury, deprivation and loss often only imperfectly expressed due to social, material and cultural conditions (Renault, 2010; Wilkinson, n.d.:1). Focusing on economically advanced societies, and, therefore, on contexts in which the basic needs of most people have been met, the social suffering of many people is expressed only hesitantly, not entirely capable of naming itself as injustice. Like Bourdieu, Renault does not equate these experiences with *la grande misère* (extreme poverty or destitution) of a class or nation. Rather, he focuses on *les petites misères*, the many anxieties borne by ordinary people who struggle to survive on low wages for exhausting work (Renault, 2010; Dejours, 1998). For Renault, these experiences cannot always be expressed as unmet expectations for rights or esteem suggested by liberal or social-democratic frameworks. Yet the focus on the hidden injuries of economic disadvantage promises to 'bring whole sections of society out of invisibility' (2017: 5). Following Bourdieu and Dejours once again, Renault substantially questions the adequacy of social rights and redistributive compromises promised by these frameworks, and therefore suggests a concept which reflects the psycho-social and non-material impacts of poverty-related suffering.

At this point, Renault further refers to the tendency of the underprivileged towards self-doubt as regards their subjective perceptions of injustice (2007a: 327). While the subjective nature of suffering also renders it challenging to evaluate from an external perspective, it is an aspect of social suffering which overlaps with its second component, namely the absence of a validating 'language of pain' in which to express one's experience. The interaction between these aspects of suffering seems to complicate the efforts by the poor to resist their existential conditions in a socially coordinated way (Sayer, 2005: 35; Lovell, 2007: 74). The point seems borne out by the fact that, despite the poor-led social movements which have emerged in recent European states, ordinary people clearly still need to survive within the existing economic division of labour. Renault's awareness of this point suggests a conception of misrecognition which is more modest, and not so 'loaded with normative expectations', as Honneth's idea (2010: 235).[3]

More specifically, the first dimension of Renault's conception of social suffering refers implicitly to the struggles of the underprivileged over symbolic capital. Associated with Bourdieu's thought, this concept refers to the advantages that the person gains through identification with, or 'recognition' according to, a particular hierarchical symbolic system or scheme of reciprocally accepted meanings relating to lifestyles, choices and beliefs (Bourdieu, 2013).[4] This concept appears crucial to Bourdieu's own exploration of the harms involved in social suffering, which involves a wider theoretical narrative associating desires for recognition mostly with the dominated (Bourdieu, 1987; Harker, Mahar and Wilkes, 2016). In this sense, Renault appears to follow Bourdieu in assuming the social suffering of the very poor to arise from their embattled efforts to partake of the criteria for prestige according to a system of social meanings which reflects the symbolic power, or the values, preferences and choices, of the socially dominant (Bourdieu, 2013; see also Lovell 2007). The paradox involved in social suffering is therefore that, while people might only experience psychological pain if they perceive injustice, it is exactly the difficulties of naming the experience as unjust, since it depends on their own perception of a need to attain the lifestyle or mode of living of the economically dominant, which seems to suggest the injustice. From this perspective, the collectively political nature of the suffering of many becomes almost inevitably obscured.

This conception of social suffering may again be illustrated by Bourdieu's ethnographic studies in *The Weight of the World* (Bourdieu and Accardo, 1999) of the experiences of conflict, precarity and immigrant ghettoisation in French suburban housing developments. These narratives mostly do not suggest the explicit resistance of the underprivileged to an economic crisis (Bourdieu and Accardo, 1999; Renault, 2017).[5] Rather, they seem to be revealed through hesitation, fatigue and world-weariness. Bourdieu's well-known discussion of these issues includes extended interviews conducted with, for example, a permanent and temporary worker at the same car factory; a steel worker laid off after 20 years and struggling to support his family on unemployment benefits; and an Algerian family who encounter racism in the suburb to which they had to relocate (1999: 100; 109; 239). In drawing from related experiences of the hidden injuries of economic disadvantage, Renault's theory highlights the lack of social unity between different sections of the underprivileged, and their subjective experiences of isolation, de-politicisation and alienation from the wider political society. While this does not mean that resistance or oppositional agency are impossible, their experiences of malaise are likely to be uncoordinated rather than grounded in solidarities with others sharing their predicament (Renault, 2007a: 331).

Ultimately, social suffering in Renault's sense therefore questions the grand narratives of resources, rights or even social esteem, and focuses instead on forms of harm which, while debilitating, do also leave open certain opportunities for resistance. As Peters expresses the point, only too often the poor and powerless may comply resignedly, along with a 'very conscious and many times discursively articulated experience of acute criticism and painful reflection on [their] social environment and the conditions of [their] existence' (Peters, 2012: 79). While these painful reflections may lead to everyday forms of resistance, they tend not to be expressed in terms of a collective moral injury. Additionally, the comparatively isolated and ununified experiences of the underprivileged are, Renault suggests, likely to be fueled by '*complexes de culpabilisation*' (tendencies towards self-blame) (2007a: 333), which follow from the ways in which modern bureaucratic states render the social hardships of many ordinary people invisible.

This first feature of social suffering, namely its hesitant expression, seems therefore constituted by the person's awareness of 'structural conditions which offer no means of respite or escape' (Wilkinson, n.d.: 6). That is, due to the overlap between social and mental structures (Renault, 2004: 4), even in the act of resisting, the poor and powerless are likely to be unclear as regards to whom or to what they should be opposed. Renault aptly illustrates this issue through a discussion 'sans' movements (the *sans-papiers*, *sans-logis*, *sans-emplois*; undocumented migrants, the homeless and the unemployed). While in one sense it is true that these groups have acted collectively, their lack of social or cultural unity or other strong grounds for commonality suggests, for Renault, the absence of the common identity needed for a concerted struggle for recognition. It is not only that these struggles are constituted through a particular lack (i.e. of legal residency, of housing or of employment) rather than a pre-existing common identity (Renault, 2007a: 328). Rather, it is also that wider neoliberal discourse, for instance, seems to deepen divisions between the unemployed and salaried workers who struggle for better working conditions (Renault, 2007a: 230), a situation which further prevents the poor or the exploited from perceiving the injustice of their situation.

These arguments lead Renault to refer again to the second feature of his concept of social suffering, namely the unavailability of a political discourse in which it may be expressed (2017: 32–33). At this stage, he draws from anthropologists Veena Das and Arthur Kleinman (Das, 1995; 1997; Das, Kleinman, Lock and Lock, 1997), who emphasise the lack of an available 'language of pain' in the aftermath of scenes of social devastation. For instance, Das focuses on the mass rapes of women at the time of Partition in India, at the moment of political independence, the horror of which was lost within public efforts to accommodate it within a discourse which justified a shared communal identity. By analogy, Renault refers to the ideological script offered in advanced European economies in which the disaffection of the poor is often reported as a social vice (2017; 107–108; Wacquant, 2008), in ways that even assertions of 'violence against the poor' raised by the political left tend to leave unaddressed. As Renault explains: '[t]he simple reference to violence and to dehumanization can take account neither of the ways in which these different elements are experienced as indissociable by [the sufferers] nor of the social and psychological dynamics which structure the drama lived through' (2017: 85–86).

One concern with this analysis is that it would overstate experiences of social suffering to suggest that there is no meaningful language in which to express their existential or intrapsychic effects; or to suggest that people who suffer in particular ways share no language of desired political transformation. For instance, the *sans* movements, or 'have-nots', do seem to have formed limited alliances on the basis of shared experiences which have enabled them to advance their claims for inclusion and for particular rights (see Chimienti and Solomos, 2011). More broadly, despite their cultural and ethnic heterogeneity, in France and elsewhere in Europe different underprivileged groups have reacted with a shared sense of grievance (Jetten, et al., 2020). Yet, despite these counter-arguments, Renault's alertness to the frequently dispersed nature of the struggles of the economically disadvantaged seems borne out by the concerns that ultimately the different *sans* movements have been divided over the objectives of their struggle (McNevin, 2009; Nandi, 2021), and the fact, as suggested by Dufour (2009), of internal disagreements as to whether to pursue social inclusion or to struggle for transformation of the wider society. From the perspective of a cosmopolitan recognition theory, the concern may be that the aim for inclusion within dominant, universalist conceptions of social justice and human rights may not enable suffering people to communicate their experience in terms of a demand for a better life from the specific perspective of their hardship.

The two features of Renault's conception of social suffering therefore seem to interlock, suggesting a lack of cohesive social unity between the underprivileged within advanced European states, a situation which complicates the emergence of their struggles for recognition. If his idea is convincing, Renault's concept suggests theoretical keys to understanding the role of social suffering further afield, within a cosmopolitan framework, an issue which I examine next. This is to say, Renault's concept of social suffering appears to move productively beyond Honneth's 'semantic bridge' conception towards a compelling concept for a cosmopolitan recognition theory aimed at dignifying the world's poor.

3.4 Social Suffering, Epistemic Injustice and an Ethos of Humanitarian Concern

As the normative implications of Renault's approach may appear uncertain at the global level, to examine its cosmopolitan implications I turn at this stage to Iain Wilkinson and Arthur Kleinman's (2016) further insights. Their account explicitly associates the social scientific study of social suffering with the historical development of a worldwide normative humanitarian ethic. More specifically, they have focused on the global dimensions of social suffering, a focus which is implicitly connected, as I shall argue, with what may be called the 'epistemic injustices' confronting the global poor (Schweiger, 2016). As will now be suggested, combining the insights of Renault, Wilkinson and Kleinman reveals the need normatively to defend forms of dynamic agency of the poor globally, which are likely to coexist with, and arise from, their social suffering. For the very poor around the world, this form of agency may be taken to suggest at least the initial starting-point for the fuller recognition struggles which would assist to dignify their lives.

Wilkinson and Kleinman begin by acknowledging that, from its disciplinary beginnings, social inquiry was geared towards improving the lives of the worst off in society. Against the sentiment-based theories of Adam Smith and David Hume, however, the growth of impartial rational choice paradigms especially in disciplines such as economics tended to concentrate on the standpoint of 'the general other' (2016: 61; see also Wilkinson, 2005), turning away from the small-scale micro-narratives of distress and disaffiliation so crucial to the humanitarian impulses of social science. Wilkinson and Kleinman's emphasis on the need to refocus attention on these narratives seems crucial. For while it may be true, as Renault suggests, that only too often the poor and powerless are likely to lack the social unity to mount a coordinated recognition struggle, Wilkinson and Kleinman seem right to suggest that the renewed focus on their social suffering promises to reveal, worldwide, alternative knowledge about humanity or concerning human needs than that which could be suggested by the impartial, 'detached spectator' of rational choice frameworks.

This interpretation seems supported by Wilkinson and Kleinman's strong focus on contemporary global forms of social suffering. Included amongst their examples is the situation of rural migrant workers in the Chinese economy, now caught up in one of the greatest internal migrations in history. In attempting to escape rural poverty, they have risked a marginal existence by losing the cultural security of their traditional *hukoku* household registration system (2016: 3). From a cosmopolitan perspective, the example highlights the fact that, beyond questions of resources, forms of suffering associated with global poverty may often involve the loss of traditional cultural identity, chronic fatigue, ritualised humiliations, depressive symptoms and disease, all effects which 'upend lives, break bodies and vex minds' (2016: 3).[6] From this perspective, social suffering should therefore be viewed globally, involving experiences which may be cruel and inhuman.

Moreover, the most profound instances of social suffering around the world may be 'ineffable' (2016: 5), or difficult to rationalise, as they persist in apparently civilised forms of life committed to human rights and social justice. That is, it may be impossible to convey these experiences in the ordinary, legalistic language of a human rights violation. As Wilkinson and Kleinman ask:

> What form of language is suited to convey the "violence" that is done to more than a billion people who are born into the rapidly expanding slum districts of the megacities of the developing world, and who are largely abandoned to work at surviving in diseased environments [...]? How do we represent the losses and ungrounded lives of the world's 50 million refugees? And how do we use the language and understanding that we do possess in order to respond?
>
> (2016: 6)

Rather than being irrational or meaningless, however, for Wilkinson and Kleinman social suffering is likely to vacillate between excessive and diminished meaning. On the one hand, people who suffer inescapably attempt to attribute meaning to the experience, as it would be unusual to suffer without any subjective consciousness of doing so, and without any attempt to rationalise the experience. On the other hand, these forms of suffering are also likely to be 'unspeakable' or 'unacceptable to consciousness' (2016: 7). Therefore, while the poor and the powerless may attempt to respond to their situations by adapting to or minimising their circumstances, the social nature of their suffering seems revealed by a tension or contradiction they are likely to perceive between the psychological experience and the ideals of their society, such as rational commitments to human rights (Wilkinson and Kleinman, 2016: 10). This apparent paradox seems reflected in the social suffering of many globally who are caught in rapidly changing social and economic labour conditions, precarious employment and unstable climatic conditions leading to the destruction of livelihoods.

For Wilkinson and Kleinman, the social scientist's focus on global forms of social suffering raises a normative call to action. Their focus intrinsically opposes 'unthinking acceptance of the way things are' (2016: 9). In this sense, the focus on global suffering alerts to the need to suggest which sort of injustice is caused by these forms of suffering. The social scientific effort to reveal social suffering seems intrinsically concerned with uncovering the alternative, and perhaps hidden and transformative, discourses of the very poor. In this sense, Wilkinson and Kleinman may be interpreted to suggest the aim of the inquiry into social suffering is to uncover what have been labelled the 'epistemic' injustices confronted by the global poor (Schweiger, 2016). This interpretation of Wilkinson and Kleinman's thought suggests that the study of social suffering could increase knowledge of human needs by attending to subaltern peoples' particular experiences of exclusion and marginalisation.[7]

To explain, Miranda Fricker's much-discussed discussion of the concept of epistemic injustice (2007) refers to a wide range of marginalised groups, emphasising how people believe testimonies of harm or disadvantage to the extent they deem their interlocutors credible. When prejudice enters these assumptions, as in the case of widespread neoliberal distinctions between the 'idle' or 'deserving' poor, Fricker's theory suggests that claims as regards material injustice are likely to become socially weakened where the poor and powerless cannot, for example, appeal to widely shared ethical intuitions concerning entitlement or desert. Significantly, Fricker outlines two forms of epistemic injustice. The first takes the form of testimonial injustice, according to which the speaker's account of their experience is deemed questionable from an external perspective. Second, hermeneutic epistemic injustices may cause the speaker to discount their own testimony due to background prejudices or cognitive biases (Fricker, 2007: 35). While it seems likely that the poor and powerless globally are likely to experience both types of epistemic injustice, Wilkinson and Kleinman seem to suggest hermeneutic epistemic injustices are likely to affect the capacities of the very poor to struggle for the recognition of their needs and identities.

This perspective seems to be borne out by Wilkinson and Kleinman's warning that claims of the rural poor worldwide are only too frequently rendered inaudible within authoritative (medical, public health-related and other professional) discourses (2016: 86). Thus, in attempting to pursue their own form of life or indigenous form of development, for example, the very poor may encounter hermeneutical injustices, owing to the dominance of externally imposed narratives of progress and modernisation. Their alternative narratives and sources of knowledge risk being obscured without a commitment to uncovering and attempting to comprehend the specific forms of their social suffering (see also Schweiger, 2014). Wilkinson and Kleinman's defence of this humanitarian ethos therefore seems to alert to the need for more attention to subjects of development in interventions to ameliorate their suffering (2016: 17). Without such emphasis on uncovering epistemic injustices and the hidden transcripts of the poor, there is a risk that the study of social suffering would perform, in their words, no more than 'an "ornamental function" in the wider reporting of social adversity' (2016: 104), a situation which would threaten to deepen the social invisibility of suffering. To acknowledge this point would be to recognise, in a further sense, Renault's idea that 'suffering can only exist for as long as it can be the subject of a demand being heard' (2017: 87).[8]

Wilkinson and Kleinman's implied focus on the epistemic injustices confronting those who suffer socially, then, might be usefully interpreted as a concern to defend a humanitarian ethos which supports the agency of the underprivileged. They signal the dangers of an excessive, even voyeuristic, concern with social suffering instanced by the international media's focus on the pain of distant others, a situation which Paul Farmer refers to as the 'mediatized politics of pity' (Farmer, 2004, cited in Wilkinson and Kleinman, 2016: 101). Also raised by Didier Fassin (2005; 2009) from a Foucauldian perspective, the risk is that much of the intense public attention to global social suffering tends to serve political aims whilst not genuinely encouraging the affluent nations to take responsibility for the harms of global poverty and the outcomes of other global crises. Wilkinson and Kleinman further allude to the risks of humanitarian discourses of aid, which have at times been taken to portray the suffering of millions worldwide from poverty as a matter of 'cosmic' misfortune.[9] As they summarise (2016: 154), the paradoxical risk is that the media's intense focus on worldwide suffering deepens this suffering by becoming 'part of a culture which both obfuscates social analysis and diminishes our capacity for human recognition' (2016: 154).

Against this 'dark' side of humanitarianism, however, Wilkinson and Kleinman point out that the major theorists of social suffering, such as Bourdieu, are profoundly aware that the language of social science may itself do symbolic violence to the poor, and thus that there are inherent risks in attempting to give a voice to this suffering (2016: 155). Despite these risks and challenges, a more genuine humanitarian ethos may emerge from a renewed focus on global forms of social suffering, one which would, for example, enable indigenous forms of knowledge and of 'development' to emerge by attending to their precise mode of their suffering and their efforts to resist seemingly colonialist conceptions of their situation (Tucker, 1999).[10]

For example, to return to an example raised in Chapter 2, positive knowledge of the agency of the poor may be gained by considering indigenous peoples' resistance to the target-setting agendas of development needs laid out by the Millennium and Sustainable Development Goals. This focus may productively engage indigenous peoples' suffering and resistance to imposed policies of development, which, as Yap and Wafene (2019) argue, have often obscured their cultural conceptions of their needs, such as the priority they attribute to living in harmony with nature.

While, as suggested previously, Renault seemed right to suggest the poor and powerless often lack a coordinated 'language of pain', Wilkinson and Kleinman also correctly seem to emphasise the productivity of the hidden forms of subaltern knowledge, embedded within experiences of social suffering, which might offer plausible paths towards uncovering the potentially dynamic agency arising from their social suffering. To be sure, while to focus on these subaltern experiences of resistance is not already to suggest the possibility of coordinated recognition struggles of the poor, these forms of dynamic agency are also not insignificant, and may provide means to dignify human lives. If this point seems plausible, the chapter turns next to a more general conception of the glimpses of dynamic agency which may be located in the context of suffering and efforts for bodily and psychological survival in the context of global poverty. Without wishing to reify these constraints, I focus on a conception of agency interpreted from Wilkinson and Kleinman's humanitarian conclusion that the study of social suffering is 'not sufficient in itself unless it leads to human action on behalf of our fellow human beings' (2016: 158). It is this focus on dynamic agency, I suggest, which constitutes the first positive tier defended in this book for protecting agency and dignity in the face of global poverty.

3.5 Survivalist, Reason-to-Value Agency and a Positive Recognition Politics in Global Poverty

So far, my discussion in this chapter has focused on the way the concept of social suffering brings into view the variety of ways people bear the frustrations of struggling for survival globally. However, given that survival struggles may frequently not amount to full struggles against injustice or for recognition, it seems vital to acknowledge, in ways both Wilkinson's and Renault's theories seemed to suggest but leave somewhat under-explored, the creative and partly transformative modes of agency which may be the by-product or side-effect of people's suffering. That is, it seems that forms of creative energy may arise from social suffering; and even if this energy arises out of economic necessity, it suggests the starting points from which recognition struggles could eventuate. Therefore, whereas thinkers such as Honneth take the experience of grievance and moral injury as the motivational core of recognition struggles, a cosmopolitan recognition theory focuses, rather, on the conception of agency which often arises from the lived contexts of social suffering within structural constraints, without necessarily assuming people consciously to wish to struggle against injustice. In these contexts, it seems worthwhile to aim to protect the creative and purposive aspects of agency which may provide the origin of collective consciousness and recognition struggles, even if these struggles might often in practice be far from guaranteed.

Awareness of this ambiguity seems vital, as it seems important to remain realistic as regards the implications of these forms of agency. While suffering can, and possibly often does, give rise to creative strategising, the risk remains that much action undertaken under serious economic constraints would either confirm the status quo or be self-defeating. Therefore, the concept which I call at this stage 'reason-to-value' agency would also consider the potentially negative outcomes of individual agency under structural constraints (Gaucher and Jost, 2011), and would accept that this conceptual focus would be unlikely to tackle the roots of the structural inequalities experienced by the very poor. However, although reason-to-value agency is unlikely to be fully liberatory, it also avoids the link between social suffering and the expression of a moral grievance, a link which, as argued earlier, seems to pervade Honneth's conception.

The advantage of this focus is that exclusively focusing on the negative outcomes of social suffering might risk stifling the content of diverse people's aspirations for a dignified life, which may only be articulated in the context of resisting structural constraints. Therefore, Schick (2009) seems right to warn of the risks of simply marking out diverse experiences of social suffering without attempting to learn from them. One avenue for this learning would be to acknowledge how the very poor around the world strive in basic but often innovative ways to maintain their dignity in everyday action (Blumenberg and Agrawal, 2014). While the concept of dignity is essentially contested (Bates, 2005; Rodrigues, 2005), it seems crucial to emphasise how human action may express purpose, intention, pride and identity, even if not all of the outcomes may be emancipatory.

More specifically, I present this form of agency according to two overlapping dimensions. Beyond a certain material baseline which seems the logical basis for human beings to live a decent human life, it would include at least a modest capacity to critique reflexively the most self-defeating consequences of one's suffering. Second, the reason-to-value agency of the poor seems to involve their capacities to prioritise and decide on trade-offs between the basic needs they may pursue in leading a life, to cite Sen's classic phrase, which they have 'reason to value' (Sen, 1990a: 112 See also, Sen, 1999: 75). Protecting these capacities seems vital because people around the world are likely to have different values and priorities which impact their survival mechanisms and how they wish to mitigate their vulnerabilities. This point is emphasised by Sen's (1990) focus on households not as sites for the simple calculation of overall wellbeing, as much development economics seems to assume, so much as the location for the negotiation of interests. In view of these insights, cosmopolitan recognition theory would acknowledge that people attempt to survive and cope differently, according to different value-priorities.

To be sure, there is likely to be a complex relationship between reason-to-value agency and the concept of a coordinated recognition struggle. While the structural constraints of severe poverty might often impede people from pursuing their central aims, their creative strategising under structural constraints might involve forming limited solidarities with others, with collective coping strategies offering the gateway to overcoming their situation more systemically. Although it seems clear the forms of agency which coexist with social suffering do not guarantee a socially transformative recognition struggle (Khader, 2009), enhancing this form of agency at least offers a realistic but nuanced defence of the elemental importance of survival, which could provide the conditions for future empowerment. That is, emphasising the productive 'tactics and trade-offs' which the very poor might make between different forms of privation (Kabeer, 2016) suggests apt initial focus for a cosmopolitan recognition theory.

The concept of reason-to-value agency may be explained by turning to consider the situation of poor single mothers, whether in developing states (Chant, 2003) or in advanced economies (Lister, 2015). The issues confronting them seem to have supported orthodox ideas that female-headed households tend to be 'the poorest of the poor' (Chant, 2003). This view could appear questionable, as while it seems clear expending one's practical and emotional energies on survival would be highly exhausting and likely to undermine one's potential for resistance, Chant (2003) also refers to the creative resourcefulness of women in developing societies, which serves to question the idea that female-headed households globally are always likely to constitute the most socio-economically vulnerable. Hence, while it seems undoubtedly important to consider the lower earning potential, heavier domestic obligations and poorer social and economic mobility affecting female-headed households due to cultural and labour market barriers (Kabeer, 2003, cited in Chant, 2003), it is also realistic to question the more general claim which often seems to arise, namely the unlikelihood that women make strategically beneficial choices in such a way which might comparatively improve their quality of life, at least in areas where they consider it most crucial to mitigate their suffering.

More specifically, Chant identifies a surprising degree of creative strategising within female-headed households which complicate standard representations of women in female-headed households as 'merely poor' (Chant, 2003, citing Walker et al., 2013). As Kabeer further argues, this standardised portrait appears to oversimplify the way poverty and in contrast well-being reproduce themselves not only through possession of resources such as money, but through rules, norms, practices and entitlements too, in a variety of arenas which may be based on the state, the market or through the 'moral economy' of kinship, rules which determine 'who gets what' and on what terms (Kabeer, 2016: 3, citing Sen, 1990). Following in this vein, Chant refers to the capacities of women for social networking in developing societies and their capacities to form solidarities with other women in similar situations, possibilities which may increase outside a traditional nuclear family structure where women are more likely to accept a dependent role. While Kabeer rightly warns of the dangers of overestimating the transformative potential of these acts, which may involve 'trade-offs between different privations' rather than fully emancipatory action, and although it seems right not to celebrate survival to an extent which de-politicises structural constraints, nonetheless the dignity arising in the context of survival seems crucial to acknowledge and further protect (see also Rodrigues, 2005).

Barbara Harris-White (2005) supports this point by vividly portraying the paradoxical continuation of agency in the context of destitution in India. She focuses in particular on the tendencies of small collectives of alms-seekers to group together to maintain small-scale caste-specific credit and insurance institutions which enable them to construct entry barriers to their settlements and work according to collectively enacted rules. While their destitution is too extreme to be structurally challenged by these actions, their activities are likely to maintain everyday forms of agency and dignity which emanate from their suffering. While focusing on the dynamic potential of reason-to-value agency should clearly not obscure from view the limitations of this form of agency in terms of enabling people to depart from poverty traps, concentrating on how people maintain identity and a sense of personal efficacy in the context of a shared situation suggests the starting point from which people may later begin to struggle for the recognition of their full humanity. At least, focusing on these everyday activities is likely to counter a certain 'blindness to the human aspect' in many mainstream studies of poverty (Sedmak, 2013: 559–560).

At the same time, the concept of reason-to-value agency would balance this positive focus with the acknowledgement that struggles to cope under structural constraints may become counter-productive. To elaborate on this point, Hoggett and Frost's (2008) analysis of the hidden psychological injuries of economic disadvantage, and their focus on the 'psychosocial subject' in welfare states, seem apt to consider. While they do not rule out the possibility of creative agency, they draw attention to the ways in which social suffering may become externalised and symbolised, especially in conditions of rapid industrialisation, which have weakened many people's potential to attain respect and esteem through traditional forms of labour. Social suffering refers, on their conception, to 'the lived experience of the social damage inflicted in late capitalist societies on the least powerful, and the intra-psychic and relational wounds which result' (2008: 440). Echoing Renault, the agency associated with suffering is likely to become paradoxical and perhaps counter-productive especially where the opportunities for traditional collective action, or 'second-order agency' (Hoggett, 2001; 2006), become increasingly remote.

From this perspective, the poor may especially express their suffering by embodying their condition. Drawing on a range of studies over 20 years in the *Journal of Health and Social Behaviour*, for example, Hoggett and Frost refer to the strong correlations between adaptive forms of coping such as through substance abuse, somatic illnesses of various kinds, addiction or neurosis (2008: 442). Social suffering may also be enacted in ways which are profoundly difficult to rationalise. Alluding to Butler's concept of 'melancholic agency' (1997, 2003), which suggests that pain is often more acute when it relates, as under slavery, to the sense that the collective history of one's group has been lost, Hoggett and Frost suggest that pain may even be enacted in the form of suicide or in the profoundly troubling forms fictionally illustrated by Toni Morrison's protagonist in *Beloved* (see Butler, 1997, cited in Hoggett and Frost, 2008: 456). In relation to global forms of poverty, the implication may be that, in the absence of a narrative sense of the achievements of one's economic class or social group, the agency which one's suffering entails may perhaps never be fully separable from its 'melancholic' dimensions.

Moreover, Hoggett and Frost rightly suggest that the human agency arising from social suffering involves perpetual risks that the sufferer might 'project' their distress into the world and on to others. In other words, people may become prone to expressing their suffering through forms of discrimination or domination, in so far as 'what I cannot bear in myself, I can always locate in the other' (2008: 452). Majid Yar (2008) exemplifies this point by suggesting that, denied recognition in the wider society, the disaffected and alienated may turn to forms of physical violence which, although counter-productive, may undeniably express active agency. While, then, the positive and negative dimensions of reason-to-value agency are often likely to be inseparable, the crucial issue normatively would be to protect the capacities of people to reflect on the ways that their choices and actions may reinforce their suffering in forms of 'double suffering' (Hoggett and Frost, 2008: 449), or actions which self-defeatingly reproduce social exclusion or shame. Despite the challenges involved in this form of agency, it still seems true that it is from the condition of a person's own valued identity, however aspirational, that they would be most likely to locate the raw material for dignifying their lives.

To recall, the concept of reason-to-value agency is clearly inspired by Sen's capabilities approach, which focuses on the significance of the person's capacity to live a life which reflects their values (Sen, 1990a). While the theoretical differences between recognition theories and the capabilities literature have been suggested previously, it is worth re-emphasising that the concept of reason-to-value agency in a cosmopolitan recognition theory would view the experiences of social suffering as further 'conversion factors' which both positively and negatively affect a person's positive freedoms (Robeyns, 2009). In this vein, the emphasis would lie more strongly than in the capabilities approach on the individual's capacity to act in the context of structural constraints, as people define for themselves the priorities they wish to pursue and which trade-offs would best support their dignity and their reasons for living. As the capabilities literature also contends, a variety of environmental and social factors affect a person's ability to transform goods and opportunities into wellbeing; and social suffering seems an important conversion factor which may strengthen or weaken the individual's potential to achieve a life they strongly value (Sen, 2005; Robeyns, 2005; Alkire 2007; 2008). Further, recognition theory suggests that this dynamic action in the context of social constraints may be viewed as building-blocks for personal dignity from which limited forms of trust become possible, and from which fuller, more socially transformative recognition struggles may emanate.

At the same time, the concept of reason-to-value agency more explicitly follows the capabilities approach in accepting as valuable choices and strategies which might seem unconventional from more typical liberal-individualist perspectives, such as women's options for homeworking in developing societies, which might enable people to act according to their kinship structures and forms of life (Hill, 2010). Agreeing with the capabilities theorists' focus on the emergence of agency under non-ideal conditions (Alkire, 2002; Robeyns, 2005), this approach suggests that these constraints and valued reasons are likely to provide key bases for human dignity, even if in relatively uncoordinated ways. Additionally, beyond the capabilities approach, these constraints may provide the basis for limited coordination with others in similar situations, around specific interests, whether for enhanced childcare facilities or homeworking opportunities to supplement formal labour markets (Abbott, 1997).[11]

The purpose of focusing on the creativity which may arise in the context of survival struggles is that these struggles often tend to reveal a person's deeper priorities, such as the value placed on traditional forms of labour in indigenous communities, which might motivate limited forms of trust with others similarity situated. Diaz de Leon (2020) exemplifies this point by suggesting how very poor migrants travelling through Mexico, whilst often separated from their traditional kinship structures, form limited solidarities with culturally or ethnically different but similarly displaced people for the purposes of mutual protection. While doing so does not structurally eliminate their vulnerabilities or their material hardships, forming a 'thin' community pragmatically enables them to mitigate specific vulnerabilities and to enhance agency, in ways which do not at the same time necessarily entail a cognitive awareness of one's situation as unjust nor obviously involve collective expression of grievance or moral injury.

As suggested previously, reason-to-value agency in cosmopolitan theory would most likely not challenge global structural inequalities, nor probably empower individuals to depart in a sustained way from the structural constraints that limit their lives. Moreover, Sabine Alkire (2002) correctly warns of the elusiveness of the concept of agency as the capacity to act according to what one has reason to value. Bandura (1995) also, connectedly, asks whether any attempt to assess a person's agency would always have to depend on a person's subjective sense of effectiveness in responding to their vulnerabilities, a difficult issue which seems to be in turn dependent on the form of life they have 'reason to value'. The potential circularity of this form of agency is highlighted still further by Yar's (2008) claim that, at times, some people may seek to mitigate the vulnerabilities they perceive through forms of violence and discrimination. One clear limitation, then, of the concept proposed is that it leaves room for potentially controversial judgements as regards a person's priorities, for instance whether they strongly value control over household finances rather than a greater overall level of income (Kabeer, 1996). The normative open-endedness of protecting this form of agency clearly brings with it some inevitable complexities in human development.

However, the advantage of the approach is that, in refraining from pre-evaluations of what must obviously count as mitigating one's vulnerabilities, it does not automatically categorise the very poor as victims, even in the absence of a coordinated recognition struggle or resistance movement. As Alkire (2002) explains, again in relation to the capabilities approach, focusing on a conception of wellbeing that one has reason to pursue responds to the idea that poverty is multidimensional, and reasons and conceptions of the good life are plural. Therefore, many of the 'proxy measures' used to evaluate poverty in very poor societies, such as number of years' schooling, employment status, health status or land ownership, will often be problematic and inconclusive (see also Naryayan, 2000). From the perspective of cosmopolitan recognition theory, too, what seems crucial normatively is a dual focus on contexts, first, where individuals seem to lose all potential for resistance to their structural constraints; and also, as suggested through the examples of homeworking in female-headed households, the protection of capacities to coordinate interests around creative strategising, which might encourage future social transformation through fuller struggles for, and over, the recognition of one's aspirations and rights.

As Sen suggests, the elaboration of basic needs may itself be quite complex. Therefore, the 'need for careful assessment of aims, allegiances, objectives etc., may be important and exacting' (1985: 204). The concept of reason-to-value agency in a cosmopolitan recognition theory accepts this idea, extending it to suggest that it is through their vulnerabilities that the person often articulates their needs. These survival tactics are likely to be limited and episodic, or based on single issues through which the poor may form limited solidarities with others based on partial trust, rather than overarching resistance movements based on the social unity to form a collective 'language of pain'. Again, in the case of some women in developing societies, some creative strategies may not increase income as such but have been thought to increase women's subjective perception of control, and hence the dignity they attribute to their lives. For some, for example, it may seem rational consciously to opt to trade-off higher overall household income through life with their spouse in order to live independently and increase their overall control over household finances (Chant, 2003).

Finally, however, it bears emphasising that the concrete normative and political implications of protecting reason-to-value agency are evidently, and perhaps inevitably, open-ended. Robust welfare provision and social rights would be significant. However, additionally, given the range of vulnerabilities confronting female-headed households, for instance, writers such as Kabeer (2016) seem right to emphasise that priority might also be given to protect women from oppressive domestic relations. Therefore, reason-to-value agency seems to entail forms of development which are responsive to the forms of vulnerability-mitigation which the very poor, only too often women in developing societies, deem valuable to make. It seems right to support these limited forms of agency, without, perhaps unrealistically, first seeking to resolve all social suffering. Protecting the reason-to-value agency of the very poor holds out hope for, even though it does not guarantee, a more sustained departure from poverty cycles through more socially coordinated forms of empowerment.[12] Without suggesting one-size-fits-all solutions, an emphasis on this concept responds to the needs of the poor to pursue their goals in an internally complex dialogue with their particular, and often particularly constrained, circumstances.

3.6 Conclusion

This chapter has asked how a cosmopolitan recognition theory might begin the task of comprehending and responding to the issues confronted by the world's poor, whilst avoiding becoming trapped in the narrations of these experiences without a normative path forward. I began from the intuition of the need to react to social suffering as a form of misrecognition. It was crucial, I argued, to unsettle Honneth's conception of misrecognition as moral injury, in such a way which assumes a semantic link between the experience of social suffering and the emergence of a coordinated recognition struggle against injustice. This insight led to a different conception of social suffering, which then suggested the complex relationship between poverty-related suffering and the everyday forms of agency exercised by individuals in coping with, and surviving, their diverse situations.

Concentrating on reason-to-value agency suggests, in summary, the need for practices of human development to focus on the values and priorities of specific individuals in the lived contexts in which they seek to mitigate their vulnerabilities. While the well-known capabilities approach already focuses on the protection of agency as the normative basis of dignifying the lives of the world's poorest millions, I extended this idea for a cosmopolitan recognition theory, in order to propose the basis for the positive recognition politics of the global poor, on the basis that resistance and the creation of meaning are often possible even in the context of material constraints. This argument is, however, raised in the context of awareness of the risk of reifying structural constraints, or regarding them as an inevitable feature of human existence. It is precisely at this stage that the limitations of a normative focus on reason-to-value agency appear, as the concept does not suggest the self-conscious emergence of fuller campaigns against social domination on which recognition theorists have usually focused. Understandably, then, it is towards the more challenging goal of empowerment in a cosmopolitan recognition theory to which I next turn attention in Chapter 4.

Notes

1 The early parts of this chapter draw from my paper, 'The Harms of Global Poverty as Misrecognition: Social Suffering, Invisibility and Alienation', in G. Schweiger (ed.), *Poverty, Inequality and the Critical Theory of Recognition* (Dordrecht: Springer, 2020).

2 The ambiguity in Honneth's discussions of this issue seem further evident in his statement that 'the experience of disrespect is always accompanied by affective sensations which are, in principle, capable of revealing to individuals the fact that certain forms of recognition are being withheld from them' (Honneth, 1995: 136). At the same time, he only alludes to the 'possibility' that the injustices done to the person will be 'cognitively disclosed' to them (Honneth, 1995: 138).

3 The idea is not that these forms of social suffering are unique to Renault's conception, but only that the relation he draws between social suffering and the condition of the economically marginalised in societies such as France render his concept especially useful to consider in the context of this chapter.

4 The idea of a struggle over symbolic capital seems to relate to Bourdieu's wider and 'negative' theory of recognition, which is exemplified by his idea that the hunger for 'recognition' is located mainly in the side of the dominated. The connected concept of symbolic power is complex and relies on the further network of ideas central to Bourdieu's thought such as 'habitus' or 'political field', Symbolic capital is itself a complex concept refers to forms of power within the system of social meanings designating superiority or inferiority, a form of power which is irreducible to one's income or culture. Indeed, in his discussions of symbolic capital, Bourdieu argues that neither brute force nor the possession of resources alone suffice for the effective exercise of power. For a more detailed discussion, see Bourdieu (2013) and Harker, Mahar and Wilkes (2016).

5 This point may be true also in the context of recent *gilets jaunes* protests in France.

6 In addition to the Chinese example, Wilkinson and Kleinman cite the situations in the textile industry in Bangladesh, in the mines of Burma and Congo, in the houses of Mumbai's slum dwellers where piecework is done night and day, in the garbage collecting in the northeastern Brazilian favelas and in the brothels of Cambodia and Lagos (2016: 3).

7 Although this point is clearly an interpretation from Wilkinson's and Kleinman's stated perspective, it seems apt given their evident sensitivity to the idea that engaging with others' suffering involves critical re-engagement with the cultural values-systems, the suppression of which might have contributed to the experience of social suffering. As they write: 'A key matter for analysis and debate concerns the involvement of lived experience in our research and thinking. This involves an examination of traditions of ontology and epistemology [...] It also calls on us to declare a standpoint with regard to the claims we are witnessing and to a greater or lesser extent contributing to cultural and political processes that impoverish people's experiences of the world' (2016: 17).

8 The literature on the study of, for instance, indigenous modes of development is relevant here. The power relations dividing the implementation of indigenous development vis-à-vis a more apparently scientific form of development associated with the West are crucial. A number of studies have been undertaken examining the contradictions between the imposition of Western, scientific models of development vis-à-vis the development practices of indigenous communities in Africa. For example, see Brockensha, Warren and Werner (1980), Kalland (2000) and Briggs (2005).

9 The question of the 'depoliticisation' of poverty even by NGOs in the postcolonial era, especially in many African states, in the sense of assisting poor pop-

ulations to live sustainably with their poverty rather than fighting the social relations which reproduce it, is a complex theme, pursued by Manji (2010).

10 In this context Anderson et al. (2005) refer to the way in which in the first 'wave' of development, which is to say externally developed, modernisation-centred models, substantially failed in relation to many indigenous groups. The second 'wave', which may be thought to consider more crucially specific forms of suffering of indigenous groups in relation to their wider societies, focuses on 'development' concentrating more clearly on their cultural values and, thus, development on their own terms. One might argue in this context, however, that focusing on the specific suffering of indigenous peoples has not led to dismantling the power-structures which produced the dominant frames of 'development' in the first instance. For further discussions of indigenous peoples' interventions in terms of defining their own development needs vis-à-vis the target-setting of the Sustainable Development Goals, see Yap and Wafene (2019).

11 Abbott (1997) in particular refers instructively in this context to the ways in which poor women in India have organised towards identifying urgent needs for recognition of their invisible informal sector income-generating activities, such as via SEWA (The Self-Employed Women's Association).

12 The relationship between everyday resistance and movements towards empowerment, and whether empowerment movements are by definition always 'socially transformative', are evidently difficult questions, both from the perspective of recognition theory, and from the point of view of the capabilities literature from which I also gain inspiration. For instance, although I have mentioned the SEWA movement in terms of women's everyday agency, in so far as the movement exemplifies women's limited form of coordination around interests in different forms of homeworking in the informal sector, some do view the SEWA movement further in terms of its potential to empower women too. See Hill,(2010). For more foundational literature on the origins of the SEWA movement in India, see Rose, (1992). For further critical discussions, see Nandy (2021).

References

Abbott, Dina (1997). 'Who Else Will Support Us? How Poor Women Organise the Unorganisable in India', *Community Development Journal* 32/3 (June): 199–209.

Alkire, Sabina (2002). *Valuing Freedoms: Sen's Capabilities Approach and Poverty Reduction* (New York: Oxford University Press).

Alkire, Sabina (2007). 'Choosing Dimensions: The Capability Approach and Multidimensional Poverty', in N. Kakwani and J. Silver (eds), *The Many Dimensions of Poverty* (NY: Palgrave MacMillan), pp. 89–119.

Alkire, Sabina (2008). 'Concepts and Measures of Agency', Oxford Poverty and Human Development Institute, OPHI Working Paper Series, Working Paper No. 9, pp. 2–23.

Allen, Amy (2010). 'Recognising Domination: Recognition and Power in Honneth's Critical Theory', *Journal of Power* 3/1: 21–32.

Anderson, Robert, Ronald Camp, Leo Dana and Benson Honig (2005). 'Indigenous Land Rights in Canada: The Foundations for Development', *International Journal for Entrepreneurship and Small Businesses* 2/2: 104–133.

Bader, Veit (2007). 'Misrecognition, Power and Democracy', in David Owen and Bert van der Brink (ed), *Recognition and Power: Axel Honneth and the Tradition of Critical Social Theory* (Cambridge: Cambridge University Press), pp. 244–246.

Bandura, A (1995). 'Exercise of Personal and Collective Efficacy in Changing Societies', in A. Bandura (ed), *Self-Efficacy in Changing Societies* (Cambridge: Cambridge University Press), pp. 1.45.

Bates, Justin (2005). 'Human Dignity: An Empty Concept in Search of Meaning?' *Judicial Review* 10/2: 165–168.

Blumenberg, Evelyn and Asha Weinstein Agrawal (2014). 'Getting Around When You are Just Getting By: Transportation Survival Strategies of the Poor', *Journal of Poverty* 18/4: 355–378.

Bourdieu, Pierre (1987). *Distinction: A Social Critique of the Judgement of Taste* (Cambridge: Cambridge University Press).

Bourdieu, Pierre, Bourdieu, Pierre and Alain Accardo (eds) (1999). *The Weight of the World: Social Suffering in Contemporary Life* (Stanford: Stanford University Press).

Bourdieu, Pierre (2013). *Outline of a Theory of Practice* (Cambridge: Cambridge University Press).

Bourdieu, Pierre and Lois Wacquant (2013a). 'Symbolic Capital and Social Classes', *Journal of Classical Sociology* 13/2: 292–302.

Briggs, J. (2005). 'The Use of Indigenous Knowledge in Development: Problems and Challenges', *Progress in Development Studies* 5/2: 99–144.

Brockensha, D., D. Warren and O. Werner (eds). (1980). *Indigenous Knowledge Systems and Development* (New York: University Press of America).

Butler, Judith (1997). *The Psychic Life of Power* (Stanford, CA: Stanford University Press).

Butler, Judith (2003). 'Afterword: After Loss, What Then?', in D. Eng and D. Kazanjian (eds), *Loss: The Politics of Mourning* (Berkely, CA: University of California Press), pp. 467–473.

Chant, Sylvia (2003). 'Female Household Headships and the Feminization of Poverty: Facts, Fictions and Forwards Strategies' [on-line]. London LSE Research Online. Available at: http://eprints.lse.ac.uk/archive/00000574. January 2006. Accessed 22.07.22.

Chimienti, M. and J. Solomos (2011). 'Social Movements of Irregular Migrants: The Struggle for Essential Rights', *Globalizations* 8/3: 343–360.

Das, Veena (1995). *Critical Events: An Anthropological Perspective on Contemporary India* (New Delhi: Oxford University Press).

Das, Veena (1997). 'Sufferings,Theodicies, Disciplinary Practices and Appropriations', *International Social Science Journal*, 49/154: 563–572.

Das, Veena, Arthur Kleinmann and Margaret Lock (eds). (2007). *Social Suffering* (Berkeley: University of California Press).

Dejours, C. (1998). *Souffrances en France: La Banalization de L'Injustice Sociale* (Paris: Seuil).

Deutsch, M. (1974). 'Awakening the Sense of Injustice', in M. Ross and M. Lerner (eds), *The Quest for Justice* (Canada: Holt, Rinehart and Winston), pp. 19–42.

Deveaux, Monique (2018). 'Poor-Led Social Movements and Global Justice', *Political Theory* 46/5: 698–725.

Deveaux, Monique (2021). *Poverty, Solidarity and Poor-Led Social Movements* (Oxford: Oxford University Press).

Diaz de Leon, Alejandra (2020). ''Transient Communities': How Central American Transit Migrants form Solidarity without Trust', *Journal of Borderlands Studies* October 37/5: 1–18.

Dufour, Pascal (2009). 'Globalization and the Collective Action of the Socially Excluded in France: At the Heart of the Margins?' *French Politics* 7: 316–314.

Eade, Deborah (2010). 'Capacity-Building: Who Builds which Capacity?', in Andrea Cornwall and Deborah Eade (eds), *Deconstructing Development Discourse: Buzzwords and Fuzzwords* (Oxfam, GB: Practical Action Publishing), pp. 203–214.

Farmer, Paul (2003). *Pathologies of Power: Health, Human Rights and the New War on the Poor*, vol. 4 (Berkeley: University of California Press).

Fassin, Didier (2005). 'Compassion and Repression? The Moral Economy of Immigration Policies in France', *Current Anthropology* 20/3: 362–387.

Fassin, D. (2009). 'Another Politics of Life is Possible', *Theory, Culture and Society* 26/5: 44–60.

Fricker, Miranda (2007). *Epistemic Injustice* (Oxford: Oxford University Press).

Frost, Liz and Paul Hoggett (2008). 'Human Agency and Social Suffering', *Critical Social Policy* 28/4: 438–460.

Gaisbauer, H., G. Schweiger and Clemens Sedmark (eds). (2016). *Ethical Issues in Poverty Alleviation* (Dordrecht: Springer).

Gaucher, David and John T. Jost (2011). 'Difficulties in Awakening the Sense of Injustice and Overcoming Oppression', in P. T. Colman (ed), *Conflict, Interdependence and Justice* (Peace Psychology Books), pp. 227–246.

Harker, Richard, Cheleen Mahar and Chris Wilkes (eds) (2016). *An Introduction to the Work of Pierre Bourdieu: The Practice of Theory* (Dordrecht: Springer).

Harris-White, Barbara (2005). 'Destitution and the Poverty of its Politics – With Special Reference to South Asia', *World Development* 33/6: 881–891.

Hill, Elizabeth (2010). *Worker Identity, Agency and Economic Development: Women's Empowerment in the Indian Informal Economy* (London: Routledge).

Hoggett, Paul (2001). 'Agency, Rationality and Social Policy', *Journal of Social Policy* 30/1: 37–56.

Hoggett, Paul (2006). 'Pity, Compassion and Solidarity', in S. Clarke, P. Hoggett and S. Thompson (eds), *Emotions, Politics and Society* (Basingstoke: MacMillan), pp. 145–161.

Honneth, Axel (1995). *The Struggle for Recognition* (London: Verso).

Honneth, Axel (2007). 'Recognition as Ideology', in David Owen and Bert van der Brink (eds), *Recognition and Power: Axel Honneth and the Tradition of Critical Social Theory* (Cambridge: Cambridge University Press), pp. 322–347.

Jetten, J., F. Mols, and H. P. Selvanathan (2020). 'How Economic Inequality Fuels the Rise and Resistance of the Yellow Vest Movement', *International Review of Social Psychology* 33/1.

Kabeer, Naila (2003). 'Gender Equality, Poverty Eradication and the Millennium Development Goals: Promoting Women's Capabilities and Participation', *Women in Development Discussion Paper* No. 13, pp. 1–24.

Kabeer, Naila (2016). 'Editorial: Tactics and Trade-Offs: Revisiting the Links between Gender and Poverty', *Gender and Development* 23/2: 189–205.

Kalland, A. (2000). 'Indigenous Knowledge: Prospects and Limitations', in R. Ellen, P. Parles and A. Bicher (eds), *Indigenous Environmental Knowledge and its Transformations* (Amsterdam: Harwood Academic Publishers), pp. 1–33.

Khader, Serene (2009). 'Adaptive Preferences and Procedural Autonomy', *Journal of Human Development* 10/2: 169–187.

Kleinman, A., G.L. Estrin, S. Usman, D. Chisholm, P.V. Marquez, T. G. Evans and S. Saxena (2016). 'Time for Mental Health to Come out of the Shadows', *The Lancet*, 387/10035: 2274–2275.

Lagon, M. and R. Kaminski (2017). 'Dignity and the Rule of Law: Governance and Alleviation of Social Suffering', in R. Anderson (ed), *Alleviating World*

Suffering (Social Indicators Research Series, Vol, 67) (Cambridge: Springer), pp. 1–14.

Lister, Ruth (2015). '"To Count for Nothing": Poverty Beyond the Statistics', *Journal of the British Academy* 3: 139–165.

Lovell, T. (ed). (2007). *(Mis)recognition, Social Inequality and Social Justice: Pierre Bourdieu and Nancy Fraser* (London: Routledge).

Manji, Firoze (2010). 'The Depoliticisation of Poverty', in Firoze Manji (ed), *Development and Rights* (Oxford: Oxfam GB Publishing), pp. 12–33.

McNevin, Anne (2009). 'Contesting Citizenship: Irregular Migrants and Strategic Possibilities for Political Belonging', *New Political Science*, 31/2: 163–181.

Narayan, Deepa (2000). *Voices of the Poor: Can Anyone Hear Us?* (Oxford: Oxford University Press).

Nandi, Rajib (2021). 'Solidarity at the Crossroads: Struggles and Transformations of Domestic Workers in Kerala', in C. Verschuur, I. Guerin and I. Hillenkamp (eds), *Social Reproduction, Solidarity and Economy, Feminisms and Democracy: Gender, Development and Social Change* (London: Palgrave MacMillan), pp. 145–167.

Peters, Gabriel (2012). 'The Social as Heaven and Hell: Pierre Bourdieu's Philosophical Anthropology', *Journal for the Theory of Social Behaviour* 42/1: 63–86.

Pilapil, Renante (2011). 'Psychologization of Injustice', *Ethical Perspectives* 18/1: 79–106.

Renault, Emmanuel (2004). 'Reconnaissance, Institutions, Injustice', *Revue du Mauss* 23: 180–195.

Renault, Emmanuel (2005). 'Radical Democracy and an Abolitionist Concept of Justice: A Critique of Habermas' Theory of Justice', *Critical Horizons* 6/1: 137–152.

Renault, Emmanuel and Jean-Philippe Deranty (2007). 'Politicising Honneth's Ethic of Recognition', *Thesis Eleven* 88/1: 92–111.

Renault, Emmanuel (2007). *The Experience of Injustice* (Armillaire: La Découverte).

Renault, Emmanuel (2007a). 'From Fordism to Post-Fordism: Beyond or Back to Alienation?' *Critical Horizons* 8/2: 205–220.

Renault, Emmanuel (2010). 'A Critical Theory of Social Suffering', *Critical Horizons* 11/2: 221–241.

Renault, Emmanuel (2011). 'The Theory of Recognition and the Critique of Institutions', in D. Petherbridge (ed), *Axel Honneth; Critical Essays* (London: Brill), pp. 207–231.

Renault, Emmanuel (2017). *Social Suffering*, trans. Maude Dews (London: Rowman and Littlefield).

Robeyns, Ingrid (2005). 'The Capability Approach: A Theoretical Survey', *Journal of Human Development* 6/1: 93–114.

Robeyns, Ingrid (2009). 'Justice as Fairness and the Capabilities Approach', in Kaushik Basu and Ravi Kanbur (eds), *Arguments for a Better World: Essays in Honour of Amartya Sen, Vol. I - Ethics, Welfare and Measurement* (Oxford: Oxford University Press), pp. 397–413.

Rodrigues, Philippe-André (2005). 'Human Dignity as an Essentially Contested Concept', *Cambridge Review of International Affairs* 28/4: 743–756.

Rose, Kalima (1992). *Where Women Are Leaders: The SEWA Movement in India* (New Delhi: Vistaar Publications).

Sayer, D. (2005). 'Class, Moral Worth and Recognition', *Sociology* 39/5: 362–387.

Schick, Kate (2009). '"To Lend a Voice to Suffering Is the Condition of All Truth"': Adorno and International Political Thought', *Journal of International Political Theory* 5/2: 138–160.

Schweiger, Gottfried (2014). 'Recognition Theory and Global Poverty', *Journal of Global Ethics* 10/3: 267–273.

Schweiger, Gottfried (2016). 'Epistemic Injustice and Powerlessness in the Context of Global Justice: An Argument for 'Thick' and 'Small' Knowledge', *Wagadu* 15: 104–125.

Scott, James C. (1990). *Weapons of the Weak: Everyday Forms of Peasant Resistance* (Oxford: Oxford University Press).

Sedmak, Clemens (2013). 'Human Dignity, Interiority and Poverty', in C. McCrudden (ed), *Understanding Human Dignity* (Oxford: Oxford University Press), pp. 559–571.

Sen, Amartya (1990). 'Development as Capability Expansion', in J. DeFilipis and S. Saegert (eds), *The Community Development Reader* (London: Routledge), pp. 319–328.

Sen, Amartya (1990a). 'Justice: Means versus Freedoms', *Philosophy and Public Affairs* 19/2: 111–121.

Sen, Amartya (1999). *Development as Freedom* (New York: Anchor Books).

Sen, Amartya (2005). 'Human Rights and Capabilities', *Journal of Human Development* 6/2: 151–166.

Thompson, Simon (2006). *The Political Theory of Recognition* (London: Polity).

Thompson, S. and G. Burns (eds). (2013). *Global Justice and the Politics of Recognition* (London: Palgrave).

Tucker, V. (1999). 'The Myth of Development: A Critique from a Eurocentric Discourse', in R. Munck and D. O'Hearn (eds), *Critical Development Theory: Contributions to a New Paradigm* (London: Zed Books).

Wacquant, L. (2008). 'Ghettos and Anti-Ghettos: An Anatomy of the New Urban Poverty', *Thesis Eleven* 94/1: 113–118.

Wacquant, Loic (2008). *Urban Outcasts: A Comparative Sociology of Advanced Marginality* (London: Polity).

Walker, Julian, Alexandre Apsan Frediani and Jean-Francois Frediani (2013). 'Gender Difference and Urban Change: Implications for the Promotion of Wellbeing', *Environment and Urbanization* 25/1: 111–124.

Wilkinson, I. (2005). *Suffering: A Sociological Introduction* (Cambridge: Polity Press).

Wilkinson, I. and A. Kleinman (2016). *A Passion for Society: How We Think about Human Suffering* (Berkeley, CA: University of California Press).

Worsdale, Rosie (2017). 'Recognition, Ideology and the Case of 'Invisible' Suffering', *European Journal of Philosophy* 26/1: 1–16.

Yar, M. (2008). "And Every Cruelty will Cloud It': On Love Damaged Selfhood and Criminal Harm', Paper presented to the seminar, 'Recognition as Love and Care', University of the West of England (January).

Yap, Mandy Li-Ming and Krushi Watene (2019). 'The Sustainable Development Goals (SDGs) and Indigenous Peoples: Another Missed Opportunity?' *Journal of Human Development and Capabilities* 20/4: 451–467.

Young, Iris (2007). 'Recognition of Love's Labour: Considering Axel Honneth's Feminism', in D. Owen and Bert van der Brink (eds), *Recognition and Power: Axel Honneth and the Tradition of Critical Social Theory* (Cambridge: Cambridge University Press), pp. 191–212.

4 Empowering against Global Poverty Across the Spheres

Durable Empowerment from Social Imaginaries to Recognition Struggles

4.1 Introduction

Even if it is true, then, that a cosmopolitan recognition theory ought to attend to the potentially dynamic forms of agency arising from the suffering of the very poor, it seems clear that the theory would need to go further. Only focusing on the concept of reason-to-value agency, as explored in Chapter 3, would not fully show how the lives of those who suffer poverty around the world may be dignified, or how this commitment would provide a stable defence against the harms of poverty. The risk, which is too often a reality, is that some of the world's poor will remain trapped in long-term poverty cycles without capacities to overcome these circumstances sustainably (Harper et al., 2003; Hulme and Shepherd, 2003). Illiteracy, malnourishment and lack of power are often reproduced intergenerationally, which make leaving the precarity and threat of poverty enormously difficult, if not impossible. Conditions of persistent malnutrition, inadequate shelter and lack of social opportunities suggest that, even in contexts where some basic needs have been met, questions of empowerment and disempowerment remain considerable challenges in the task of poverty alleviation.

In this chapter, I move on to consider the empowering recognition struggles which might assist the very poor meaningfully to protect themselves against continually returning to poverty cycles of this kind. While concepts of agency or empowerment are likely to overlap, there are nonetheless differences between the concepts, which leads to a further distinction between two tiers of a cosmopolitan response to global poverty. Whereas Chapter 3 suggested that the first tier involved supporting reason-to-value agency as the gateway to the recognition struggles of the very poor, the second tier would more clearly consider the empowered recognition struggles the very poor might undertake in a socially coordinated way, to solidify control over their lives to protect their needs, interests and capacities in a future where access to assets and opportunities may be ambiguous. This chapter, therefore, defends this second stage of a cosmopolitan recognition theory by referring

DOI: 10.4324/9781003045038-5

to a concept which I label, extending Jay Drydyk's discussion (2008) in the field of development ethics, inter-sphere durable empowerment.[1]

As this conception of empowerment appears vital to defend the resolve of individuals and communities against what recognition theorists would view as pathologies of unjust social structures, this chapter attempts to locate this concept especially in Charles Taylor's much-debated liberal recognition theory. While it is not unlikely the concept could also be defended through the resources contained in alternative recognition theories such as Fraser's or Honneth's, Taylor's theory (1994) seems most apt owing to his long-standing sensitivity to the ways in which inequalities tend to reproduce themselves culturally. To acknowledge this point seems crucial, given the likelihood that the sources of the real disempowerment of the very poor globally may be cultural and social, rather than only connoting an economic issue or a question of lacking legal rights. Considering Taylor's recognition theory in this debate therefore seems compelling, despite its more usual application to questions of multiculturalism, national identity and language rights in his native Quebec (Levy, 2010; Smith, 1994; Smith, 2004).

The focus on Taylor's recognition theory seems additionally appropriate given that the central purpose he attributes to struggles over recognition is their ability to transform society towards greater justice, an aim which seems consistent with the emancipatory objectives of a variety of social groups. For Taylor, truly emancipatory recognition struggles tend to exemplify empowerment construed as a capacity to impact one's situation and to influence social change. In this sense, his recognition theory promises to provide a critical standard for evaluating national and international development policies which aim to tackle the disempowerment of the poor. This defence of empowerment seems also bolstered by Taylor's comparatively recent reflections on the concept of modern social imaginaries, an idea through which he has emphasised a modern self who becomes capable of conceptualising social change by reflecting on their values and status in different domains of social and political life (Taylor, 2004, 2007). Considering these two areas of Taylor's thought suggests a conception of recognition struggles which supports 'inter-sphere durable empowerment'. As will be argued, the idea offers a critical framework for considering the empowerment potential of development initiatives such as microcredit programmes around the world, which are so often regarded as improving the lives of poor women in developing societies especially.[2]

My discussion will proceed as follows. After proposing a definition of inter-sphere durable empowerment in Section 4.2 in terms of its psychological, social and normative dimensions, Section 4.3 first examines Taylor's concept of social imaginaries to explore the crucial background to his substantive recognition theory. As the concept of modern social imaginaries refers to the informal range of symbolic understandings which structure a society's organisation of different (cultural, political and economic) spheres, this layer of Taylor's thought seems to support the psychological and social dimensions of the conception of empowerment defended in this chapter. Section 4.4 then relates this idea to Taylor's better-known recognition theory and its relevance to the struggles of the very poor from the perspective of a cosmopolitan recognition theory. I suggest that Taylor's conception of recognition struggles presupposes and supports inter-sphere durable empowerment, particularly its normative dimension which emphasises the the needs of the oppressed to form collective consciousness of injustice and to react against this injustice in a coordinated way. The chapter closes with a critical examination of the empowerment potential of microcredit programmes which have been implemented in developing societies to empower poor women especially. The contradictory effects of these initiatives for the women in question suggest the need further to examine the relationship between empowerment's different forms of power in a cosmopolitan recognition theory, a task which is undertaken in the following, and final, chapter.

4.2 Agency, Inter-Sphere Durable Empowerment and Many Paths to Development

The concept and ideal of empowerment, then, seems immediately highly relevant to responding to global poverty through a cosmopolitan recognition theory. Without understanding the empowerment potential of struggling for recognition, it becomes unclear how these struggles could fully support the dignity of the very poor around the world. Clearly, however, much depends on the meaning of empowerment; and to outline an initial definition, I again turn to approaches developed within the capabilities-inspired literature on human development (Alkire, 2008; Crocker, 2008). While it seems fair to say that this literature does not always firmly distinguish the concepts of agency and empowerment (Ibrahim and Alkire, 2007; Kabeer, 1999; Galie and Farnworth, 2019), Jay Drydyk (2008, 2013), however, has offered a strong and useful distinction which holds that, in contrast to bare agency, sustainable empowerment would usually involve a stable capacity to effect change in one's life. As he explains, the United Nations' Human Development projects have often extolled the value of empowering the poor, projects which are not best understood solely in terms of expanding agency. As distinguishing between these concepts therefore seems vital, Drydyk's distinction is worth considering, before proposing a definition of empowerment relevant to cosmopolitan recognition theory which will aim to extend his definition.

Drydyk begins by arguing that the simple exercise of bare agency would not signal a poor person's real capacity to influence social norms and structures to form a secure capacity to control their life (2008: 234). Of course, as the previous chapter's discussion of reason-to-value agency highlighted, it is important to acknowledge that the poor are not passive victims but are capable of responding dynamically to their social context. However, simply supporting the human capacity to mitigate one's vulnerabilities in order to survive social suffering would inevitably fall short when considering serious poverty around the world (Card, 2014). While purposive activities related to coping and 'treading water' are ethically significant, these acts are unlikely to lessen the longer-term insecurity and precarity of life. Drydyk (2013), therefore, rightly suggests that conflating agency with empowerment misses a central feature of empowerment, which concerns a question of 'power-over', or the stable influence one is able to exercise over existing power-relations. To return to the previous chapter's example, while the women in female-headed households might trade-off security gained through marriage for greater control over household finances, their actions may be strategic but not empowered if they have little or no control or influence over the norms necessitating these choices. If domination is at least in key part a matter of being prone to arbitrary and potentially discriminatory norms, which becomes more likely without stable access to adequate nutrition and access to resources, it seems clear domination could entrench poverty in disempowering ways (Haugaard, 2012, 2015).

If, therefore, domination is likely to be disempowering (Martins, 2022;Stewart 2000),[3] it seems vital for a cosmopolitan recognition theory to focus on the long-term personal security and empowerment of the poor, even in circumstances where their assets and opportunities may fluctuate (Drydyk, 2008: 234). Drydyk further suggests that empowerment, almost by definition, would need to be durable or long-lasting; it should not be understood as simply exercising more basic agency from moment to moment.[4] Additionally, a closer examination of the human development literature in fact reveals some key distinctions between the concepts in developing countries, especially in analyses of the 'microcredit' initiatives mentioned earlier. For example, Naila Kabeer begins by highlighting the reasonable view that the availability of small business loans expands a person's options in the informal labour market, for example. However, while this expansion of options seems to support freedom construed as negative liberty, microcredit programmes have also been thought to contain the potential to empower poor women in developing societies especially, by providing them avenues to contest power-relations as regards to significant issues, or at 'critical control points', such as, perhaps most clearly, in the sphere of work (1999: 445). There may be different 'critical control points' in a person's life, with control in the political realm, for instance, usually achieved through civil and voting rights. By strengthening the person's 'power-over' in these different spheres of life, Kabeer's analysis seems to reinforce Drydyk's argument that durable empowerment should involve a standing capacity to influence existing power structures in order 'to make gains prevail' (2008: 232). That said, a difficult question confronting this definition of empowerment would be to demonstrate how a person's increased power-over could become more self-sustaining, or how these 'gains would prevail', in Drydyk's terms, in the sense of ensuring the individual's lasting sense of control over their life. To respond to this question, I seek to expand Drydyk's definition of empowerment in terms of assets and opportunities, by highlighting a number of further issues which seem extremely relevant to durable empowerment but to which Drydyk refers only indirectly.[5]

First of all, durable empowerment might be further defined by its social component, in the sense that becoming empowered may be understood usually to involve a social process which develops through making the greater control, influence or opportunity secured in one sphere potentially impact and transform one's control and influence in another. While it is not clear how overall gains in empowerment across different life-spheres could obviously be calculated or compared interpersonally, Koggel (2009) seems to defend this social, inter-sphere process by emphasising, first, that there is likely to be no single state of being empowered. Rather, it is more relevant to consider incremental pathways to overcoming disempowerment (see also Koggel, 2007). In this context, it becomes especially important to be able to use one's gains in one life-sphere to impact one's status and control in others, in order to gain greater stability in contexts where empowerment is almost never an all-or-nothing matter. For instance, in evaluating the empowerment potential of particular labour options in poor societies, it seems necessary to consider the different relationships which these opportunities constrain or enable. In poor rural economies, for example, the empowerment potential of opting for subsistence farming often seems to be discounted in official measurements of empowerment, as it seems to relate only to the informal and community sphere. This is despite the fact, as Koggel suggests, pursuing this opportunity may lead a person to much greater influence and control within the local community than taking up more training opportunities in the formal labour market, for instance. Hence, the real empowerment potential of this option seems to depend on how far it increases the person's social and political influence more broadly. Connectedly, in the case of family planning measures to tackle poverty in parts of Mexico, Koggel observes that realistic evaluations of women's empowerment would most likely depend on how far these policies enable women to expand their control and influence in household decision-making where large families have a strong cultural value (2009: 255).

While it seems clear that these considerations do not provide a sure way of calculating overall increases in the empowerment of any person or group, they suggest that the process of increasing one's overall empowerment is likely to involve an inter-sphere process, one which involves translating the influence gained, say, from a new labour opportunity into greater control in the domestic realm. This point is indirectly supported by Drydyk's suggestion that paths to durable empowerment usually flow through a system of relationships (2008: 233). For the very poor around the world, the relevant relationships may even be as broad as to include the status of the person's nation in relation to the operations of multinational corporations and international markets, large-scale relationships which have implications for the cohesion of families and communities. While these relevant relationships may thus be complex, they reinforce the concept of empowerment as a person's capacity to translate their influence between different 'spheres of justice', to invoke Michael Walzer's idea (1984).

Additionally, it seems necessary to extend the definition of durable empowerment to include a component which Drydyk also mentions indirectly, namely a strong inward or psychological aspect, exemplified by a person's capacity to conceptualise social change. Although to focus on human psychology almost inevitably lacks the rigour and objectivity of an approach which focuses mainly on material asset holdings or resources, a psychological focus has been central to feminist analyses of empowerment in developing countries (Cornwall and Edwards, 2010). As these feminist contributions suggest, it is an aspect which is often sidestepped in the development ethics literature with a strong international policy focus, not least due to the difficulties of measuring or even discerning a person's mental state or subjective perception of control over their future. However, this focus on what some intersectional feminist writers have labelled 'conscientization', or the intrapsychic or psychological form of empowerment, seems highly relevant to a person's capacity to influence key decisions in their lives. Significantly again, this insight seems to be reinforced by numerous studies of the empowerment of women of colour in the USA (see Summerson-Carr, 2003; Gutierrez and Lewis, 1999; Kieffer, 1984).

A definition of durable empowerment relevant to global forms of poverty would also, I suggest, need to consider the fact that as a capacity empowerment is inevitably normative, in the sense that becoming truly empowered would probably involve a growing consciousness of the forms of discrimination confronting one's social groups. Drydyk makes the associated point that empowerment should not be equated simply with the person's increased capacity to satisfy desires in a straightforward Hobbesian self-interested sense, as, if so, a person may be taken to be empowered where their preferences have been adapted to oppressive conditions (2008: 232). Again, thinkers writing from an intersectional perspective, and especially from the perspective of women of colour, insist that empowerment should involve the person's growing consciousness of the political and structural constraints under which they choose, and, in particular, the need to make their choices with the transformation of these structural constraints in mind (Kieffer, 1984; Gutierrez, 1990). From this perspective, when one is poor and powerless, becoming empowered might therefore involve acting not only with 'power-over' assets and opportunities but with collective consciousness or 'power-with'.[6]

While each of these three (social, psychological and normative) components of empowerment evidently requires further explanation, especially as regards its role in recognition theory, it seems right to assume their relevance to the broad and deep problems of global poverty in the current world. Drydyk's explicit and useful idea of empowerment as the capacity to 'make gains prevail' may therefore be extended to suggest that the concept would involve a person's capacity, *through participating in individual and collective decision-making across different life-spheres, to imagine and secure the future transformation of injustice.* This definition extends Drydyk's conception, especially through its normative emphasis on the formation of collective awareness and the need for the future transformation of injustice. Empowerment is, thus, construed as a capacity to make choices which are likely to contest or question structural constraints or injustices. If this concept seems plausible as the value defining the second, more comprehensive stage of a cosmopolitan recognition theory aimed at dignifying the world's poor, the main sections of this chapter will take on the task of grounding this concept in one particularly influential approach in contemporary philosophies of recognition.

4.3 Charles Taylor's Modern Social Imaginaries: Towards Empowerment Between the Spheres

More specifically, it seems possible and necessary to locate the defence of durable empowerment in one of the most pioneering recognition theories in recent years, namely the liberal theory of Charles Taylor (1994). In doing so, I draw first on Taylor's expansive thought more broadly. The psychological and inter-sphere dimensions of empowering the poor and powerless seem well supported by considering Taylor's long-standing concern with processes through which modern people achieve a critical consciousness of their identity. In particular, Taylor's recent discussion of the concept of 'modern social imaginaries' suggests insights into what may be called the modern individual's 'recognizer-status' (Laitinen, 2003), or their self-conception as a person capable of engaging in recognition struggles by reflecting on their status in particular spheres of social and political life. This area of Taylor's thought provides critical insights into how the imaginative capacities of the oppressed have been mobilised historically, including through anti-feudalist movements, the campaigns through which the Third Estate peasants of *ancien régime* France raised their revolutionary demands, and the progress of trade unions in nineteenth-century Europe (Taylor, 2004: 30).

Of course, in introducing Taylor's concept of the modern social imaginary, the question arises as to whether he intends this examination to bear any connection with his normative recognition theory (Steele, 2017). On the surface, the concept seems to be presented as a matter of narrative history or as an ontological description of modern societies. That said, Taylor typically does not draw overly strong distinctions between his historical works and his normative philosophy; and there seem advantages in drawing from his account of modern social imaginaries to highlight the imaginative and social resources which enable, or even propel, people in modern democracies to imagine and eventually act for social change. For Taylor, this imaginary domain historically provided the oppressed with hopes for emancipation, in contrast with the psycho-social resources available to people of hierarchical societies who conceived their situation as part of God's design (2004: 23).

Interpreting Taylor, the strongly emancipatory nature of the modern social imaginary therefore seems to suggest social and psychological support for emancipation and empowerment, almost by definition.

To clarify Taylor's version of this concept, Adams, Blokker, Doyle and Smith (2015) emphasise the parallels between his conception and Habermas' idea of the 'life-world', as both of these prominent ideas suggest the social grounding of a person's imagination but not in such a way which simply reiterates or reproduces social norms. Taylor emphasises the fact that ideas latent in one's social world are often logically prior to the emergence of normative principles and one's capacity to theorise them (2017: 1046). In fact, for Taylor, each society could have more than one social imaginary, the normative entailments of which are likely to be interpretively open. Barack Obama's mobilisation of the American imaginary surrounding race in his 'A More Perfect Union' speech in 2008 provides a contemporary example, perhaps in a way which emphasises the potentially controversial nature of modern imaginaries (Steele, 2017: 1046). Presenting one overarching 'modern' social imaginary in his recent writings, Taylor's emphasis lies on how this framework has influenced a number of disparate movements for liberation or emancipation, highlighting, in one sense, how psychological change often precedes active struggles over one's material interests (Cornwall and Edwards, 2010). Construing Taylor's concept in this sense emphasises the idea that empowering the poor to struggle against their condition is likely not to be only a question of providing more basic resources, improved local and national governance or developing pro-poor markets (Brown, 2005, cited in Drydyk, 2008: 239). While these material provisions may in context be vital, Taylor's concept emphasises personal and collective capacities to imagine change (Eyben, Kabeer and Cornwall, 2008).

While writers such as Ricoeur (2007) and Castoriadis (1998) have also suggested accounts of modern social imaginaries, Taylor's version seems distinctive for being both individualist and collectivist. For Taylor, these two foci arise due to the centrality of the idea of the social contract in at least the modern Western imaginary, a system of exchange for mutual benefit which confers security in exchange for allegiance to the common good. At the same time, he contends that all societies, including the pre-modern, contained social imaginaries, and that, as a result, 'humans operated with a social imaginary well before they got into the business of theorizing about themselves' (2004: 25).[7] For Taylor, however, the modern, Western social imaginary has special significance, as through the thought of Grotius, Rousseau, Locke and Tocqueville it suggests the shared but almost unconsciously lived background assumptions of everyday life which underlie conceptions of nationhood in many modern democracies.[8] Acknowledging a debt to Anderson's *Imagined Communities,* Taylor also alludes, however, to the likelihood of alternative social imaginaries, and hence alternative paths to human development in a globalising world. While conceding he must leave it to others to spell out the details of these 'multiple modernities' (2004: 195), he focuses on how the capacities of the disenfranchised in particular are inevitably formed genealogically, in a manner which reflects his historical method in his earlier masterwork, *Sources of the Self* (1992).

Crucially, then, Taylor is centrally concerned with the imaginative, psychological capacities of modern individuals and the inter-sphere nature of the modern social imaginary. In his account, three distinct spheres are crucial to the modern Western imaginary. The first is popular sovereignty, which emphasises the principle of civic participation; the second, the democratic public sphere which includes a respect for political rights; and the third, the autonomous sphere of the modern market regulated by the norm of entitlement (2004: 17). For Taylor, the modern economic sphere, regulated by impartial individualism, is distinct from the political, which expresses the idea of power founded on the collective consensus of free subjects (Stock, 2006). Different conceptual resources and normative principles which emerge from these spheres, such as principles of political freedom and equality of economic opportunity, suggest a tension between regulative ideas which modern individuals would need to negotiate (2004: 40–41).[9]

The empowerment potential derived from these ideas in the 'imaginary' domain seems confirmed by Taylor's observation that it was by reflecting on their social imaginary that nineteenth-century trade unionists struggled for labour justice, by conceptualising themselves as part of their society's 'long march' (2004: 22), and by challenging their social realities on the bases of principles of mutual service and mutual respect (2004: 12). While this point may, debatably, raise concerns as to whether Taylor presents too homogenising narrative of modern progress, as though all human development is likely to have one pre-conceived telos (Yack, 2005), for his own part Taylor seems aware that the practical entailments of the principles of popular sovereignty, equal opportunity and political rights cannot be fully predicted in advance (Taylor, 2004: 23).

Evidently, there are limits to how far Taylor's concept of a modern social imaginary may be taken as the basis for empowering the very poor; and it seems crucial to acknowledge the contextual and material preconditions which would be needed for people to struggle in an empowered way against injustice. It seems realistic, however, to take this area of Taylor's thought to indicate the norms through which an empowered self, or a 'recognizer' subject in modernity, emerges (Laitinen, 2003). This is a self who is able to reinterpret the ideas latent in their social imaginary to conceptualise the possibility of social change across different spheres of life. Again, Taylor seems to highlight this potential by referring to women's historical campaigns for equal pay for equal work (Taylor, 2004: 32; Blum, 1991), political campaigns which emerrged from their newly gained status as political equals. Thus, the inter-sphere nature of modern empowerment seems reflected in Taylor's underlying observation that the 'horizontal' normative ideas in modernity intrinsically differ from the 'vertical' assumptions of pre-modern imaginaries which focused not on individual agency but the divinely ordained order (2004: 32).

Significantly, the social and psychological dimensions of modern empowerment as interpreted from this area of Taylor's thought may even hold insights when international development policies are considered. To suggest why, it is worth turning to Hickel's (2014) critique of recent development policies undertaken by the UK Department for International Development (DFID), the IMF and the World Bank, which have prominently focused on increasing women's labour participation (Roberts, 2014; Chant, 2016; Wilson, 2015; de Haan, 2017). According to Hickel, the programmes undertaken by Nike and Goldman Sachs in collaboration with the World Bank have in particular assumed a correlation between increases in women's labour participation, progress in national growth and poverty alleviation. Hickel's concern is that the predominant faith in the empowerment potential of focusing on providing young women in poor societies with labour options risks being reductive, forgetting the full personhood of the very poor, and, in the language of this chapter, failing to recognise the psychological and social bases of the empowerment of the young women.[10] That is, the equation between economic freedom and empowerment seems overly simplistic, as it may underestimate the way in which the women may continue to be disempowered owing to wider political factors, such as structural adjustment and national debt. Additionally, although the point may be debatable and would ideally require much further examination, Hickel also challenges these policies for implying that, at most, kinship, culture and the domestic spheres act as hindrances to empowerment (2014: 1356), rather than supporting the young women's own capacities to reconceive the relationship between these spheres, or to use their economic freedom to influence their status in the different areas of life.

In this sense, these policies may seem to undermine the very conception of selfhood which Taylor's modern social imaginary suggests, namely a modern subject who negotiates their status within power-relations in different spheres of life. While being in many ways an unconventional application of Taylor's examination of modern social imaginaries, this area of his thought seems to raise the question of how far the young women benefiting from the World Bank programmes may use their economic freedom politically, for example to contest unjust power-structures[11] more broadly. This concern has been echoed by capabilities writers, who have also asked how genuinely or comprehensively these official programmes do empower individuals or groups (Frediani et al., 2019; Clark, 2012). While it clearly provides no panaceas in these debates, a focus on Taylor's concept of modern social imaginaries seems to provide the backdrop for a strong normative claim for the need for a more participatory or recognitional approach to the question of empowerment. Crucially, it suggests the capacity of a person as a recogniser of value to reflect on and to translate their influence and control between culture, the market and the public sphere as potentially divergent spheres of life.

4.4 Furthering Durable Inter-Sphere Empowerment: From Recogniser-Subjects to the Dialectics of Recognition

While Taylor's expansive conception of modern social imaginaries therefore seems to provide some crucial background ideas relevant to durable empowerment, my main focus now turns to his substantive recognition theory. It is here that Taylor's theory seems to defend a conception of recognition which provides core support for all three components of durable empowerment outlined previously, especially its normative aspect, which involves the capacity to choose with consciousness of collective injustices experienced by one's social groups. In a strongly universalist theory which seems compelling from the perspective of worldwide poverty, it is crucial that Taylor conceptualises social transformation as one of the core objectives of struggling for recognition.

Two initial premises in Taylor's recognition theory particularly suggest the idea that people become 'durably empowered' through the process of struggling for recognition. The first is the significance which Taylor attributes to the human need for mutual recognition, which may be met only through dialogue or through the particular 'languages' or frameworks of value in which people define their identities (1994: 32). Second, these frameworks or discourses are also likely to be plural in peoples' lives, as, in modernity, it is through different normative languages that human beings realise their natures as 'self-interpreting animals' (1994: 32; Taylor, 2017 [1985]). For Taylor, these languages enable modern individuals to reflect on and potentially to challenge the norms and practices governing the different life-spheres. In this sense, achieving mutual recognition with others is likely to involve invoking one's status in one sphere, to transform one's status towards greater equality and mutuality in other domains of life. This point seems to have special relevance for global poverty, because, as I aim to emphasise, Taylor conceives the goal of recognition struggles not to be to solidify pre-existing static identities but rather to pursue the cultural and even the potential economic change which results from the encounter with differences (1994: 32).

More specifically, Taylor's theory of recognition depends on the idea that a person's struggle to affirm their authentic identity is intrinsically empowering, in that doing so strengthens one's self-concept and one's 'inner self' (1994: 41).[12] Additionally, the end-point or telos of struggling for recognition would be normatively empowering in the sense of enabling the person to contest pre-given social norms, if they seem to withhold sufficient recognition, with the aim of expanding justice in the future. This interpretation of Taylor's liberal recognition theory, however, admittedly raises the concern that, from the perspective of the poor around the world, struggling for the recognition of one's needs and capacities, which modern structural inequalities may deny, is always likely to be arduous under the liberal principles of autonomy Taylor prioritises. I shall respond to this concern more fully shortly. For now, Taylor's emphasis on critical reflection on and potential contestation of the values of different spheres would at least render the poor and powerless less prone to adopt a mode of living and self-image which they do not subjectively endorse. The theory seems to defend the idea that democratic societies should listen to the arguments which they may raise for social rights or redistribution. Although, once again, an overall solution to the dire issues of poverty worldwide could not be guaranteed by this process, it seems reasonable to suppose that Taylor's recognition theory potentially supports the 'power-within' (Cornwall and Edwards, 2010) of the very poor, by offering grounds to protect human capacities to counter outward rationalisations for a socially inferior status or the distributive outcomes which leave them prone to domination. In sum, Taylor's core aim seems to be to suggest a conception of empowering recognition struggles which is in some ways similar to global justice conceived as republican non-domination (Bohman, 2015; Schuppert, 2014).[13]

To support this interpretation fully, it is worth returning first to Taylor's essential claims in his essay, 'The Politics of Recognition' (1994), in which he focuses on the person's need for recognition first by referring to the narrative nature of formation of modern selfhood. For Taylor, people are 'dialogical selves' (1994: 32), 'strong evaluators' who form an understanding of their identity through considering their life-goals by reacting to significant others in their lives. This process forms part of the individual's dialectical, Hegelian struggle for the other's acknowledgement, and which, in the favourable case, results in a state of comparative equality or mutual recognition, a goal which Taylor views as a universal human need, irrespective of specific group affiliations. To support this universal need, Taylor suggests the unique modern significance of the political sphere (1994: 43), with political recognition being mainly confirmed through equal subjective rights. Consistent with his conception of modern social imaginaries, however, Taylor is also highly aware of the different spheres of social life in which people form their identities narratively. These extra-political spheres of recognition, which evoke but go beyond Honneth's conception of the three modes of recognition,[14] suggest that 'we understand the formation of identity and the self as taking place in a continuing dialogue and struggle with significant others' (1994: 32).

It is perhaps curious that, after raising this point, Taylor then devotes the rest of his essay to the idea of political recognition as equal rights (Thompson, 2006: 22). This seeming faith in the political sphere as the main venue of recognition seems paradoxical, as Taylor, in contrast with more standard liberal writers, is very conscious that the other spheres also contribute to a person's overall state of recognition. For example, he gives much significance to women's private-sphere struggles against sexist stereotyping and to Fanon's description of the ways colonialist tropes pervade the self-conception of colonised peoples through inferiority complexes (1994: 64, 65). These issues reiterate his keen awareness that political parity is not the sole objective of empowered recognition struggles (1994: 62).[15] Rather, recognition struggles would be most empowering for the disenfranchised when they go beyond pursuing political recognition as an end-in-itself, and when they aim, as in practice they most commonly do, for a revaluation by the modern subject, the 'recognizer', of the values and statuses of different spheres.

Exactly how people would form capacities for critical reflection on their status within different recognitive spheres is a complex issue, which will be further discussed in the next chapter. For the moment, my main aim is to emphasise the centrality of the issue of empowering inter-sphere reflection to Taylor's conception of recognition struggles. This point seems confirmed by Taylor's repeated focus on the idea that the act of struggling for recognition enables people to avoid enthrallment to the pejorative self-images internalised through others' attitudes (1994: 49). In states which already guarantee political equality, these self-images seem likely to arise from informal attitudes outside the political sphere. Therefore, while political dignity may be both instrumentally and intrinsically valuable, the objective of recognition struggles is broader, as what Rawls calls the 'fair value' of a person's political dignity will often depend on informal interactions with families, communities, the market as well as the political sphere. While, to be sure, people may more easily re-negotiate their control over the different venues of recognition if they securely possess political rights, the significance of empowered recognition struggles from Taylor's perspective seems to involve weakening the focus on political parity and focusing instead on a person's search for identity through the different spheres.[16]

This point also appears reflected in Taylor's distinction between different forms of political recognition. In one sense, Taylor strongly defends the idea that the public culture of modern democracies necessitates universal dignity; but this focus should be balanced, he argues, with a politics of difference which valorises concrete differences. Explicitly although briefly, he suggests that responses to material poverty should fall within the universalist sphere, in the form of social rights. He expresses the point in the following way:

> Naturally, the actual detailed measures justified by this principle [of universal dignity] have varied greatly, and have often been controversial. For some, equalization has affected only civil rights and voting rights; for others, it has extended into the socioeconomic sphere. People who are handicapped by poverty from making the most of their citizenship rights are deemed, on this view, to have been relegated to second-class status, necessitating remedial action through equalization.
>
> (Taylor, 1994: 37–38)[17]

At this point, Taylor seems to recommend redistributive rights for the poor to alleviate second-class citizen status. While he therefore seems to follow Honneth's synthesis of maldistribution as a form of misrecognition, he is also aware that overall equal recognition may involve a continual re-evaluation of which issues belong in the sphere of legal rights and of the issues that ought to be construed as 'political'. Taylor's steady focus on the needs of minority cultures for group-specific rights attests to the need for this social reevaluation. While, for Taylor, the cultural inequalities confronted by the Quebecois in Canada may entail cultural rights (1994: 52),[18] for the very poor difference recognition could be taken to entail pro-poor group-differentiated rights as well as, potentially, different policies aimed at their empowerment.

To appreciate the openness of Taylor's conception of difference recognition, then, it is worth reinforcing the idea, suggested previously, that his main concern is not to justify the confirmation of existing identities. Although he aptly asks in relation to the search for identity, 'what is more legitimate than one's aspiration that it never be lost?' (1994: 40), it seems important to suggest that, in many cases the poor do not, as may be true of many cultural minorities, struggle to preserve a historically authentic group identity. As suggested previously, for many social groups the aim of a politics of difference may not be to affirm a denigrated identity but rather to struggle against what Renault (2017) calls the invisibilisation of their social suffering. As regards the indignity the very poor may feel on account of this social invisibility, Taylor's continual concern with the informal and cultural bases of oppression again seems significant. Some such modes of cultural oppression affecting the poor are vividly highlighted by Vivian C. Adair, an American who describes herself as a 'poverty class scholar', who depicts her own and her sister's childhood as one in which they were 'shamed and humiliated in our ragged and ill-fitting hand-me-downs [...] our very bodies signaling our Otherness' (Adair, 2005: 823, cited in Lister, 2015: 143). The implications of this point for the difference-recognition of the very poor are complex. On the one hand, while Lister resists the idea that empowering the poor would normally involve the assertion of a disenfranchised identity, Deveaux (2018, 2021), as suggested earlier , seems to support difference-recognition for poor-led movements, arguing that international poverty-alleviation programmes should consider the identity claims of, for instance, the Landless Rural Workers' Movement in Brazil (MST), the Bangladeshi poor mobilisation organisation, Nijera Kori, and the Indian pavement dweller movement.

Without forcing a decision between the different interpretations of difference-recognition in the case of global poverty, a core point would be that informal, cultural inequalities may undermine the dignity and agency needed for the poor-led social movements identified by Deveaux to emerge at all. To recognise this point leads us to consider Taylor's added defence of the third, normative dimension of durable empowerment. Whether or not the poor and powerless struggle for the recognition of special welfare rights, for instance, for Taylor it seems crucial to the act of struggle that people become conscious of injustice and aspire to transform society towards greater justice. Again, Taylor's explicit discussion of campaigns for cultural recognition prove instructive, as it is clear they are not uniquely associated with securing political rights. Rather, there may be different modes of resisting dependency (1994: 62),[19] as subaltern groups struggle to move their societies towards a common culture which embodies greater justice (1994: 67). Whereas at times Taylor seems to conflate the issue of creating a more just society with the specific aim of changing societal standards of aesthetic appreciation, by valorising different non-Western cultures' artworks in terms of a Gadamerian 'fusion of horizons' (Taylor, 1994: 67; Zurn, 2003: 530),[20] still the aim of focusing on the standpoints of very poor, on their needs and their life-goals, would seem to be to expand the wider society's responsiveness to the injustices involved in poverty. In this sense, Taylor's conception of the recognition struggles of the poor, whether for welfare rights, pro-poor differentiated rights or participatory development policies which enable their voices to be heard, would be strongly normative. The purpose of their recognition struggle would be to contest and challenge constraining social and economic norms.

At this stage, however, the tensions in Taylor's theory identified by writers such as Habermas (1993) become compelling. If the deeper aim of recognition struggles is to enable disadvantaged groups, such as the poor, women and ethnocultural minorities, to have their voices heard, Habermas' concern is that difference recognition in some instances will inevitably conflict with Taylor's proceduralist sphere of universal dignity, grounded in liberalism's focus on individual autonomy. Civil society inevitably contains, Habermas warns, a vast number of voices making claims, some in relation to the market or labour norms and others as regards dominant cultural values, which some will inevitably view as violating their authentic needs and identities. For Habermas, one cannot listen to and 'recognize' the voices of all oppressed groups whilst still maintaining a neutral public sphere which guarantees equal subjective rights. However, while Habermas proposes a distinctive alternative which enables subaltern voices to emerge involving the co-originality of the 'life-world' and the political sphere, Taylor is more cautious, and is t highly conscious of the fact that liberal democratic societies are not neutral with regard to difference. Liberalism is a 'fighting creed' (1994: 62), one which must openly confront the question of the limits it must draw on publicly endorsed views and perspectives. Therefore, whilst recognition struggles are normatively empowering, they cannot all be supported, an issue which, following Maeve Cooke's analysis, raises the question of how far the articulation of needs and identities by poor-led movements could be supported under liberalism:

> ...The laws of the state, even when they aspire to complete neutrality amongst substantive conceptions of the good, are ultimately connected to institutions and practices which are not neutral structures, but rather themselves express particular views about the self and the good. [For example], the institution of the market reflects a particular view of selfhood and the good, in that it emphasizes the value of economic efficiency

> (a value challenged by deep ecologists, for instance), and characteristics such as self-sufficiency, thus discriminating against [...] those who fail to attain it due to circumstances beyond their control.
>
> (Cooke, 1997: 270)

In response to this point, while Taylor's theory surely confronts a challenge of locating a standard against which to evaluate the claims, articulations of needs and subjective experiences of the poor, some of which may call into question liberalism's philosophical assumptions as regards the priority of individual autonomy, he is nonetheless acutely aware that the normative response to those who appear to call one's boundaries into question cannot simply be dismissiveness. As he urges, however arduous it may be, there must be an ongoing attempt to engage the voices of the disenfranchised, on the basis of a 'presumption for equal respect' (Taylor, 1994: 66; Cooke, 1997: 282). It is in this perhaps additional sense that, for Taylor, contemporary liberalism is best viewed as a fighting creed.

4.5 Revisiting Microcredit: Durable Empowerment through Dignity, Identity Politics and Back

As this chapter previously suggested, significant debates have arisen within development ethics concerning the effects of microcredit loans on power-relations within cultures and households. In countries ranging from India and Bangladesh to diverse African states, these loans have been praised for their empowerment potential (Kabeer, 2001; Mahmud, 2003). In contrast with top-down forms of development assistance and philanthropy, the extension of loans to women in poor countries especially has often been thought to strengthen not only their financial status and labour options but also their self-concepts and sense of self-efficacy (Fernando, 2004; Guérin, 2011; Guérin, Kumar and Agier, 2013). Given the role of these initiatives in encouraging empowerment, this final section of the chapter takes space to ask whether these programmes support the recognition struggles of the very poor, even though externally implemented policies would not usually be viewed as the means through which recognition-claims are raised. This interpretation seems worth pursuing, however, given how strongly the empowering potential of these loans has been suggested to enable the poor to contest an inferior position or social subordination in different areas of life. As I aim to show, viewing microcredit from the perspective of Taylorian recognition struggles highlights complexities with the normative dimension of empowerment, specifically the idea of collective consciousness or 'power-with'. These complexities inevitably turn the emphasis back, when considering global poverty, to the need to understand the relationship between the psychological and normative dimensions of durable inter-sphere empowerment.

To arrive at this conclusion, I first consider the positive gains which seem to have been offered by microcredit programmes (Ali and Hatta, 2012;

Guérin et al., 2013). These policies seem to especially highlight the social, inter-sphere dimension of empowerment, as supported through Taylor's recognition theory. For example, by raising financial status and creating new labour options for the poor, the objective has been to empower very poor communities through greater control over their more general life-conditions. However, a more careful analysis of the effects of these initiatives seems to question their potential to assist, in Taylor's phrase, the project of placing the 'I' in the 'we', the dialectic through which people come to regard each other as moral equals overall, despite their differences (1994: 48–49).[21] As suggested previously, it will often be ambiguous whether increasing a person's power-over in one domain or sphere would necessarily increase their overall empowerment. This point is significant, as recently the positive benefits of microcredit have been queried, with Mahmud (2003) suggesting the outcomes depend on highly contextual variables. Whether microcredit enables women to exert more control over household financial decisions, for example, will often depend on their initial situation before receiving the loans; and it seems that increased financial capacity does not always translate into gains in terms of decision-making control more broadly.

Additionally, as regards the normative dimension of empowerment, or the capacity of the poor women receiving the loans, for example, to increase their critical consciousness of the injustices which affect their lives, the empowerment potential of microcredit, to some, has seemed further doubtful. According to Serene Khader's (2014) recent analysis of the programmes implemented in Bangladesh, microcredit's tendency to expand welfare agency, conceived in terms of a capacity to act according to one's seeming wellbeing interests, has often not been accompanied by an increased capacity for feminist agency, for reasons which will be explained. If Khader is correct, it might be harder to view these policies as genuinely supporting the empowering recognition struggles of poor women.

To explain, Khader raises core dilemmas over whether these policies genuinely lead to greater control by the loan recipients in the critical decisions in their lives. Her concerns reflect the fact that, especially where the recipients of the loans are female, feminist concerns have been raised in relation to the increased risks of domestic violence, in situations where male household members believe their authority to be challenged by the increased financial status of their spouses (Schuler et al., 2017). Naila Kabeer responds to this situation by counter-arguing that, whilst these potential side-effects cannot be discounted, they should not dispel faith in the longer-term empowering potential of microcredit, as these side-effects are likely to be temporary effects of changes in the status quo within households, which should not be thought to detract from the overall positive consequences of these loans (Kabeer, 2001, cited in Khader, 2014: 242). In response to this debate, Khader voices the concern that, even if Kabeer's argument is compelling, the policies may be disempowering at a different level if they do not lead women to greater feminist consciousness which enables them to think, act and choose with a sense of 'power-with', or for the longer-term benefit of their social groups. For instance, if the women do not utilise their increased financial status to question their subjection to apparently oppressive cultural norms, such as *purdah* or female seclusion, for Khader microcredit will not have increased what I have called the normative component of their empowerment. If one chooses to submit to oppressive norms, the greater labour options presented by microcredit, such as homeworking, risk reinforcing patriarchal norms in a way that would fail to support the agency of women as a social group (Khader, 2014: 242).

While this argument seems to reflect very real concerns, and while it seems right to question the empowerment potential of microcredit if it leads to an acceptance of an inferior social status domestically or culturally, the dilemma seems to invite the further question of what it would mean for the very poor to develop collective consciousness or an awareness of prevailing social injustices. As has been discussed, where the affiliations of such a large constituency as those who are economically disadvantaged are likely to be plural, as keenly reflected in Renault's discussion of the 'have-not' movements in Chapter 3, the real normative question may be which group affiliations or structural constraints the individual should hold in view when making empowered social choices. The complexity of this issue is highlighted by Khader's recognition of the paradox that, if the availability of microcredit encourages women to conform to apparently self-subordinating self-seclusion, empirically this choice increases their social status or cultural recognition, through conformity to traditional norms (Khader, 2014: 230). While they gain in cultural recognition, however, Khader questions the idea that this situation has been genuinely empowering for the women, to the extent that they have seemed not to act with critical consciousness of the frequently gendered nature of norms of seclusion.

This apparent paradox, however, appears to open up further questions as to what constitutes critical consciousness, in a world where, for social change to occur at all, people often make complex trade-offs. While the formation of feminist consciousness should not be played down, it seems necessary to acknowledge the uneven and sometimes hidden pathways through which the disempowered often progress towards empowerment (Cornwall and Edwards, 2010). The point seems significant from the perspective of a critical recognition theory, as the crucial issue may not be the paradoxical trade-offs involved in particular choices but whether an empowered attempt to struggle for recognition is raised by expanding the options-set of the very poor, which, all things considered, expands equal dignity and mutuality across different spheres of life. As complex human beings, the poor women receiving microcredit would presumably wish to consider the dignity achieved through expanded labour options, their interests in maintaining cultural identity, and, reasonably, their collective interest in improving the status of women as a social group. Therefore, when evaluating the role of microcredit in the empowering recognition struggles of the poor, it seems crucial to adopt an expansive and flexible view of the normative basis of empowerment, which is likely to bear a complex relationship with the psychological component of empowerment.

I shall return to this relationship in the following chapter. For now, to return to Khader's example, a further reaction would be that the choice of the poor women to opt for *purdah* need not necessarily indicate disempowerment, whereas a choice which leads to greater susceptibility to domestic violence or significantly weaker control over household decisions may amount to clearer indicators. For some women, whether rich or poor, keeping faith in community norms may be a self-aware and even political choice. As Taylor's recognition theory highlights, people are 'strong evaluators' who choose to act from the starting point of a cultural horizon which designates some choices as more or less worthy (1994: 40, 1992). From this perspective, a person conceivably could comply with community norms whilst increasing their consciousness of the structural constraints underlying their choices and of the need to alter these structural constraints. Studies of the empowerment of women of colour bear out this point by suggesting that the question of 'power-with' is not a question of choosing a particular community for whom one acts, but rather thinking multiple axes of race, gender and class position and underlying economic structures simultaneously. If a similar point may be suggested as regards the multiple (cultural, gender or other) affiliations of the poor, the normative component of empowerment then seems complex. For the very poor globally, the normative form of empowerment seems crucially related to the psychological dimension of empowerment, conceived as a complex imaginative ability to hold in view different axes of subordination in the process of choosing and deciding (Hill-Collins, 1990).

In sum, although this discussion of microcredit as a facilitator for women's empowered recognition struggles has been only too brief, the issues raise core questions concerning the normative dimension of empowerment, perhaps most acutely in the form of the question, 'power with whom?' Are choices only empowered if they enable the person to choose to act for the betterment of particular groups with whom they identify? It seems especially complex to respond to this question without returning to focus on what some feminist writers in particular have called 'conscientization', or psychological, dimension of empowerment, which would assist the very poor and powerless to mobilise their capacities to struggle for mutual recognition. Therefore, with the three conceptions of empowerment in view, it seems that a cosmopolitan project of dignifying the world's poor would view the normative question of 'power with whom?' as raising the need for a deeper account of the psychological capacities of the poor to conceive the possibilities of social transformation in the context of the different structural constraints experienced.

4.6 Conclusion

This chapter has aimed to develop a potentially more complex layer of a cosmopolitan recognition theory than that developed previously. I moved on from considering the protection of reason-to-value agency as the gateway to the recognition struggles of the poor, towards a conception of recognition understood as the means through which the very poor empower themselves against the domination which risks trapping them in cycles of poverty due to structural constraints. After presenting a three-dimensional conception of durable empowerment as a resource for cosmopolitan recognition theory, I explored this idea from the perspective of Charles Taylor's liberal recognition theory and of his more recent concept of modern social imaginaries. While Taylor's conception of recognition struggles highlighted the three (psychological, social and normative) dimensions of empowerment through his emphasis on the narrative self, strong evaluation and the cultural nature of oppression, in conclusion I drew attention to the complexities of the normative dimension of empowerment in particular, conceived in terms of the formation of critical consciousness of injustice, complexities which are especially emphasised by recent debates concerning feminist agency in relation to microcredit loans.

As the crucial dilemma appeared to arise in relation to the normative dimension of durable empowerment, my exploration in this chapter seems to invite the further question of whether the concept, as least as grounded in Taylor's liberal recognition theory, under-describes the relationship between its psychological and normative dimensions. This normative dimension involves, I have suggested, a critical consciousness of unjust structures and oppressive social norms which form the background to one's choice and action. If inter-sphere durable empowerment does entail forming critical consciousness of the need to choose in such a way that is likely to increase justice for one's social groups, the dilemma remains as to how the different forms of power within empowerment relate to one another. More generally, a core question seems to arise as to the role of group consciousness in the empowered recognition struggles of the very poor. For this reason , the next and final chapter turns to the recent controversy between Honneth and French philosopher Jacques Rancière concerning the politics of recognition versus disagreement in the context, especially, of Rancière's longstanding focus on the historical identity of the very poor as the uncounted and the excluded.

Notes

1 Specifically, Drydyk (2008) defines durable empowerment in terms of the following conditions: strategic decision-making in life-choices; capacities for decision-making and influence; and the capability to make those gains prevail. The first section of this chapter aims to extend this definition.

2 To explain briefly, 'microcredit' is generally regarded as linked with the wider phenomenon of 'microfinance', the purpose of which is to offer access to capital for individuals who have been previously not been eligible for financial services. In enabling the very poor, and often especially very poor women, to access financial capital, microcredit facilities have been conceptualised as a means of stimulating economic growth in very poor societies. At the same time, the objective of

increasing the availability of these services has also been to empower individuals and groups (Kabeer, 2001). As the literature surrounding the development potential of microcredit programmes has been so vast globally, it is almost inevitable this chapter will not be able to cover all the relevant issues and debates. However, for the purpose of this chapter, I draw not only from Kabeer's (1999) wide-ranging study of microcredit and empowerment in Bangladesh, but also the wider studies of microfinance in developing societies including Isserles (2003), Fernando (2004) and Guérin (2008).

3 In particular, Martins (2022) refers to domination as being one of the faces of power, alongside coercion and manipulation, a form of power over others which can lead to disempowerment.

4 Card (2014) correctly observes that in some obvious ways the concept of survival is a 'multiply ambiguous concept'. On the one hand, as an activity it involves certain skills ('skilled survival'), which people invoke in order to save themselves and keep going. However, the noun 'survival' also seems to refer to what remains, what is not defeated or destroyed. What Card calls 'remainder survival' may also be a very important source of dignity and agency for the poor, but in a different sense than 'skilled survival'. The overall idea, however, is that these forms of survival are unlikely to be fully empowering, a point explored in Chapter 3.

5 I summarise Drydyk's explicit criteria for durable empowerment in footnote 1.

6 In using these terms, I draw from wide-ranging theoretical approaches to power, most particularly Allen (1998) and Haugaard (2012). Whilst many of the existing discussions emphasise 'power-over' and 'power-with' as relevant to empowerment, as will be discussed, it seems vital to incorporate within the definition of durable empowerment the further notion of 'power-within', an idea which is implicit in Cornwall's (2008) discussions of women and human development in very poor countries.

7 As Steele (2017) suggests, the social imaginary refers to the background normative ideals against which a person would be able to conceive possibilities for the future, which are not usually expressed in terms of theories so much as in terms of images, stories, legends and narratives. However, these stories are potentially what legitimise their campaigns for future justice . This sense of legitimacy might seem ineffable or ungrounded from the perspective of people with different narrative understandings of social life.

8 While the concept of the 'social imaginary' was introduced earlier by Castoriadis and Ricoeur in different ways, Taylor later developed his conception in conversation with a number of thinkers, including Craig Calhoun, Dilip Gaonkar, Benjamin Lee and Michael Warner (see Calhoun et al., 2014). His own conception is mainly presented in Taylor (2004), the major source from which I draw in this section.

9 In particular, the later parts of Taylor's essay quite vividly depict the disparity between the principles of different spheres which the modern individual appears to need to negotiate. As he writes, 'action in the political sphere has to take account of the integrity of the other forms, and the goals which people seek within them' (2004: 41).

10 Logically, of course, Hickel's argument is not necessarily gender-specific. However, Hickel's emphasis on young women especially seems crucial and understandable, as policies encouraging their labour participation have been at the centre of some of the World Bank's development policies over some time.

11 This point seems reinforced by Eyben, Kabeer and Cornwall (2008) who contend that, while single acts of defiance against social norms may appear empowering, the outcomes are only empowering if they genuinely change the influence or the overall control a person a person may be able to exert over their life-situation.

12 Taylor's reference in this context is, more particularly, to authenticity in the cultural thought of Herder, as well as to the horror of dependency in the thought of Rousseau.

13 Again, the point appears to draw the connection between Taylor's and Rousseau's thought, which is unsurprising also, given Taylor's frequent references to Rousseau's political thought. As he argues, 'I thought that Rousseau could be seen as one of the originators of the discourse on recognition' (1994: 44).

14 More specifically, while Honneth foregrounds different spheres in which recognition operates, namely in the intimate, labour and political spheres, as discussed in Chapter 1, and while he often clarifies how these spheres inter-relate, he does not specifically suggest why this inter-relation is significant or valuable for people pursuing recognition.

15 This point is reflected in Taylor's critique of a purely proceduralist rights-based liberalism which fails to consider the balance which should be struck between the cultural goals of a nation and its commitment to equal, generic rights (see Taylor, 1994: 60).

16 This point evokes Cornwall and Edwards' (2010) idea of empowerment as essentially involving negotiations which very poor women in particular may undertake within different spheres of social and political life. I return to this point in connection with the final section's discussion of microcredit programmes.

17 Moreover, for Taylor, as for Honneth as suggested in Chapter 1, this progressive assertion of welfare measures and socioeconomic rights as a mode of recognition for the very poor represents part of the historical development of modern societies' own progress, by expanding ideals in ways which were at first controversial to many within modern, Western societies (Taylor, 1994: 39).

18 As indicated earlier, a very large literature now exists concerning Taylor's commitments to group-differentiated rights, especially in his native Canadian context. As my objective at this stage is mainly to contest the idea that Taylor is principally concerned with fixed or reified cultural identities, I do not discuss Taylor's commitment to cultural rights as such in depth. For a fuller discussion of Taylor's conception of cultural recognition, see Patrick (2000) and Hirvonen (2012).

19 Taylor draws evocatively at this stage on Fanon's existentialist study in *The Wretched of the Earth*. The key objective of mutual recognition seems, on this basis too, to be avoidance of overall dependency, or enthrallment to the opinions of others.

20 Taylor's emphasis on different cultural forms of art is understandable given his more general emphasis in his essay on cultural differences, and, specifically, the forms of equal respect which would challenge collective ideas of worth, value and appreciation.

21 As Taylor writes, 'The struggle for recognition can find only one satisfactory solution, and that it is in a regime of reciprocal recognition amongst equals. Hegel follows Rousseau in finding this regime in a society in which there is an 'a we that is an "I"' and an 'I that is a we' (1994: 48–49).

References

Adair, Vivian C. (2005). 'US Working Class/Poverty Class Divides', *Sociology* 39/5: 817–834.

Adams, Suzi, Paul Blokker, Natalie Doyle and J. A. Smith (2015). 'Social Imaginaries in Debate', *Social Imaginaries* 1/1: 15–52.

Ali, Isahaque and Zukarnain A. Hatta (2012). 'Women's Empowerment or Disempowerment through Microfinance: Evidence from Bangladesh', *Social Work and Policy* 6/2: 111–121.

Alkire, Sabine (2008). 'Concepts and Measures of Agency', Oxford Poverty and Human Development Initiative (OPHI), Working Paper no. 9. (2008-01-01).

Allen, Amy (1998). 'Rethinking Power', *Hypatia* 13/1: 21–40.

Blum, Linda (1991). *Between Feminism and Labour: The Comparable Equal Worth Movement* (Berkely: University of California Press).

Bohman, James (2015). 'Domination, Global Harms and the Priority of Injustice: Expanding Transnational Republicanism', in Barbara Buckinx, Jonathan Trejo-Mathys and Timothy Waligore (eds), *Domination and Global Political Justice: Conceptual, Historical and Political Perspectives* (London: Routledge), pp. 83–99.

Brown, S. (2005). 'Applying Q Methodology to Empowerment', in D. Narayan (ed), *Measuring Empowerment: Cross-Disciplinary Perspectives* (Washington, DC: World Bank), 197–215.

Calhoun, Craig, Dilip Gaonkar, Benjamin Lee, Charles Taylor and Michael Warner (2015). 'Modern Social Imaginaries: A onversation', *Social Imaginaries* 1/1: 189–284.

Card, Claudia (2014). 'Surviving Poverty', in Diana Tietjens-Mayer (ed), *Poverty, Agency and Human Rights* (Oxford: Oxford University Press), pp. 21–42.

Castoriadis, Cornelius (1998). *The Imaginary Institution of Society* (Cambridge: Cambridge University Press). The reference is given as Castoriadis (1988) in the reference list. I have amended this item to 1998 in the reference list.

Chant, Sylvia (2016). 'Galvanizing Girls for Development? Critiquing the Shift from "Smart" to "Smarter Economics", *Progress in Development* 16/4: 314–328.

Clark, D. A. (ed). (2012). *Adaptation, Poverty and Development: The Dynamics of Subjective Wellbeing* (Basingstoke: Palgrave MacMillan).

Cooke, Maeve (1997). 'Taylor, Habermas and the Politics of Recognition', *Political Theory* 25/2: 258–288.

Cornwall, Andrea (2008). 'Unpacking Participation: Models, Meanings and Practices', *Community Development Journal* 43/3: 269–283.

Cornwall, Andrea and Jennifer Edwards (2010). 'Introduction: Negotiating Empowerment', *Ids Bulletin* 41/2: 1–9.

Crocker, David (2008). *The Ethics of Global Development: Agency, Capability and Deliberative Democracy* (Cambridge: Cambridge University Press).

De Haan, Arjan (2017). 'The Win-Win Case for Women's Economic Empowerment and Growth: Review of the Literature', Institute for the Study of International Development (ISID). GroW Working Paper series, GWP-2017–03, Concept Paper. Available at: http://grow.research.mcgill.ca/publications/working-papers /gwp-2017-03.pdf. Accessed 10.11.22.

Deveaux, Monique (2018). 'Poor-Led Movements and Global Justice', *Political Theory* 46/5: 698–725.

Deveaux, Monique (2021). *Poverty, Solidarity and Poor-Led Social Movements* (Oxford: Oxford University Press).

Drydyk, Jay (2008). 'Durable Empowerment', *Journal of Global Ethics* 4/3 (December): 231–245.

Drydyk, Jay (2013). 'Empowerment, Agency and Power', *Journal of Global Ethics* 9/3: 249–262.

Eyben, Rosalind, Naila Kabeer and Andrea Cornwall (2008). 'Conceptualising Empowerment and the Implications for Pro-Poor Growth', *Institute for*

Development Studies. Report to the DAC POVNET on Empowerment. September 2008, pp. 2–35.

Fernando, Jude (2004). 'Microcredit and Empowerment: Visibility without Power', in J. Fernando (ed), *Microfinance: Perils and Prospects* (London: Routledge), pp. 187–238.

Frediani, A. A., D. A. Clarke and M. Biggeri (2019). 'Human Development and the Capabilities Approach: The Role of Empowerment and Participation', in D. Clark, M. Biggeri and A. A. Frediani (eds), *The Capabilities Approach: Empowerment and Participation* (London: Palgrave MacMillan), pp. 3–36.

Galie, A. and C. R. Farnworth (2019). 'Power-Through: A New Concept in the Empowerment Discourse', *Global Food Security June* 21: 13–17.

Guerin, Isabelle (2008). 'Markets, Freedoms and the Illusions of Microcredit: Patronage, Caste, Class and Patriarchy in Rural South Asia', *The Journal of Development Studies* 53/5: 741–754.

Guérin, I. (2011). 'The Gender of Finance and the Lessons of Microfinance', in Beatriz Amendariz (eds), *The Handbook of Microfinance* (Singapore: World Scientific Books), pp. 589–612.

Guérin, Isabelle, Shantosh Kumar and Isabelle Agier (2013). 'Women's Empowerment: Power to Act or Power over Other Women? Lessons from Microfinance', *Oxford Development Studies* 41/1: S76–S94.

Gutierrez, E. (1990). 'Working with Women of Color: An Empowerment Perspective', *Social Work* 35: 149–153.

Gutierrez, E. and E. Lewis (1999). *Empowering Women of Color* (New York: Columbia University Press).

Habermas, Jurgen (1993). 'Struggles for Recognition in Constitutional States', *European Journal of Philosophy* 1/2: 128–55.

Harper, Caroline, Rachel Marcus and Karen Moore (2003). 'Enduring Poverty, the Conditions of the Childhood Lifecourse and Intergenerational Poverty' *World Development* 31/3: 535–554.

Haugaard, Mark (2012). 'Rethinking the Four Dimensions of Power: Domination and Empowerment', *Journal of Political Power* 5/1: 33–54.

Haugaard, Mark (2015). 'Domination and Agency', *Journal of Political Power* 8/1: 1–14.

Hickel, Jason (2014). 'The 'Girl-Effect': Liberalism, Empowerment and the Contradictions of Development', *Third World Quarterly* 35/8: 1355–1370.

Hill-Collins, Patricia (1990). 'Black Feminist Thought in the Matrix of Domination', *Black Feminist Thought: Knowledge, Consciousness and the Politics of Empowerment* (London: Routledge), pp. 221–238.

Hirovonen, Onmi (2012). 'Taylor and the Problem of Recognizing Cultural Groups', *Distinktion: Journal of Social Theory* 13/1 (Recognition, Invisibility and Social Disrespect): 109–124.

Hulme, David and Andrew Shepherd (2003). 'Conceptualising Chronic Poverty', *World Development* 31/3: 403–423.

Ibrahim, Solava and Sabina Alkire (2007). 'Agency and Empowerment: A Proposal for Internationally Comparable Indicators', *Oxford Development Studies* 35/4: 380–403.

Isserles, Robin G. (2003). 'Microcredit: The Rhetoric of Empowerment, the Rhetoric of Development as Usual', *Women's Studies Quarterly* 31/3–4 (Fall/Winter): 38–57.

Kabeer, Naila (1999). 'Resources, Agency and Achievements: Reflections on the Measurement of Women's Empowerment', *Development and Change* 30: 435–464.

Kabeer, Naila (2001). 'Conflicts over Credit: Re-evaluating the Empowerment Potential of Loans to Women in Rural Bangladesh', *World Development* 29/1: 63–84.

Khader, Serene (2014). 'Empowerment through Self-Subordination: Microcredit and Agency', in Diane Meyers (ed), *Poverty, Agency and Human Rights* (Oxford: Oxford University Press), pp. 223–248.

Kieffer, C. (1984). 'Citizen Empowerment: A Developmental Perspective', in J. Rappart, C. Swift and R. Hess (eds), *Studies in Empowerment: Steps Towards Understanding Action* (New York: Hayworth Press), pp. 9–36.

Koggel, C. (2007). 'Empowerment and the Role of Advocacy in a Globalized World', *Ethics and Social Welfare* 1/1: 8–21.

Koggel, Christine (2009). 'Agency and Empowerment: Embodied Realities in a Globalised World', in Sue Campbell, Letitia Meynell and Susan Sherwin (eds), *Embodiment and Agency* (Pittsburgh: Pennsylvania State University Press), pp. 250–268.

Laitinen, Arto (2003). 'Social Equality, Recognition and the Preconditions for a Good Life', in *Social Equality Today* (November): 1–26.

Levy, J. T. (2010). 'Multicultural Manners', in M. Seymour (ed), *The Plural States of Recognition* (Palgrave Politics of Identity and Citizenship Series) (Basingstoke: Palgrave MacMillan), pp. 61–77.

Lister, Ruth (2015). '"To Count for Nothing": Poverty Behind the Statistics', *The Journal of the British Academy* 3: 139–165.

Martins, Nieno Ornelas (2022). 'Social Positioning and the Pursuit of Power', *Cambridge Journal of Economics* 46/2: 275–292.

Mahmud, Simeen (2003). 'Actually how Empowering is Microcredit?', *Development and Change* 34/4: 577–605.

Patrick, Morag (2000). 'Liberalism, Rights and Recognition', *Philosophy and Social Criticism* 26/5: 28–46.

Ricoeur, Paul (2007). 'Ideology and Utopia', in *From Text to Action: Essays in Hermeneutics* (Evanston: Northwestern University Press), pp. 308–324.

Roberts, A. (2014). 'The Political Economy of "Transnational Business Feminism": Problematizing the Corporate-Led Equality Agenda', *International Feminist Journal of Politics* 17/2: 209–231.

Schuppert, Fabian (2014). *Freedom, Recognition and Non-Domination: A Republican Theory of (Global) Justice* (Dordrecht: Springer).

Schuler, Sidney Ruth, R. Lenzi, S.H. Badal and L.M. Bates (2017). 'Women's Empowerment as a Protective Factor against Intimate Partner Violence in Bangladesh', *Violence against Women* 23/9: 1100–1121.

Smith, Nick (1994). 'Charles Taylor, Strong Hermeneutics and the Politics of Difference', *Radical Philosophy* (Autumn) 68: 19–27.

Smith, Nick (2004). *Charles Taylor: Meanings, Morals and Modernity* (John Wiley and Sons).

Steele, Meili (2017). 'Social Imaginaries and the Theory of Normative Utterance', *Philosophy and Social Criticism* 43/10: 1045–1071.

Stock, Femke (2006). 'Imaginaries Imagined: A Discussion of Charles Taylor's "Modern Social Imaginaries"', *Ars Disputandi* 6/1: 230–238.

Stewart Angus (2000). *Theories of Power and Domination: The Politics of Empowerment in Late Modernity* (London and New York: Sage Publications).
Summerson-Carr, E. (2003). 'Rethinking Empowerment Theory Using a Feminist Lens: The Importance of Process', *Affilia* 18/1 (Spring): 8–20.
Taylor, Charles (1994). 'The Politics of Recognition', in A. Gutman (ed), *Multiculturalism: Examining the Politics of Recognition* (Princeton: Princeton University Press), pp. 25–74.
Taylor, Charles (1985). *Philosophical Papers Vol. 1: Human Agency and Language* (Cambridge: Cambridge University Press).
Taylor, C. (1992). *Sources of the Self: The Making of the Modern Identity* (Cambridge: Harvard University Press).
Taylor, Charles (2004). *Modern Social Imaginaries* (Duke: Duke University Press).
Taylor, Charles (2007). 'On Social Imaginaries', in Peter Gratton and John Panteleimon Marioussakis (eds), *Traversing the Imaginary: Richard Kearney and the Postmodern Challenge* (Evanston: Northwestern University Press), pp. 29–47.
Taylor, Charles (2017 [1985]). 'Self-Interpreting Animals', in *Martin Heidegger* (London: Routledge), pp. 55–86.
Thompson, Simon (2006). *The Political Theory of Recognition: A Critical Introduction* (London: Polity Press).
Walzer, Michael (1984). *Spheres of Justice: A Defence of Pluralism and Equality* (London: Basic Books).
Wilson, Kalpana (2015). 'Towards a Radical Reappropriation of Gender, Development and Neoliberal Feminism', *Development and Change* 46/4: 803–852.
Yack, Bernard (2005). 'Modern Social Imaginaries', *Ethics* 115: 62–633.
Zurn, Christopher (2003). 'Identity or Status? Struggles over 'Recognition' in Fraser, Honneth and Taylor', *Constellations* 10/4: 519–537.

5 Regarding the Suffering of Others

Rancière on Recognition, Disagreement and Empowering Forms of Power

5.1 Introduction

The previous chapter suggested the pivotal but complex role of the concept of empowerment in dignifying the lives of the poor through a cosmopolitan recognition theory. In particular, it was suggested that the three dimensions of durable inter-sphere empowerment seemed to leave a number of questions open-ended. Although I argued that empowering oneself in the context of deep, global forms of poverty would normally involve forming collective consciousness or power-with, crucial questions seemed to remain regarding how this consciousness could be formed where the experience of poverty would not necessarily unite people in terms of a stable or unified community of interest. At the same time, it does not seem implausible to suggest that forming a certain collective consciousness, or historical awareness of group injustice, would be crucial to enabling the very poor and the excluded to struggle for inclusion, pursuing a conception of the good life which is truly their own. Justifying inter-sphere durable empowerment, therefore, appeared to involve combining the different forms of power, namely power-over, power-within and power-with, to enable the poor and excluded to articulate their priorities in a participatory dialogue over human needs.

In order to further clarify the relationship between these various components of empowerment, this final chapter concentrates more specifically on the interaction between the psychological and normative dimensions of the concept. To do so, I engage the thought of French philosopher, Jacques Rancière, whose ideas I interpret in a way which will, I hope, clarify the relationship between these forms of power in the potentially empowering recognition struggles of the very poor. This interpretation derives especially from Rancière's recent debate with Honneth concerning the nature of recognition-claims (Honneth and Ranciere, 2016). Rancière contributes unconventionally to recognition theories by distancing his defence of the inner or psychological empowerment of the poor from any stable conception of collective identity. Specifically, he emphasises the capacity as one involving the ability to imagine alternative forms of suffering and modes of living to one's own, and to conceive one's own situation, such as poverty or

DOI: 10.4324/9781003045038-6

economic exploitation, as related to different communities and their distinctive forms of suffering. His approach to recognition-claims, therefore, might even be thought to involve a moment of 'dis-identification', an idea which draws from his wider concepts of 'dissensus' or 'disagreement' (Rancière, 1999; 2001), concepts which refer to a person's resistance to their situation against prevailing norms. While many challenging questions clearly arise concerning the evolution of this capacity in the context of problems such as poverty or inequality, questions which have led some to label Rancière's thought a-political or overly 'aesthetic' (e.g. Dillon, 2003), I defend his core conception of psychological empowerment, whilst also suggesting a movement beyond his explicit theory to clarify the relationship between this imaginative capacity and the formation of collective consciousness of historical identity. Taken as a whole, I suggest Rancière's unconventional contribution to recognition theory (Deranty, 2003) contains significant insights into the deep exclusions the poor may experience in inscribing their claims on the political agendas of their societies. By avoiding the identitarian focus of some mainstream recognition theories, Rancière convincingly portrays recognition as a matter, for the poor and powerless, of becoming conscious of the exclusions of the existing order.[1] In this sense, his thought productively focuses on the capacities of the very oppressed to raise a claim for a new or better universalism. This is so even though, I argue, his theory might be further balanced with a specific conception of a collective memory of injustice on the part of the disenfranchised.

To further explain, in contrast with the later Frankfurt School writers' emphasis on the value of self-realisation, Rancière insists on a radical conception of equality, or what he classically calls 'the equality of speaking subjects' (1999: 29–30). He does so through his core concept of the 'distribution of the sensible' (*le partage du sensible*) (2011, 1999: 17), which refers to the way in which societies typically pre-specify the range of speech and bodies which are effectively perceptible, and those whose experiences are unacknowledged. For Rancière, as the needs and concerns of the very poor are often likely not to be fully perceived within their wider society, truly empowering recognition-claims would involve questioning the existing social and political order in order newly to inscribe their needs and priorities on the political agenda. Therefore, in Rancière's terms, to raise an empowering recognition-claim would not involve a purely negative assertion of a suffering identity but an original proposal, a radical demand for inclusion which would question current conceptions of universality. In this sense, the most radical recognition-claims would not aim for reconciliation with prevailing social norms so much as the assertion of a new and better cosmopolitan universalism. While defending some of Rancière's core insights, I also contest his tendency to under-theorise the ethical importance of group identities, and, in the terms of the argument of this book, the relationship between the psychological and normative dimensions of durable empowerment. As will be argued, fully durable empowerment, which would enable the poor and powerless to think, choose and decide in such a way that secures a stable departure from cycles of poverty, would most likely involve forming collective consciousness of historical injury.

My discussion is organised as follows. Section 5.2 outlines the background of Rancière's interpretation of the presentation of 'the poor' in Western philosophy, whom he takes to be repeatedly portrayed as excluded, and therefore prevented from formulating their own suffering as an injustice. In turn, this predicament prevents them from pursuing a conception of the good which they have fully assessed for themselves. Section 5.3 explores Rancière's application of this idea in his recent debate with Honneth (Honneth and Rancière, 2016), an analysis which leads to my focus in Section 5.4 on Rancière's concept of the 'distribution of the sensible' and its implications for the struggles of the very poor worldwide to contest the limitations of official conceptions of development and progress. As suggested previously, Rancière provides a compelling conception of empowerment as a matter of exposing the limitations of the current recognition order, empathetically by contrasting one's own social suffering with others' and aligning one's condition with the suffering of different groups. While accepting Rancière's strong universalism, Section 5.5 concludes by aiming to transcend his non-identitarian conception of recognition to establish the significance of collective consciousness in the recognition struggles of the poor, especially by distinguishing the idea of consciousness of historical injury from the question of authentic group identity.

5.2 The Philosophers and Their Poor: Rancière and the Disenfranchised Beyond Equality Politics

The origins of Rancière's recent contribution to recognition theory may be usefully located in his early writings, *The Philosopher and His Poor* (1983). Prefacing his later defence of a radical conception of equality also, in these early essays Rancière sought to explain a logic of exclusion running throughout Western thought. For Rancière, throughout the Western canon the question of political inclusion appears to depend on conceptions of reason which continually presuppose a social class which remains excluded and uncounted, namely 'the poor'. From this reading of Western thought, equality of the poorest, subaltern classes may be hard won where their historical exclusion is the very basis of the inclusion of others.

Rancière's early thought emphasised, more specifically, how classical philosophers from Plato onwards presupposed the political exclusion of a particular class as a condition of asserting the priority of those with the capacity to reflect and to contemplate. Political order in the *Republic* classically expresses a fundamental contrast between those who rule by natural capacity on one side, namely the philosopher-kings, and the workers, whose natural capacities seem to justify their exclusion from political affairs. For Plato, it is the artisan's assumed natural propensities which justifies denying them the leisure-time to think. The philosopher's disdain for capitalism is, from this perspective, rationalised by the imperative of each to do his or her own business in a utilitarian division of labour,[2] with the masses consigned to commerce in a way that instrumentally preserves the status quo. In Andrew Parker's reading of Rancière, therefore, 'in Plato's *Republic* the ersatz is first and foremost the artisan, who can do only one thing at a time [...] since he has been given the time to do only one thing, his trade and nothing else' (Parker, cited in Rancière, 1983: xiv). Yet, despite the efforts of this political design, the 'artisan remains a problem which the philosophers cannot master in their own terms' (Parker, cited in Rancière, 1983: xv). As trades are diverse, the artisan may exchange one trade for another, and even risks political subversion through intellectual engagement. For this reason, the philosophers, as the engineers of souls and of society, must uphold the order through myth.[3]

For Rancière, the disempowerment of the artisan is later confirmed more relentlessly by Marx, for whom 'the poor' presents not as the working class so much as its disappropriation as the proletariat, the non-class tasked with making revolution (Rancière, 1983: 34). If the proletariat becomes the agent of history, 'it is not because it "creates everything" but because it is dispossessed of everything – not only of the "wealth" it "created" but especially of its "creative" power, i.e. the limits of the "dedicated" worker realizing himself in "his" product' (Rancière, 1983: 80; Marx and Engels, 1976: 4/37). For Rancière, Marx's proletarian, whom the revolution perpetually awaits, therefore loses his identity as an agent to the progress of history in which all projects of self-realisation would be obsolete, as would be so under communism. As such, for Rancière, the later Marx instrumentalises the proletarian in a certain sense by denying his internal plurality and subordinating him to the exclusive task of advancing history.

While, for reasons of space, these synopses inevitably oversimplify Rancière's analysis, they nonetheless indicate his highly provocative interpretation of the history of Western thought. Time and again, the poor and the uncounted are reduced to a singular purpose which denies the fundamental essence of being human, and therefore their fundamental equality. For Rancière, this reductiveness and denial of human equality is eventually also reiterated by Bourdieu (Rancière, 1983: chapter 9, citing Bourdieu, 1987). On the one hand, Plato's exclusion of the artisan depends on the propagation of an ideology, 'that magnificent myth, that noble lie' (Plato, 1987: Book III, 415a). In late modernity, however, this logic of exclusion becomes reconfigured but no less potent. For Bourdieu, the noble lie resurfaces in the form of class ideology. Although its true nature is in principle knowable, its ideological nature remains concealed from the 'the poor' and finds expression only in the hesitant and paradoxical forms of social suffering, such as those explored in Chapter 3. For Bourdieu in *Distinction* (1987), capitalism's myths concerning privilege and entitlement are effective because the only means for emancipation is to enter 'the game of bourgeois passions'

(Rancière, 1983: 200), emulating the privileged in a struggle over recognition which ultimately expresses domination.[4] For Rancière, Bourdieu's thought remains trapped in narrating this process rather than challenging it politically. While allowing the theorist the means to acknowledge the possibility of opposition and resistance, inevitably the poor and the excluded do not set the terms of recognition:

> An anti-Platonic myth of the separation of souls. But in what, really, does its anti-Platonism consist? For one cannot see what possibility of doing something else than their "own business" was won there by the artisans. The denunciation of the *scholē* also denounces the *parvenu*, who arrogates to himself the leisure to study that he does not have.
>
> (Rancière, 1983: 169)

For Rancière, genuine liberation would involve suggesting how the poor themselves might offer a philosophical critique of the ideology from within, in such a way that would counter the tendency of Bourdieu's ethnographies to confirm the inequities they reveal, and in such a way that the theory of the judgement of taste, for example, would not simply end by confirming the 'demonstrable efficacy of domination' (Rancière, 1983: 177).[5] For Rancière, the outcome of the Western philosophical narrative is that from Plato onwards, the noble lie maintains its disempowering grip.[6] This dimension of Rancière's thought seems already to reveal a strong critique of relying on a framework of recognition as the means to empower the very poor. On this conception, to struggle for inclusion according to existing social criteria produces only the option of interpreting the poor and powerless from the perspective of pure rational choice, with all its complexities, or, otherwise, simply reiterating, again in Rancière's words, 'the implacable necessity of the relations of production and domination' (Rancière, 1983: 284).

5.3 Honneth, Rancière and Global Poverty: Between Recognition and Disagreement

Rancière's seemingly far-reaching reading of Western philosophy seems immediately to suggest that he would, then, resist the language of recognition in theorising global forms of poverty; and he seems right, at least, to avoid equating the struggle for recognition with a capitulation to ideological conceptions of worth and taste according to Bourdieu's theory. In fact, however, Rancière's orientation to recognition struggles is more complex, and may be highlighted through his comparatively recent debate with Honneth. This dialogue strongly suggests Rancière's desire to reconfigure the concept of 'recognition' where, following his earlier thought, some are substantially excluded from the dominant recognition order. Specifically, Rancière introduces to the debate over recognition his long-standing commitments to concepts of 'disagreement' or 'dissensus' in order to outline a conception of what Chapter 4 identified as the psychological dimension of empowerment. Therefore, whereas I argued previously that this component in modern societies would be likely to emerge through the ideas latent in Taylor's modern social imaginary, Rancière complicates this picture by suggesting that frequently the very poor encounter severe obstacles in inscribing their claims on the political agenda. His approach to recognition-claims emerges especially in response to the following issues: (a) universal justice in recognition-claims; (b) the question of identity; and (c) whether social suffering should be viewed as the motivational source for recognition struggles. I suggest that Rancière's *universalist, non-identitarian and non-grievance–based* conception of recognition indicates a particular conception of power-within or the psychological component of durable empowerment. The universalist and non-grievance–centred aspects of this conception are most compelling from the perspective of analysing global poverty.

Turning first to the question of universal justice in recognition-claims, Rancière insists on his long-standing premise that, while all political demands aim towards understanding, the claims of the poor and the excluded are especially prone to misunderstanding (Rancière, in Honneth and Rancière 2016: 85). This is owing to their originality; they are likely to express a previously hidden, denied or suppressed conception of universal justice rather than a reinterpretation of their society's norms. It is for this reason they are both rare and prone to *mésentente*.[7] Here Rancière seems to confirm a point raised previously in this book concerning the challenges the poor and powerless might confront in establishing a language according to which they could articulate the injustice of their suffering. For Rancière, this is because the claims of the excluded tend to 'designate [...] a permanent struggle to enlarge the restricted form of universalism that is the rules of the game' (2016: 84). This point evokes Rancière's insistent point that emancipation, when one has been socially excluded, will often involve articulating a new conception of equality. For example, in response to the protests in the French *banlieues* of 2005 by low-income youths in localities disproportionately affected by poverty and crime (Body-Gendrot, 2016),[8] Rancière warns of the risks of asserting a marginalised identity in a violent or insurrectionary manner, in the form of a 'military confrontation' rather than in an attempt rationally to demonstrate one's equality with others. For Rancière, demonstrating discontent in this militant manner risked only entrenching the youths' sense of marginalisation rather than, as they might have, 'construct[ing] a time and space that could be shared', or a new conception of the universal (2016: 70–71; Gundogdu, 2017).

Although Rancière's response to this incident is complex and bears further comment, for the moment my main purpose is to emphasise how the point seems to highlight a key difference between his own and Honneth's conceptions of recognition. Rancière insists that the most empowering recognition struggles would not simply express one's sense of imperfect reward according to a given society's recognitive norms. For Rancière, this focus would only confirm what he takes to be the conservative nature of the more usual conception of recognition, a point which he emphasises as follows:

> In the usual sense, recognition [...] means: I identify this voice, I understand what it tells me, I agree with his or her statement [.... However], the point I would like to make is how far does the concept that makes "recognition" the object of a struggle depart from the two presuppositions in the usual meaning of the term, namely the identification of pre-existing entities and the idea of a response to a demand? How far does it depart from an identitarian conception of the subject and from the conception of social relations as mutual?
>
> (Rancière, in Honneth and Rancière, 2016: 85)

Essentially, these questions emphasise Rancière's concerns with Honneth's tendency to assume that people who struggle for recognition are for the most part attempting to achieve a form of reconciliation with the social order. To recall, rejecting the Hobbesian constitution of the individual in self-interest, Honneth takes recognition struggles to originate from the need to construct relations of confidence, respect and esteem with others, a claim which seems to suggest this desire for social reconciliation. In contrast, or Rancière, although it may be true that some justice-claims take this form, the most radical recognition struggles will usually aim to exceed the givens of a society's distribution of respect and esteem. To recall Chapter 1, Honneth defends the potential universalism of his recognition theory by assuming the normative principles underlying advanced capitalist societies to relate in a deeper, abstract way to a general, anthropological conception of the human being (Honneth, 1995; Honneth, in Honneth and Rancière, 2016: 86). Although, in this sense, he aims for a theoretical bridge between the universal or transcendent and the immanent or particular, for Rancière this manner of accessing the universal will be unsatisfactory, as it would not highlight the radical nature of the claims of the poor and powerless.

As this claim seems difficult to assess fully without applying it to an example of a concrete global struggle against poverty, which will be undertaken later in this chapter, for the moment it is worth granting Rancière this possibility, especially as it leads to the second feature of his conception of empowering recognition struggles, namely their non-identitarian nature. At this stage, Rancière reacts to the tendencies of mainstream recognition theories to overstate existing identities as the grounds of social struggle. For Rancière, one should avoid conceptualising the historical struggles of African-Americans for equal political respect, for example, or the struggles of minorities for special rights purely as campaigns to confirm existing identities (Rancière, in Honneth and Rancière 2016: 87). Analogously, any identity for which the poor and the excluded struggle would be original, as they should not be understood purely as raising a straightforward claim for welfare redistribution or social rights. Although, again, this point may in some ways be debatable and controversial, it would seem to reflect Rancière's legitimate desire to avoid what might be called, following Wendy Brown's terminology in the context of her study of identity politics, a 'wounded attachments' conception of recognition (Brown, 1994), one based on the desire to vindicate or demand compensation for an under-valued historical identity. Rancière's resistance to this conception seems to be explained by asking how, if all subjectivity, suffering and struggle occurs in order to affirm already-existing identities, any recognition struggles would genuinely transform society, or its understanding of subjectivity and suffering.

Although this seems to be a genuine and valuable question, at the same time Rancière's critique seems focused on claims raised on the basis of authentic cultural identity, to which, as previous chapters have shown, major recognition theorists such as Honneth and Taylor are not in fact strongly committed. As Rancière concedes, Honneth's conceptions of the self and of identity are in fact quite dynamic. To this extent, Rancière's critique seems best understood as a more general wariness of the risk of the conservative nature of these frameworks, or as a warning of the slide towards a static form of ideological recognition, according to which women, for example, may be extolled only or mainly as housewives. While Honneth does take seriously the dangers of this form of ideological recognition, critics such as Patchen Markell (2009) seem to reinforce Rancière's concern that any reconciliatory conception of recognition risks curiously sliding into disrespect, in the sense of creating the standing risk of only acknowledging people for virtues which are socially significant to possess or for labour which is involuntarily performed, in a way which again evokes the risk that recognition amounts to a form of domination. Rancière, therefore, seems right to ask whether the 'process [of struggling for recognition] requires a concept of the subject which questions the identity model more radically, a subject calling into question the wrong done by all forms of inclusion in terms of identity' (Rancière, in Honneth and Rancière, 2016). Again, although the point seems to be a fairly general criticism of the risks inherent in any political value, it leads Rancière productively to counter-assert the need for a radical expression of equality rather than a straightforward confirmation of existing identities or social roles (Rancière, 1989). In fact, for Rancière, this novel expression would be a demonstration to oneself over and above any demand one imposes on others or the wider society.

I shall argue eventually that Rancière's critique of identity in the recognition struggles of the poor is likely to be problematic from the perspective of a cosmopolitan recognition theory. As a first reflection on Rancière's critique, for now, it is worth emphasising that both Honneth and Fraser avoid focusing too heavily on identity-movements, such as campaigns concerning gender and multiculturalism, as discussed in Chapter 1.[9] Hence, Rancière's argument seems in some ways overstated and not the strongest basis on which to raise an alternative conception of recognition. It does, however, lead Rancière to identify a further feature of recognition struggles, which seems highly significant, and which he rightly takes to differentiate his theory from Honneth's. This is the idea that the most empowering recognition struggles would not be understood mainly or only as a protest against one's own social suffering. An emancipated recognition struggle would not mainly assert a negative grievance, according to Rancière, as doing so would only confirm inequality. Rather, this form of struggle would ambitiously express what he terms a 'logical demonstration of equality' (1995: 47). This is clearly a demanding idea, which may even appear implausible and impractical from the perspective of very poor, the marginalised or socially excluded. The idea that one should enact one's equality in front of the world at large may seem to underestimate the extent of structural constraints. To recall, in response to the uprisings after the acts of police repression in Clichy-sous-Bois, Rancière argued that the demonstrators risked self-defeatingly reproducing their exclusion. What would have been truly radical and emancipatory, as Rancière earlier suggested more generally in *On the Shores of Politics*, would have been to attempt to 'escape from a minority' (Rancière, 1995), to reach out to another world, to exceed the givens of one's social and economic identity and to act in ways that expressed one's rationality. For Rancière, doing so would have offered a means of reconstituting the universal or a common world with others. On the one hand, while one should not underestimate barriers imposed by structural constraints, it also seems plausible to suggest that, for those whose lives are limited by their ideological recognition as destitute or disposable, real emancipation would involve disputing these categorisations (see Ilcan and Lacey, 2011).

While provisionally accepting Rancière's idea, then, that emancipation may often involve moving beyond grievance, it is still worth noticing that some other theoretical ambiguities seem to arise from his central ideas. As Chambers (2014) and Norval (2012) ask, is it plausible to suggest that the recognition struggles of the poor or powerless arise wholly from outside of the given recognition order? As Norval (2012) further suggests, Rancière's idea seems beset by the challenge that he seems to want to portray democracy as a ruptural break with the prevailing order. However, in an ambitious claim for inclusion, the democratic experience must always also show how this challenge reconstitutes that order, so that a new claim does not always constitute a full break with prevailing norms. While I will return presently to these issues, for now I provisionally support the potential of Rancière's strongly universalist and non-grievance-centred conception in the context of global poverty, while remaining doubtful that empowered recognition struggles could involve the very poor distancing themselves completely from collective consciousness or action according to a group identity.

5.4 Empowering the Global Poorest: Power-Within as Identification with the Universal?

As Rancière, therefore, appears to raise some crucial disagreements with better known conceptions of recognition, his critique lays the foundations for his more substantive conception of the psychological component of empowerment, an approach which seems highly relevant from the perspective of global poverty. Specifically, Rancière appears to understand this capacity as a power empathetically to engage other modes of living and suffering as the precondition for pursuing one's own conception of the good life reflectively. Although it is admittedly a complex idea, this argument seems to offer some crucial insights into the psychology which would probably be needed politically to struggle against the threat of continual cycles of poverty, by forming consciousness of one's situation not only as a matter of economic hardship but as a form of injustice. Additionally, Rancière's idea seems, as I aim to show, highly dependent on the concept of the 'distribution of the sensible', an idea on which he frequently relies to suggest how certain forms of injustice remain unperceived societally as exclusions or injustices (Rancière, 2009: 12).[10] While it would probably overstate the issue to suggest that empowerment always takes the form of actively questioning the given recognition order, this focus on the perceptible field, raising the question of which injustices are readily discerned as such as such, seems a significant idea.

More specifically, to examine his argument fully, it is worth separating Rancière's conception of the psychological power central to empowerment in terms of two components. The first and somewhat unusual dimension consists in using one's imagination to engage different forms of human suffering, a process which seems to involve distancing oneself from one's own experience. The second component involves translating what has previously been unheard or not perfectly understood into a legitimate political demand, or, according to Rancière at least, a new universality. For Rancière, the move from exclusion to inclusion involves a further move between 'voice' and 'speech' in Aristotle's sense (Aristotle, 1965). While I will argue that Rancière's thought does suggest significant insights into how hierarchy and inequality may be challenged (2001: 10; 12), an argument which seems productive for debates concerning global poverty, difficulties also arise in wholly distancing this form of empowerment from the issue of existing group identities.

To arrive at this conclusion, it is worth turning back to the dialogue between Rancière and Honneth. For his part, Honneth does not dispute Rancière's focus on the perceptible field, or the 'distribution of the sensible', as crucial to recognition theory (Honneth, in Honneth and Rancière, 2016: 103).[11] As he suggests, it seems crucial to acknowledge existing recognition orders permit inequalities and that in the resulting distributions, some remain substantially excluded and hence 'the part without the part' (see Rancière, 1999). On the other hand, Honneth takes the conflation of recognition struggles with campaigns to alter this perceptible field to be overstated or exaggerated, given there are many meaningful but non-revolutionary interpretive conflicts over the norms of any recognition regime (Honneth and Rancière, 2016: 103), as exemplified by the struggles which were explored over the interpretive meanings of love, rights and esteem in

Chapter 1. For Honneth, in nineteenth-century European first-wave feminist movements, for example, women sought inclusion within the dominant political forms of recognition in campaigns which, while not revolutionary, still suggested a significant intervention (2016: 104).

In whichever way these two thinkers interpret the role of the 'distribution of the sensible' in recognition struggles, however, what seems more crucial to their theoretical disagreement is their lack of consensus over the role of social suffering. It is this point which highlights the distinctiveness of Rancière's conception of recognition. As argued in Chapter 3, Honneth insists on a likely semantic connection between the person's subjective experience of social suffering and their desire for political change. Put differently, campaigns for change will always be linked to some form of discontent with the existing order. Rancière's rejoinder is interesting in that, rather than disagreeing outright with Honneth, he shifts the emphasis from one's own social suffering to an imaginative power to connect existentially with the suffering of others. He concedes that social suffering will always be likely, given the tension that always exists in a society which distributes rewards differentially and the underlying fact of human equality (Rancière, in Honneth and Rancière, 2016: 113). People who are oppressed or excluded will inevitably suffer as they wish to 'seize the inner contradiction of the political order' (2016: 115).

However, for Rancière the core issue is that this suffering is likely to remain a-political unless one mobilises an inner power to 'reach out to another world', as he described in relation to the post–Clichy-sous-Bois demonstrations (see Rancière, 2006).[12] In this context, Norval (2012) rightly suggests that Rancière's theoretical points are often best illuminated through his historical examples. For instance, he refers to Jeanne Deroin's historical landmark decision to run as a candidate for the *Assemblée Nationale* in 1849.[13] As Rancière explains: '[s]he did so in order to construct another world, another relation between the domestic and political space' (Rancière, in Honneth and Rancière, 2016: 118). The inner resources which led to Deroin's action seem to confirm the first component suggested earlier in Rancière's conception of the inward capacity needed for empowerment. That is, her action seemed fueled by her awareness of injustices outside her own subjective experience. Aligning her campaign with different forms of suffering, including those of working-class men, children and convicts, enabled her to conceive her feminist demand truly as a claim for a better world. Furthermore, her proposal also seems to reflect the second feature of Rancière's understanding of this imaginative capacity. By proposing to run for election, she attempted to enact, or in Rancière's terms 'logically to demonstrate', a different world, one in which, as her contemporary George Sand suggested, her candidature as a woman would have been exceptional at a time before women had been formally enfranchised. Her action therefore seemed to highlight the possibilities of a more rational, more universally inclusive world, rather than, as Rancière suggested in response to the Clichy-sous-Bois demonstrators, engaging in an antagonistic military confrontation.

Rancière, therefore, reacts to Honneth by asserting the importance of an imaginative capacity which tends towards the 'invention of other ways of being, including other ways of suffering' (Rancière, in Honneth and Rancière, 2016: 125).[14] Although some of Rancière's critics accuse him of impracticality and of underestimating the depth of structural inequalities, it does not seem implausible to believe that this wider consciousness might serve as a catalyst for developing one's sense of one's material situation as part of a wider world which ought to be transformed. In rather dense reasoning, Rancière argues that: 'it is through the appropriation of the suffering of the other that there is an overcoming of the situation' (2016: 125). The reason for this, for Rancière, lies in the larger questions of inclusion and exclusion which one begins to consider by attempting to comprehend different forms of suffering, as one asks who is or is not socially entitled to this or that form of suffering. From this perspective, it is not that the different forms of suffering become interchangeable, or that one literally or even metaphorically experiences others' pain or sense of exclusion. However, it seems conceivable that the distance one gains from the intense particularity of one's own situation enables one to conceptualise suffering not just as a negative subjective state but in terms of questions of universal justice or injustice. As Rancière insists, 'you also have to exchange your suffering against another, which at this point is precisely a kind of symbolic suffering' (2016: 125).

This rather complex process describes what Rancière (2009; 2014) means by 'subjectification', dis-identification, or even what one might label a 'de-recognitional' moment in recognition struggles. Rancière further illustrates this argument by referring to workers' movements in nineteenth-century France, in which, he contends, to mobilise themselves the workers had to re-imagine their suffering. They had to view themselves as suffering not only from a lack of money or from poor life-conditions but rather from 'broken time' and, hence, an inability to undertake different experiences, for example to engage novels which depicted the suffering of the sons of the bourgeoisie who do nothing, a different suffering to which they were not entitled (Rancière, in Honneth and Rancière, 2016: 126). Compelling though it seems, this idea of dis-identification raises a number of critical questions, such as the plausibility of generally assuming knowledge of other forms of suffering to lead to the capacity to distance oneself from one's own situation. One question may be whether Rancière means to refer to a strong sense of ambivalence as regards one's inherited identity, the capacity to view all forms of suffering as equivalent, and hence a strong form of impartiality. In a sense, it seems true that a person could increase their capacity to view the world differently by conceptualising their suffering or their mode of exclusion or oppression as one form amongst others. This wider knowledge might enable the givens of one's situation to seem not inevitable but as one situation which motivates a struggle for universal justice. Therefore, in a weak sense, to broaden one's view may be considered part of the empowerment process, enabling one to form a conception of oneself as part of a larger whole, as an equal amongst others.

If, however, dis-identification involves no longer prioritising the group-based origin of one's own inequality, this claim appears much less convincing. Moreover, at this point some of the key objections which have been raised against Rancière's philosophy seem very relevant. Jodi Dean (2011), for example, argues that the idea of the 'presupposition of equality' which the poor should logically demonstrate through this dis-identificatory politics comes to seem 'more akin to a fantasy', without an analysis of the social conditions and the institutional contexts which maintain hierarchies and constrain collective struggles for equality. Peter Hallward (2009) similarly argues that Rancière's focus on the intermittent moments of the individual's dis-identification with their condition appears disconnected, counter-intuitively, from the broader social dynamics through which collective struggles are typically raised. In some ways, these critiques may seem to underestimate the subtlety of Rancière's conception of emancipation as a process occurring over time inwardly rather than achieved through a one-time confrontation with institutions of power (see Rancière, 2011). Hence, while retaining doubts about a strong conception of dis-identification as impartiality, it seems plausible that the inner psychological component of empowerment might involve a weaker sense in which thinking in terms of universal justice involves distancing oneself from one's own subjective suffering.

That said, however the idea of dis-identification is construed, Gundogdu (2017) seems correct to voice a connected concern as to the strong distinctions seemingly presumed by Rancière between viewing one's suffering as emanating from a specific group identity and the radical newness of a particular claim. I shall return shortly to this tension in Rancière's thought when focusing on a particular example of a cosmopolitan struggle against destitution. For now, there seem reasonable grounds for taking up the weak impartialist interpretation of Rancière's idea of dis-identification, on the grounds that the psychological openness to different ways of suffering could fuel one's motivation to struggle for justice. As Shaw (2017) argues, Rancière's radical political proposals seem reflected in the Black Lives Matter movement's attempt to reconceptualise justice as a more substantive conception than the procedural, due process idea usually associated with liberalism. Yet in interpreting this movement in terms of Rancière's theory, it also seems crucial to acknowledge that the defenders of Black Lives Matter have strongly resisted the forgetfulness of specific historical injuries. As a number of commentators have suggested, the central critique has precisely been that the 'due process' conception of justice was one which historically legitimised injustices against African-Americans (Havercroft and Owen, 2016; Hooker, 2016). Therefore, while Rancière's strongly universalist, cosmopolitan conception of empowerment seems productive in view of the structural constraints of the very poor, if interpreted in terms of a weak capacity to think beyond one's own suffering, it still seems doubtful whether the poor and powerless could forget a history of exclusion in the course of their recognition struggles. Expanding on this issue next, I turn more deeply to the relationship between the inner, psychological capacity suggested by Rancière and the idea of power-with, as a matter of the recollection of historical injury.

5.5 Combining the Forms of Power: The Empowerment of the Poorest in the Sardar Sarovar Project

In this concluding section, I pursue the above analysis in terms of a particular international struggle to maintain livelihood and subsistence, in order further to understand the complex relationship between the two central forms of power in durable empowerment, namely the psychological and the normative. To recap, although Rancière's conception of recognition struggles departs from an identitarian approach which draws on stable concepts of group consciousness, it would also seem surprising if his framework were fully to discount any conception of collective identity. In examining this point, I suggest moving beyond Rancière's conception of dis-identification by highlighting the unsettled boundaries between the uncounted and the counted and between, on the one hand, a radical challenge to the status quo arising from the disadvantaged, and, on the other, a struggle based on historical memory of a denigrated identity. The need to unsettle these distinctions is highlighted well by the high-profile dispute concerning the Sardar Sarovar project in India, which decimated the livelihoods of many of the region's rural poor in the name of a particular conception of development. This controversy has been incisively documented by the Booker Prize-winning novelist Arundhati Roy in *The Cost of Living* (1999), who comments on what she regards as one of the great illusions of India's quest for economic progress, namely the massive dam projects which promised modernisation since Independence. While the project has long been rationalised on grounds of its resource-benefits to urban areas, up to a million of the local rural poor, primarily Adivasis and lower-caste groups, have been either forcibly displaced or rendered destitute.[15] In her explicitly political writings, Roy has emphasised the paradoxes of one of Sarovar's most ambitious projects, the Narmada Dam, by raising the rhetorical question: 'how can the "market" put a price on things – food, clothes, electricity – when you don't know how much it cost, and who paid for it?' (1999: 7).

Especially well known in development and ecological studies, the controversy surrounding the Narmada Dam provides a crucial practical lens for cosmopolitan recognition theory, as it involved a coordinated opposition movement including a coalition of activists who together challenged the conceptions of development and progress advanced by the Indian state and the World Bank (Sangvai, 2000; Baviskar, 1995). Employing a range of tactics including Gandhian non-violent protest, the strongest resistance was raised by the Narmada Bachao Andolan (NBA) or the 'Save Narmada Movement', of which Roy has been a vocal spokesperson. The Narmada is well known for being the fifth largest river in India, which runs for over 1,300 kilometres through the states of Madhya Pradesh, Maharashtra and Gujarat. According to Bose (2004), over 250,000 people have been forced to relocate, whilst over a million have seen their livelihoods disrupted or erased. Proponents of the Narmada Valley Development Plan promoted the benefits of increased drinking water, irrigation and hydroelectric power to the nearby urban areas, advances which have come at the cost of the rural poor whose livelihoods have been disrupted if not destroyed through the implementation of this official conception of development (Bose, 2004: 136).

It seems useful and plausible to interpret the campaign which arose in terms of Rancière's conception of recognition, in so far as those disadvantaged by this policy raised and expressed their concerns politically and internationally. Even if, as will be explained, ultimately their struggle did not succeed, the concerns of the rural poor did gain significant exposure at both regional and state levels in India (Sangvai, 2000). From the perspective of Rancière's theory, the rural poor and their defenders may be conceptualised as the uncounted, whose mode of living seemed not to figure in the Indian state's conceptions of development. In this context, the solidarity of figures such as Roy seemed crucial, as through their collective efforts a claim was raised, in a petition which reached India's Supreme Court to dispute the forcible movement of the rural poor to urban areas pursuing precarious work driving rickshaws and other urban occupations (Routledge, 2003). While the high-profile collaborators were clearly not the marginalised, the excluded and the uncounted, their contributions raised an alternative vision of justice for the poor and powerless politically and internationally, especially by connecting this dispute to a broader resistance to the effects of neoliberal globalisation.

That said, their status outside the affected communities of the rural poor themselves seems also to raise the question of whether empowering the global poorest should mobilise a specific sense of group consciousness from the perspective of the communities involved. As previously suggested, Rancière's strong cosmopolitan universalism suggests otherwise, as it contests identitarian conceptions of recognition. From his perspective, as has been discussed, real empowerment would consist in asserting a more universalistic conception of value, in such a way which offers a new basis for a common life with others. While the NBA did, in this vein, seem to offer an alternative, ecologically-focused conception of development to that advanced by the World Bank, it also seems crucial to recognise that the Narmada controversy overwhelmingly affected poor low-caste and Adivasi groups. Ayten Gundogdu (2017), therefore, correctly questions Rancière's demanding distinctions between the defensive reassertion of a disenfranchised identity and the proposal of a new universalism. As it seems right to unsettle this distinction, I conclude with the possible need to combine the Rancièrian conception of the psychological component of empowerment with a more open, future-oriented conception of historical collective identity.

This conclusion may be highlighted by considering the criticism Roy received for seeming to assume the ability to speak for the rural poor. Significantly, Roy responded by insisting that the Narmada controversy did not raise a rigid question of group identity but rather questions concerning the effects of neoliberal modernisation projects on social and ecological justice concerns. In this sense, Roy seemed to assert the 'de-recognitional' moment of Rancièrian recognition struggles. As she states in *Power Politics*, through policies such as Narmada, the country has lain witness to 'road gangs of emaciated labourers digging a trench to lay fibre optic cables to speed up our digital revolution' (Roy, 2001, cited in Bose, 2004: 147), a situation which affects the moral and political world inhabited by all. While the question could also be how far the contributions of figures such as Roy did empower the people whose lives were displaced, disrupted or destroyed, the coordinated challenge to international development policy seemed empowering, in so far as, as Todd May (2008) argues, from a Rancièrian perspective, real political activity occurs not simply by writing to elected representatives, an avenue which seem to remain within the current economy of sensibility. Rather, for Rancière, empowerment is a matter of presupposing one's equality by affirming a new universality. In this sense, the NBA's advocacy of alternative conceptions of development may be conceived as expressing the equality of the disenfranchised as speaking subjects (Routledge, 2003).

Even if this point is accepted, the Narmada dispute also seems to highlight the difficulties of a pure distinction between a dis-identificatory moment in recognition struggles and the defensive assertion of a historically disenfranchised or denigrated identity. In fact, it seems plausible to suggest more broadly that many campaigns arising over redistribution and recognition are frequently likely to involve a complex relationship between a campaign operating within a particular system of values and political objectives which exceed that scheme of value, raising a more radical demand for a better world. For Rancière, as has been shown, it would be the latter which is truly empowering. And, in fact, it seems right to suggest that in the Narmada dispute, coalitions of the rural poor were emphasising the insufficiency of surface reallocations made by the state according to the dominant conception of development, such as attempts to relocate the rural poor to the urban areas. This is despite the difficulty of suggesting whether, in these contestations, the very poor concretely 'presupposed' or 'demonstrated' their equality. This ambiguity evokes the critiques of Rancière considered previously for not fully conceptualising the structural inequalities and constraints which may often in practice prevent this rational demonstration. However, if Rancière's conception may be aligned with Fraser's (Fraser, in Fraser and Honneth, 2003) conception of 'deconstructive' rather than 'affirmative' recognition struggles, at least it could be suggested that the movement's challenge to neoliberal conceptions of development seemed vital.

More deeply than this, however, it seems problematic to distance the empowerment of the very poor wholly from collective consciousness or power-with. It seems problematic, that is, to assume that forming an inner capacity to imagine the future transformation of injustice would not at least strategically involve poor communities maintaining some form of collective historical memory. As regards collective consciousness, it seems Rancière defends only the most diffuse sense of power-with, which he seems to construe as the capacity of the poor and powerless to reconstitute in relation to their political communities in a truer, better conception of universal justice (Rancière, 1999: 59).[16] For, to recall Rancière's key example, in response to the riots after Clichy-sous-Bois, he (2006) argued that a more inspired, universalistic political strategy might have involved, for instance, producing an image which symbolically tethered the administrative number for their *arrondissement*, number 93, to the image of *a tricolore*. While Rancière's underlying point seems comprehensible, in the sense of rightly indicating the need to overcome a purely grievance-centred politics, it seems unrealistic to suggest that in the Narmada controversy, for instance, the poor disengaged from their inherited identities, or that they should have done so. Although the effectiveness of many challenges to policies which deepen poverty and destroy livelihoods might well depend on an inspired claim for a different universality, it also seems crucial they do not rule out a focus on the historical dimensions of group identity, as there is a need to know who further may partake of the dialogue concerning needs and rights and who was previously excluded. This is not to undermine Rancière's defence of dis-identification. However, it is to suggest that many such struggles, as Rancière himself appeared to suggest in his early explorations of the objectives of the proletarian class to give themselves a name and to speak for themselves (Deranty, 2014: 35, citing Rancière, 2007), often arise from particular historical injustices experienced by particular communities. In this sense, they are likely to draw on historical memory, even if they ultimately wish to defend a more open, and what Fraser (Fraser and Honneth, 2003; see also Fraser, 2010) would call 'transformative', account of collective identity.

Therefore, while Roy seemed correct to insist the Narmada movement should not be viewed as one affecting Adivasis in isolation (Roy, cited in Bose, 2004: 151), it seems equally crucial not to disregard the collective identity of those whose lives were undermined or seemed uncounted previously. It does not seem misconceived to suggest real transformative political activity will often involve attempting to re-think justice and offering a universalistic critique of particular power-structures. Plausibly, the shift towards this new universality might assist the rural poor to conceptualise alternatives, thereby supporting their rights to choose their mode of living. It also seems right not to conceive their struggle as a precursor to reclassification, implying a rigid conception of what the rural populations in this example should choose or how they should live.

At the same time, it seems less plausible to make the stronger claim that the anti-Narmada struggle, for instance, would only involve 'a purely negative moment in the politics of equality' (May, 2008: 50). Construed in this way, recognition struggles would seem to amount to liberal autonomy; but it does not seem to be through liberal autonomy alone that people become politically empowered. Rancière suggests that presupposing one's equality concerns an ability, again in May's words, to 'consider and carry out life-project [...] and to participate in the construction of a life' (2008: 59). However, as the Narmada dispute exemplifies, it also seems important to make room for the '*collective* assertion or expression based on the presupposition of equality' (May, 2008: 64, my emphasis). Thus, Rancière's seeming desire to distance his conception of empowerment from all stable notions of identity seems overdrawn (Gundogdu, 2017). For the historically excluded, it seems true, in Rancière's phrase, that '[the struggle for recognition] is the demonstration of a struggle for equality which can never merely be a demand upon the other – but always, simultaneously, a proof given to oneself. This is what emancipation means' (1995: 48). However, even according to the weak conception of dis-identification proposed earlier, it is likely that some commitment to specific group identities could be maintained, and, in practice, doing so may be especially significant for poor communities around the world.

More specifically, even if it would be right to emphasise that raising a demand for a better world should not involve the romantic assertion of 'authentic' group identity, there is likely to be a weaker distinction than Rancière's theory appears to suggest between raising a demand for a better world and the defensive assertion of a denigrated identity. This point seems especially crucial in the Narmada Dam dispute. As Routledge (2003) explains, the struggle against neoliberal conceptions of development exemplified not only a struggle against poverty and material inequality, but also a struggle over practices and meanings of everyday life (see also Escobar, 1992). In resisting the neoliberal conception of development, for example, a strong strand in the opposition movement was the need to preserve a threatened Adivasi culture (Bose, 2004; Agarwal, 2000). As Baviskar (1995) argues, some within this dispute pointed to the risks of 'strategically essentialising' Adivasi identity through the political presentation of indigenous modes of development as the polar opposite of the state's and international community's modernisation policies, and, in doing so, running the risk of reifying the question of Adivasi identity. In this context, Rancière appears correct to suggest that 'politics (that is, the simple effects of domination by the rich) causes the poor to exist as an entity' (1999: 14). While this point seems rightly to suggest the strongly imagined nature of group identities, complex questions seem to arise as to how this imagined conception relates to a real memory of historical injustice motivating an opposition movement.

An issue which arises from this situation, then, is that the weakly dis-identificatory conception of the inner capacity in empowerment is likely to involve a historically and politically conscious conception of group identity in practice, even if that conception might be comparatively open and non-essentialist. In the Narmada dispute, for instance, the formation of collective consciousness could keep in mind the dilemmas involved in representing the gender, class and caste-based divisions within any conception of disadvantaged identity.[17] For those whose livelihoods were affected by the Narmada project, it seems correct to suggest, with Rancière, that forming this sense of collective identity will not be rigid but would involve forming connections with others, and, therefore, imagining alternative ways of being and suffering, and to engage 'the ability of each of us, in concert with others, to engage in the reflective construction of lives' (May, 2007: 60).

It seems at this stage worth generalising from the Narmada controversy to make connections with the insights of feminist development ethicists, such as Kabeer (1999) as discussed in Chapter 4, who conceive empowerment not so much as the exclusive preservation of identity for its own sake, so much as the individual's capacity to mobilise their inner resources over the sources of existing power, which may involve preserving 'emic' cultural values in non-essentialist ways. Whereas some have claimed that subaltern groups should purposefully mobilise their group identity and values to advance their distinctive claims for justice and development, this form of strategic essentialism (Spivak, 1993) may be both conceptually and practically problematic. As Sylvain (2014) argues in the context of debates concerning the San struggles for their rights to their traditional territories in the Central Kalahari Game Reserve in Botswana, the risks involved in strategic assertions of group identity suggest that a pathway should be found between an approach which questions all collective identities as political or historical fictions, as exemplified by a pure (for instance, Derridean) deconstructive view; and the countervailing trap of too easily accepting strategic essentialism in Spivak's sense. Sylvain rightly warns that the pure deconstructionist view risks failing to view questions of group identity as genuinely political questions, whilst the trap of strategic essentialism is that it seems to presume, in a politically insincere way, a broader context in which indigenous or other group identities are thought of as primordial and essential. Sylvain rightly suggests that this insincerity tends to reproduce the logic of those fixed identities.

In contrast with both approaches, and in a way which might seem productive in campaigns against destitution such as the Narmada dispute, Sylvain (2014) seems right to follow Hale (2006) in defending a politicised conception of group identity, which may assist the poor and dispossessed as they aim to inscribe their claims upon their political agendas. In other words, the formation of collective consciousness of a historically injured identity is often likely to form a component of the struggles of marginalised or dispossessed communities. It may inform the equality they presuppose when, in Norval's (2012) phrase, they raise Rancièrian recognition struggles and aim to 'write a name in the sky'. While it seems crucial to bear in mind the ways that states have relied on the rigidity of existing group identities to trap indigenous peoples in potentially restrictive self-understandings, and have even used the political language of recognition as a code for implementing paternalist interventions (Povinelli, 2002; Coulthard, 2004), Sylvain seems right to suggest that the deconstructive turn in recognition theory, especially where claims concerning recognition and redistribution overlap, should not involve forgetting historical group oppression for the sake of offering a new conception of justice or development. Where the memory of collective historical injustice is maintained, redistributive claims and challenges to state and international policies of development might encourage a strongly political conception of power-with, not one which is cynically or strategically essentialist or one which is, in contrast, unrealistically tied to romantic conceptions of authentic group identity. However, it is a consciousness of the need to remember the injustice while presupposing one's equality and writing a new name in the sky.

5.6 Conclusion

The aim of this chapter has been to extend the previous chapter's understanding of inter-sphere durable empowerment in debates concerning global poverty, especially in terms of its psychological and normative components. In doing so, I focused especially on the dialogue between Axel Honneth and Jacques Rancière. Focusing especially on the universalising recognition-claims of the poor and uncounted, I suggested a particular conception of psychological dimension of durable empowerment seemed to arise from Rancière's thought. By concentrating first on Rancière's early focus on the exclusions of the poor through the Western philosophical canon, it seemed that the capacity for dis-identification identified by Rancière, however ethically significant for a cosmopolitan theory, should not be considered opposed to the collective consciousness of oppression in contesting national and even international development initiatives. While Rancière correctly questions and destablises assertions of unified pre-given identity, I concluded that the weak version of 'dis-identification' should be aligned with a politically conscious conception of historical injury. Doing so could be productive in availing the poor and powerless with the flexibility in their struggles over recognition to focus on new universalities and new articulations of cosmopolitan justice.

Strong defenders of Rancière's approach might, of course, wonder whether clinging to historical memory would only disable the poor and the disenfranchised from what he urged after the urban riots in France nearly two decades ago, namely that they attempt, insistently, to 'draw the line of escape, the line of universalization' (2009: 282), or to act outside of their experience of grievance. Only by doing so, he argued, would they demonstrate an equality which one must presuppose as a human being. Whilst Rancière's fears concerning regressive conceptions of group identity are not wholly misplaced, especially in light of the many situations in which collective identity has either been politically manipulated or mired people in unproductive resentment, at the same time retaining historical memory need not be synonymous with the strongly wounded-attachments conception of recognition struggles opposed in Rancière's critique of mainstream theories. In other words, the remembrance of historical injury need not be equated with the demand for compensation for grievance or restoration of a fixed identity. While, practically, there may surely be ambiguities in distinguishing the wounded-attachments conception from a more open, future-oriented but still historically aware conception of collective consciousness, it is the latter which seems crucial to durable empowerment in a cosmopolitan recognition theory. At least, it seems difficult to see how the poor and the powerless would demonstrate their equality in a historical or social void.

Finally, given the focus on reciprocity in a cosmopolitan recognition theory, some ambiguous issues surely remain as to how far the empowering recognition struggles of the poor would need first to be acknowledged by those who are included. Kabeer, for example, rightly asks how far progress in empowerment depends on the social acknowledgement of inclusion by the already counted. In Rancière's language, the question may be to what extent a particular recognition struggle succeeds in altering the perceptible field. Furthermore, there are difficult questions as to what the poor or powerless may concretely do in order to 'enact' their equality in the world over which they often have little control. As Naila Kabeer asks, should empowerment be evaluated according to the amount of structural change effected, or in terms of the effect of this structural change on individual agency? Or should empowerment be measured, as Batliwala (1993) suggests, by increases in the person's capacity to choose within an 'expanded framework of information'? Whilst these are inevitably complicated questions, I hope to have defended a conception of empowerment which depends on opening up new options and new opportunities, not through the forgetfulness of historical oppression, but, perhaps unexpectedly, through reacting to it in a creative, empathic way. Obviously, the relationship in this chapter envisaged between the forms of power in durable empowerment re-confronts challenges continually directed at Rancière's theory to explain how one might 'presuppose' equality in a world of often deep structural constraints. As testimony to the obstacles in this process, the Sardar Sarovar project discussed in this chapter, despite the withdrawal of World Bank funding in 1993 as a result of the ecological concerns raised, was resumed by the Indian state in 2000, with the extended dam height of 121.92 metres reached in 2006. While the anti-Narmada movement had been empowering, in the sense that the people of the Narmada Valley seemed to inscribe their claims against the official conception of development on the political and even international agenda, ultimately it is not clear that their proposal of a new 'line of universalization' led to a better life from their point of view.

Notes

1 It seems important to bear in mind that Rancière's references to 'the poor' should not be interpreted too literally. In *Ten Theses on Politics* (2001), he clarifies that the 'the poor' does not necessarily designate an economically disadvantaged part of the population so much as the class of person whose views do not count, or whose views are not included. Therefore, while the metaphorical nature of the term should be borne in mind, it seems plausible to apply Rancière's thought to issues of global poverty, given that so frequently the claims of the very poor around the world remain unheard.

2 As Rancière summarises: 'So, there is only one principle of exclusion. Plato's *Republic* does not decree that one cannot be a shoemaker and a citizen at the same time. [...] It does not exclude anyone by reason of the baseness of his job, but simply establishes the impossibility of holding more than one job at a time. It knows only one evil, but this is the absolute evil: that two things be in one, two functions in the same place, two qualities in one and the same being' (1983: 8).

3 As Rancière (1983: 8) cites Plato's *Republic*: 'While all of you in the city are brothers, we will say in our tale, the deity who fashioned you mixed gold in the makeup of those fit for rule, for which reason they are most precious. In that of the defenders he mixed silver, and iron and brass in the makeup of the ploughmen and craftsmen'.

4 The original French edition of *The Philosopher and His Poor* appeared earlier than the English translation which is cited in this chapter. For this reason, Rancière often appears to cite texts, such as those of Bourdieu, which were published earlier than the English translations of Bourdieu which I cite in this chapter.

5 At this stage I state Rancière's critique rather uncritically mainly for the purpose of providing the background for his later theory. As raised in Chapter 3, however, there is more debate concerning the political effects of Bourdieu's methodology and political commitments than Rancière's critique seems to acknowledge. See, for example, Croce (2019).

6 Rancière seems at this point to draw the potentially controversial conclusion that, while the social scientist may engage the task of 'demystifying' ideology, this project is destined to be politically ineffective (1983: 212–213).

7 Significantly, the French title of Rancière's (1999) publication, *Disagreement*, has a dual meaning in French, with *mésentente* suggesting both 'disagreement' and 'misunderstanding'.

8 The uprisings of 2005 arising across many French suburbs involved a series of insistent protests which were sparked by incidents of police repression in Clichy-sous-Bois, a northern French suburb, and which resulted in the violent deaths of particular youths of North African origin. During the ensuing events, some 10,000 cars were burned, 233 buildings were damaged and an estimated 4770 people were arrested. In this section, I draw especially from Gundogdu's insightful discussion of Rancière's perspective on this issue (Gundogdu, 2017: 207). In particular, Gundogdu cites an interview given by Rancière in August 2006, in which he described these uprisings as a 'real rebellion against certain states of things', but where the protestors offered 'no real political proposition' which would, he argued, have demonstrated an ability to think not only from a subjective, first-person standpoint but from a perspective which is more impartial and universalist (cited in Gundogdu, 2017: 208). Rancière's responses to these uprisings are expressed in key part in his interview with Truls Lie in *Le Monde Diplomatique* (Rancière, 2006).

9 It is worth adding that Honneth openly agrees with Rancière on the issue that, in most recognition struggles, the marginalised or disenfranchised often do attempt

to distance themselves from a formerly restrictive or pejorative conception of their identity (2016: 108).

10 More specifically, Rancière states, 'I call the distribution of the sensible the system of self-evident facts of sense perception which simultaneously discloses the existence of something in common and the delimitations which define the respective parts within it' (2009: 12).

11 As Honneth argues: 'I find it extremely convincing to say that our way of perceiving the world is regulated by certain existing normative principles, so that our way of perceiving the world, the way of being able to see what "is the case" in the social order, is structured by the pre-given political categories and normative principles which allow the justification of inequalities and asymmetries' (Honneth, in Honneth and Rancière, 2016: 115).

12 At this stage, Rancière suggests that 'there is no homology, no continuity from the suffering of individuals in a given situation to the construction of a subject as such. This also means, it is not only a question of suffering; it's a question of the construction of different universes, giving a different perceptual status and also different capacities to those who are included in the world' (Rancière, in Honneth and Rancière, 2016: 122). Here, of course, complex questions arise as to how people form the conditions for evolving the imaginative capacities he identifies.

13 It is worth remembering, however, that Deroin's attempt to run as a candidate was ultimately rejected. Thus, the fact that person might 'presuppose' or 'enact' their equality in the world at large does not necessarily entail that this 'enactment' is accepted by others. See Scott (1996).

14 Given his fairly complex argument, it is worth stating Rancière's words more fully on this point: 'I have in mind a letter of the joiner Gauny to one of his friends telling him he had to learn a new way of suffering. He recommends to his fellow worker to read the romantic novels, Chateaubriand's *René*, for instance [...] The point of reappropriating the suffering of the other is that it is through the appropriation of the suffering of the other there is an overcoming of the situation' (Rancière, in Honneth and Rancière, 2016: 127).

15 The dam projects are only one out of an array in India's development policies since Independence which have, according to some studies, brought massive costs to the rural poor. Fernandes and Thukral (1989) estimate that at least 15 million people have been displaced by projects for economic development since Independence.

16 In *Disagreement*, for example, Rancière raises the example of the historical strikes by French tailors who expressed their equality in the only way that they could, namely by utilising their collective power to force the wider society to acknowledge their equality. As Todd May summarises, 'demonstrations like these are expressions that unify those who are oppressed and those who act alongside them and on their behalf as a single subject' (2008: 55). It is this sense of 'democratic unity', or 'power-with', which the claims of the poor raise, from Rancière's perspective. Similarly, Rancière refers to the demonstrators in May 1968 Paris, who declared, against all the evidence, that 'we are all German Jews'. In his terms, these demonstrators were attempting to expose the gap between their political identity and any other kind of group identity they happened to possess (Rancière, 1999: 59).

17 Activist and anthropologist Gael Omvedt was especially vocal as regards Arundhati Roy's contribution to the NBA project, claiming that 'there is nothing wrong with going out to organize people [...] with rallying world opinion. NBA has succeeded in giving great power to a "no-big-dam" position and in putting a big question mark before whole issue of "development". You have every right to support them. But, in doing so, please think about one thing: when you go

as leaders to the people in the valley, what are the consequences for them of the arguments that you make? What does it mean when you put your own arguments, either explicitly or implicitly, in their mouths?' (Omvedt, Gael. 'Dams and Bombs-11', Editorial, *The Hindu* 5 August (1999)).

References

Agarwal, A. (2000). 'Preface', in R. Bissell, S. Singh and H. Worth (eds), *Maheshwari Hydroelectric Project: Resettlement and Rehabilitation* (Mandeshwari: Narmada Bachao Andolan), pp. 1–3.

Aristotle, trans. A. L. Peck (1965). *Historia Animalium (Vol. 1)* (Cambridge, MA: Harvard University Press).

Batliwala, Sriatha (1993). *Empowerment of Women in South Asia: Concepts and Practices* (Colombo and New Delhi: Asian-South Pacific Bureau for Adult Education).

Baviskar, Amita (1995). *In the Belly of the River: Tribal Conflicts over Development in the Narmada Valley* (Delhi: Oxford University Press).

Body-Gendrot, Sophie (2016). *The Social Control of Cities: A Comparative Perspective* (Oxford: Blackwell).

Bose, Pablo (2004). 'Critics and Experts, Activists and Academics: Intellectuals in the Fight for Social and Ecological Justice in the Narmada Valley', *International Review of Social History* 49: 133–157.

Bourdieu, Pierre (1987). *Distinction: A Critique of the Judgement of Taste* (Cambridge, MA: Harvard University Press).

Brown, Wendy (1994). 'Wounded Attachments', in *States of Injury: Power and Freedom in Late Modernity* (Princeton: Princeton University Press), pp. 52–77.

Chambers, Samuel (2014). 'Jacques Ranciere and the Problem of Pure Politics', *European Journal of Political Theory* 10/3: 303–326.

Coulthard, Glen (2004). 'Introduction: Recognising Identities, Imagining Alternatives', in Harry Englund and Francis B. Nyamnojh (eds), *Rights and the Politics of Recognition in Africa* (London: Zed Books), pp. 1–29.

Croce, M. (2019). 'The Levels of Critique: Pierre Bourdieu and the Political Potential of Social Theory', *Sociologica* 13/2: 23–35.

Dean, Jodi (2011). 'Politics without Politics', in Paul Bauman and Richard Stamp (eds), *Reading Ranciere* (London: Continuum), pp. 73–94.

Deranty, Jean-Philippe (2003). 'Jacques Rancière's Contribution to the Ethics of Recognition', *Political Theory* 31: 136–156.

Dillon, Michael (2003). 'De(void) of Politics? A Response to Jacques Rancière's 'Ten Theses on Politics'', *Theory and Event* 6/4. https://muse.jhu.edu/pub/1/article/44781

Escobar, Arturo (1992). 'Imagining a Post-Development Era? Critical Thought, Development and Social Movements', *Social Text*, 31/32: 20–56.

Fernandes, W. and E. G. Thukral (eds) (1989). *Empowerment of Women in South Asia: Concepts and Practices* (New Delhi: Indian Social Institute).

Fraser, Nancy. (2010). 'Injustice at Intersecting Scales: On "Social Exclusion" and the "Global Poor"', *European Journal of Political Theory* 13/3: 363–371.

Fraser, Nancy and Axel Honneth (2003). *Redistribution or Recognition? A Political-Philosophical Exchange*, trans. J. Golb, James Ingram and Christiane Wilke (London: Penguin Random House).

Gundogdu, Ayten (2017). 'Disagreeing with Rancière: Speech, Violence and the Ambiguous Subjects of Politics', *Politics* 49/2 (April): 188–219.

Hale, Charles (2006). 'Activist Research v Cultural Critique: Indigenous Land Rights and the Contradictions of Politically Engaged Anthropology', *Current Anthropology* 21/1: 96–120.

Hallward, Peter (2009). 'Staging Equality: Ranciere, Theatocracy and the Limits of Anarchic Identity', in Gabriel Rockhill and Philip Watts (eds), *Jacques Ranciere: History, Politics and Aesthetics* (Durham, NC: Duke University Press), pp. 140–158.

Havercroft, Jonathan and David Owen (2016). 'Soul Blindness, Police Orders and Black Lives Matter: Wittgenstein, Cavell and Ranciere', *Political Theory* 44: 739–763.

Honneth, A., J. Ranciere (2016). *Recognition or Disagreement: A Critical Encounter on the Politics of Freedom, Equality and Identity* edited by Katie Genel and Jean-Phillipe Deranty (New York: Columbia University Press).

Ilcan, Suzan and Anita Lacey (2011). *Governing the Poor: Exercises in Poverty Reduction, Practices of Global Aid* (Montreal: McGill-Queen's Press).

Hooker, Juliet (2016). 'Black Lives Matter and the Paradoxes of US Black Politics: From Democratic Sacrifice to Democratic Repair', *Political Theory*, 44/4: 448–469.

Kabeer, Naila (1999). 'The Conditions and Consequences of Choice: Reflections on the Measurement of Women's Empowerment', United Nations Research Institute for Social Development, Discussion Paper 108 (August).

Markell, P. (2009). *Bound by Recognition* (Princeton: Princeton University Press).

Marx, Karl and Friedrich Engels (1976). 'The Holy Family', in *Collected Works* (New York: International Publishers).

May, Todd (2007). 'Jacques Ranciere and the Ethics of Equality', *Substsance* 36/2: 20–36.

May, Todd (2008). 'Active Equality in Contemporary Politics', in *The Political Thought of Jacques Ranciere: Creating Equality* (Edinburgh: Edinburgh University Press), pp. 142–188.

Norval, Aletta (2012). "Writing a Name in the Sky': Ranciere, Cavell and the Possibility of Egalitarian Inscription', *American Political Science Review* 106/4: 810–826.

Plato (1987). *Republic*, trans. Desmond Lee (Harmondsworth: Penguin).

Povinelli, Elisabeth A. (2002). *The Cunning of Recognition: Indigenous Alterities and the Making of Aboriginal Multiculturalism* (Durham: Duke University Press).

Rancière, Jacques (1983). *The Philosopher and His Poor* (Durham: Duke University Press).

Rancière, Jacques (1989). *Nights of Labour: The Workers' Dream in Nineteenth Century France* (Philadelphia: Temple Press).

Rancière, Jacques (1995). *On the Shores of Politics*, trans. Liz Heron (London: Verso).

Rancière, Jacques (1999). *Disagreement: Politics and Philosophy*, trans. Julie Rose (Minneapolis: University of Minnesota Press).

Rancière, Jacques (2006). Interview with Truls Lie, 'Our Police Order, What Can be Said, Seen and Done', *Le Monde Diplomatique*. Available at http://www.eurozine.com/articles/2006-08-11-lieranciere-en.html.

Rancière, Jacques (2007). *La Parole Ouvrière* (Paris: La Découverte).

Rancière, Jacques (2009). *The Politics of Aesthetics: The Distribution of the Sensible* (London and New York: Continuum).

Rancière, Jacques (2011). 'The Thinking of Dissensus: Politics and Aesthetics', in Paul Bowman and Richard Stamp (eds), *Reading Rancière* (London and New York: Continuum), pp. 1–17.

Ranciere, Jacques (2014). 'Politics, Identification and Subjectivization', in John Rajchman (ed), *The Identity in Question* (London: Routledge), pp. 63–70.

Routledge, P. (2003). 'Voices of the Damned: Discursive Resistance amidst Erasure in the Narmada Valley, India', *Political Geography* 22: 243–270.

Roy, Arundhati (1999). *The Cost of Living: The Greater Common Good and the End of Imagination* (New York: Modern Library).

Roy, Arundhati (2001). *Power Politics* (London: South End Press).

Sangvai, Sanjay (2000). *The River and Life: People's Struggle in the Narmada Valley* (Mumbai and Calcutta: Earthcare Books).

Scott, J. W. (1996). *Only Paradoxes to Offer: French Feminists and the Rights of Man* (Cambridge, MA: Harvard University Press).

Shaw, Devin Zane (2017). 'Disagreement and Recognition between Ranciere and Honneth', *Boundary* 2. Available at https://www.boundary2.org/2017/03/devin-zane-shaw-disagreement-and-recognition-between-ranciere-and-honneth/. Accessed 16.10.22.

Spivak, G. C. (1993). 'In a Word: Interview with Ellen Rooney', in *Outside, in The Teaching Machine* (New York: Routledge), pp. 1–26.

Sylvain, Renée (2014). 'Essentialism and the Indigenous Politics of Recognition in Southern Africa', *American Anthropologist* 116/2: 251–264.

Conclusion

Dignifying the World's Poor: Cosmopolitan Justice, Recognition Theory and Beyond

According to a recent report produced by the Food Security Information Network through a partnership between UNICEF, the World Food Programme and other international organisations, in 2019 183 million people worldwide were classified as being in a 'stressed' condition in terms of food security, or at the cusp of acute hunger and at risk of slipping into a 'crisis' phase or worse if faced with an event such as a pandemic (Food Security Information Network (2022). In response to what is likely to be one of the most intense humanitarian problems confronting an ever-globalising world, which has left populations of developing countries confronting increasingly fragile livelihoods and conditions of precarious material life (Valensi, 2020; Sumner et al., 2020), this book has attempted to draw from both recent and long-standing theories of recognition to support the rights and dignity of the very poor globally. My guiding aim throughout has been to defend universal human needs for recognition, to address the harms of social invisibility or forms of poverty-related social suffering worldwide. The arguments seem especially vital considering how persistently solutions to these predicaments have seemed to elude official policies of international development and aid (Saefullah, 2019), and how far, at least in pre-pandemic years, worldwide poverty as a global issue continually became secondary to older international themes such as peacemaking, and more recently emerging foci such as terrorism and global climate change (Hulme, 2010).

It is not that these issues are mutually distant or unconnected. At the time of writing, the United Nations' World Food Programme reports humanitarian and poverty-related crises of extreme proportions in Afghanistan, for example, which have been more complex and severe since the Taliban took control, with an estimated 18.9 million Afghans not consuming enough food and with the country on the brink of economic collapse (Khan, 2021). Meanwhile, the poverty-related effects of the Russian invasion of Ukraine have also been extreme. The situation has reportedly left one in three families without sufficient food, rising to one in two in some Eastern and Southern areas, especially those on the front-lines.[1] Confronted with these situations,

DOI: 10.4324/9781003045038-7

it seems unlikely, and perhaps to misunderstand the role of normative political philosophy, to hope that arguments from this field could intervene to suggest total, once-and-for-all solutions. The hope may prove excessive in a global context of intensifying food scarcity in the wake of global health crises, war, civil conflict and ever-threatening climate degradation.

While, of course, some political philosophers in this field have, as explored in Chapter 1, urged for radical and extensive international reform (Pogge, 2007, 2007a), arguments which remain enduringly significant, it also seems a vital role for political philosophers to offer arguments for normative values, which in this book I have presented in terms of particular conceptions of agency and empowerment. To be sure, conceiving these values from the perspective of recognition theory ought to be viewed in the context of the wide global, structural power-relationships affecting the life-conditions of the very poor in a globalising world, such as the global trade practices which have significant implications for labour opportunities in the developing world. As Iris Young's allied 'social connection' model of global responsibility clarifies, the global network of market and trade practices mutually implicate the affluent with the poor around the world in chains of ethical responsibility (Young, 2006, 2010; Little, 2019). As the issues concerning international trade and labour practices clearly have implications from the perspective of recognition politics, had space permitted the ethics of multinational corporations and sweatshop labour would have been a much-needed additional practical focus in this book, to further support the arguments from agency and empowerment. As these connected global ethical issues could not have been tackled also in a book of this length, however, and with the parameters of a single philosophical project in mind, in conclusion I take the limited remaining space to reflect on the broader policy-related implications of the arguments presented, suggesting how the value-commitments of the proposed approach might further or supplement existing avenues for poverty alleviation and sustainable development worldwide. In closing, I also comment on some pressing issues almost inevitably left open-ended, including more precise issues of moral duty and obligation in the context of chronic and ongoing global poverty.

6.1 Cosmopolitan Recognition Theory: Rights, Empowerment and Development Practice

First, therefore, my recognition-theoretical defence of concepts of reason-to-value agency and durable inter-sphere empowerment ought not to be taken to be absolutely at odds with more familiar defences of the international human rights of the poor which clearly guide human development policy initiatives, such as in terms of the social rights specified under the UDHR to an adequate standard of health and wellbeing.[2] In fact, the core material interests identified by international covenants, and pursued by many humanitarian NGOs, will often be crucial, not least because their protection and fulfilment would symbolise the meaningful recognition of the dignity of the lives of the poor. As Chapter 1 discussed, in regards to international human rights as one of Honneth's forms of recognition, however, it seems necessary to remain cautious of reifying these rights, for instance by construing social rights as ends-in-themselves, as at times seemed the case in Pogge's (2005) extension of Rawlsian contract theory. As reflected in my discussion in Chapter 2, these approaches might risk forgetting the normative significance of concrete struggles worldwide to define the content, meaning and priority of these rights and needs in dialogues with one's interaction partners such as one's fellow citizens, and the more pro-active view urged by writers such as Monique Deveaux (2021) to conceptualise the poor as 'agents of justice'. The struggle against reifying either social rights or the 'global poor' should not be viewed as an argument against viewing, however, social rights as provisional fixed points within international programmes of development policy and aid. As absolute moral entitlements of the very poor, especially in situations of emergency rescue and crises of hunger, it seems clear their urgent fulfilment, whether through international aid, cash transfers or other means, would take a certain priority over what often seems to be a longer-term 'human development' aim of encouraging the poor to struggle over recognition. As Chapter 2 suggested, participatory, human-development–oriented poverty alleviation strategies, which would include the struggles of the very poor around the world to define their needs and priorities, seem to constitute certain pathways for poverty alleviation, as distinct from emergency food security programmes (Audet, 2015; Buchanan-Smith and Maxwell, 1994; Rubenstein, 2007). Yet decisions over whether to pursue 'emergency assistance' and 'development through recognition' clearly points to tense and difficult conceptual questions which I raised in relation to the Singer Solution to global poverty in Chapter 2. Through these debates, the approach defended continually alerts to the need to avoid reifying global poverty as such.

In terms of the broader value of durable empowerment defended as the internal purpose of the recognition struggles of the very poor, it is worth bringing again into focus, as I did indirectly in Chapter 4 by raising discussion of the World Bank development initiatives in collaboration with Nike and Goldman Sachs, the fact that recently these organisations have prominently invoked the discourse of empowerment in their poverty alleviation strategies (World Bank, 2000; Narayan, 2002; Fox, 2017; Prugl, 2017; Klugman et al. 2014). However, as I hope to have suggested through my earlier explorations, the two understandings of empowerment do differ. It seems fair to say that the United Nations and World Bank's focus on empowerment as a tool for poverty alleviation appears to conceive the concept of empowerment predominantly in terms of 'power-to', which, especially from certain feminist perspectives in the development ethics literature, may be thought to play down the more collectivist and subversive forms of power central to the concept (Taylor, 2004; Cornwall and Brock,

2005). In contrast, then, with this dominant and influential approach which seems to equate processes of empowerment with asset-holdings and labour opportunities, cosmopolitan recognition theory focuses alternatively on empowerment as found in solidarity with communities arising from shared experiences of indignity and social suffering. That is to say, when struggling for the recognition of one's needs and rights different forms of power are in question; and a person's actions may be as much a reaction to material deprivation as to development assistance which might be experienced as imposed. Therefore, while the perspective which has been defended does not necessarily oppose existing international policies geared towards empowerment, to focus on the concept of recognition is to alert to the need not to de-politicise or de-psychologise the concept of empowerment itself. This point explains the book's focus on human capacities to cope, survive and to transpose status, influence and control across different spheres of life, as argued in Chapter 4, capacities which may well prove vital from the perspective of the world's poor.

Overall, then, as my objective has been to offer a normatively-inspired reflection on policies relating to global poverty rather than a concrete policy recommendation as such, one main concern arising with the proposed approach is that the defence of the empowerment of the very poor world-wide should not assume the concept of empowerment to be synonymous with macroeconomic stability, privatisation or liberalisation (cf. Cornwall and Brock, 2005: 1045). Doing so would risk only supporting the initiatives of donor agencies, for instance, to engage in projects of capacity-building which may not, in specific contexts, reflect the priorities or protect the real vulnerabilities of the economically disadvantaged (Aslop, 2004). Again, this point was illustrated by my brief discussion of the collaborative initiatives of the World Bank in Chapter 4. Additionally, and this is to re-invoke point which I explored in the third chapter's discussion of Iain Wilkinson and Arthur Kleinman's (2016) link between social suffering and humanitarianism, to acknowledge the essential contestability of the terms 'development' and 'progress' could itself form an important act of recognition. This point is highlighted especially by the activities of uncovering the epistemic standpoints of poor subaltern communities, suggested in Chapter 3, as well as the disputes over the Narmada Dam in India, explored in Chapter 5. In fact, had space in this book permitted, much more detail would have been devoted to the contestation which indigenous peoples in particular have raised against dominant conceptions of prosperity, modernisation and development as key cosmopolitan recognition struggles in the current world.[3] The ongoing campaigns of the very poor around the world for the recognition and retention of their own historical modes of landholding, against what have often been aggressive neoliberal development policies, seem to reinforce Taylor's key argument (1994: 32), again as raised in Chapter 4, that due recognition is not just a courtesy which we owe others. Rather, in many cases, it is a vital human need.

6.2 Global Poverty, Duties to Support and Cosmopolitan Moral Theories into the Future

While there may therefore be more frequent contradictions between official conceptions of empowerment and the real empowerment of the very poor around the world than is often acknowledged, the concern may persist that responding to forms of global poverty through the concepts of social suffering, recognition and misrecognition ultimately tends to play down the strong correlativity assumed by rights-based approaches between the fundamental entitlements of the poor and multi-layered national and international obligations. A point raised previously in Chapter 1, the concern may be that what one gains through the flexibility of a recognition-based approach, which focuses on the social suffering, indignity and denigration experienced by the very poor, may be counteracted by its ambiguity in specifying concretely moral and political duties to respect, protect and fulfil subaltern and poor communities' needs. To be sure, as David Ingram argues in his incisive, recent study of the current global situation of unmet need, poverty and world crisis, it seems reasonable to assume

> most people would agree that living in a world where one third of the world's population lives in severe poverty, in both absolute and relative terms, [...] suffices to generate a duty to assist them on the part of higher income countries (HICs).
>
> (2018: 12)

Yet, in contrast with rights-based approaches, especially those which, as explored in Chapter One, have focused on social rights associated with welfare provision and resource-redistribution, it is in the nature of the case that it will not always be immediately clear how the poor might be protected globally to increase their capacities for creative strategising, as suggested in Chapter 3; or, perhaps more complexly, how they might be encouraged to empower themselves through recognition struggles, as suggested through Chapters 4 and 5. At this point, the positive, normative implications of reason-to-value agency and durable empowerment are inevitably complex. This is partly because my purpose, in invoking the examples of microfinance in Chapter 4 and the Sardar Sarovar project in India in Chapter 5, was to suggest that the recognition struggles of subaltern, marginalised or very poor communities are often raised in resistance to state-based and international conceptions of prosperity, advancement and development. Therefore, while it may be true that the argument presented does not offer one-size-fits-all answers to the operational question of how states or the international community may best support the central values defended, it is hoped that the defence of the value-commitments in themselves provide a critical lens through which to reflect on particular poverty alleviation strategies. This is especially as my defence of these norms suggests a further point raised by Ingram, namely the need for care, as a rights-based approach to achieve the goals of development may cause coercive forms of paternalism, such as loan agreements which impose stringent structural adjustment conditions or forms of family planning assistance in poor societies. Although these approaches may support rights, Ingram rightly argues, they may be problematic from a broader social justice, or recognition-based, perspective (Ingram, 2018: 10).

Moreover, while the lack of a strict or very definite correlation between recognition and obligation might at first seem a drawback of a cosmopolitan recognition theory, a further observation would be that, in fact, such ambiguities might equally affect rights-based approaches to global poverty (Grugel, 2009).[4] With this said, recognition theories are also obviously moral theories, with ethical implications. As moral theories, a cosmopolitan recognition theory could not refrain from suggesting that, in the name of reciprocal recognition, states and the international community should not undermine human beings' legitimate struggles against the social invisibility of their hardships. After all, in characterising societies which withhold recognition from large sections of their populations as pathological, as Honneth depicts in *The Struggle for Recognition*, there seems to be an implied imperative to restructure these societies, just as nineteenth-century feminist movements in Europe rightly demanded, and eventually achieved, social reforms in education, access to labour opportunities and voting rights. Hence, although I questioned the universalisability of Honneth's three modes of recognition in Chapter 1, nonetheless it is significant to emphasise that Honneth has for his part strongly argued that his own recognitional norms imply moral obligations, therefore raising the question of which actions and policies would secure greater recognition in his sense. For Honneth, the Hegelian origins of recognition theory clearly necessitate these moral obligations:

> The moral rights and duties that correspond to each of the circumscribed forms of recognition follow from the specific structure of the relation-to-self which is, as it were, first to be created or strengthened [...] It is this internal link with particular duties and rights that makes it all the more possible to speak of a "morality of recognition"; the relations of recognition which we have so far viewed in terms of the functional aspect of the constitution of practical relations to the self, are by their very nature *formed so that they incorporate moral actions*
> (Honneth, 1997: 35, my emphasis)

While the passage above does suggest the need to protect human beings from social invisibility or non-recognition, and that this need generates moral obligations, it also seems fair to say that the duties flowing from recognition theories would be more theoretically and practically open than those associated with rights-based justice, especially confronted with complex global problems within developing states and societies which may not always have stable, functioning welfare provision, and when the many dimensions of poverty-related suffering are considered. Furthermore, as regards the correlation between recognition and obligation, another core point would be that, as with other participatory, human development-oriented approaches, a recognition-based approach to global poverty almost inevitably emphasises the active participation of the poor, rather than only support in the form of monetary donation to charitable assistance or philanthropy. Finally, it may be significant to suggest that normative political philosophy is not, in itself, policy analysis. Of course, considering the suffering involved in the voicelessness of the poor around the word brings to one's attention, relentlessly, the question of which forms of acknowledgement and reciprocity would provide compensation for this suffering, and in which forum this compensation and rectification may be given. Where recognition is considered primarily as legal rights, then the ethical implication might be perfect duties to secure the good associated with the right, such as shelter, adequate nutrition, labour conditions or educational opportunities. However, where the form of misrecognition is social suffering, where human beings struggle against the harms of alienation, disaffection and social invisibility, as I hope to have shown through the different chapters, the correlative obligations are likely to be more challenging, diffuse and wide-ranging. One of the essential reasons for this is that when groups have been historically and socially invisible for too long, they have clearly suffered an epistemic injustice. Logically, knowing which measures which would be needed to assist them to improve their quality of life would be complex; and the corresponding moral obligations, almost by definition, could not be summarised by theoretical fiat.

This point may be emphasised well, in closing, by referring again to the fraught controversies arising around the empowerment potential of microcredit programmes, as discussed in Chapter 4. Although these policies have been pursued on the basis of their empowerment potential for poor women especially, the more direct question might be whether the programmes should be viewed as inhibiting the empowered recognition struggles of the women, if they do not increase their feminist consciousness through their increased economic activity and labour options, as discussed previously. Development ethicists have been deeply divided on this question, with some suggesting these initiatives assist women to use their increased financial status to contest unequal power-relations in the home, by exerting greater control over household financial decisions (Aruna and Jyothimayi, 2011). Others (Bateman and Chang, 2012; Bateman, 2010) have contended that microfinance amounts to a dangerous and corrosive implementation of neoliberalism at the local level, in such a way that may be especially problematic for poor women. From the perspective of durable inter-sphere empowerment in this book, it may seem both reasonable and pragmatic to support microlending practices, insofar as they inspire and facilitate possibilities for empowerment. However, the complex preconditions for the emergence of poor women's recognition struggles are likely to involve more diffuse but complex social bases, such as social freedom from violence, access to reproductive and health provision, opportunities for land and property ownership, as well as political influence. These complex social bases and support to assist their own struggles are likely to be dependent in the real world on states as well as development agencies (see Klugman et al., 2014). In these situations, arguments for recognition-based responsibilities clearly do not suggest a finished story for the empowerment of the poor and powerless in the world. Progress towards the self-realisation of the world's poorest is likely to be ongoing, incremental and contextual.

Ultimately, then, when the question of pro-poor recognition is considered in a highly uncertain world, the question of which policies, initiatives and programmes will on balance produce positive gains in terms of supporting creative agency and sustainable empowerment suggests an ongoing responsibility on the part of the better off to listen to the voices of the poor. From the normative perspective of recognition theory, perpetually, as I have argued, one must view oneself and the other as ethically connected and as mutually obliged.

Notes

1 United Nations World Food Programme, Afghanistan emergency Appeal by the World Food Programme. See https://www.wfp.org/support-us/stories/families-afghanistan-need-help?utm_source=google&utm_medium=cpc&utm_campaign=14343279763&utm_content=127819179082&gclid=EAIaIQobChMI3YXl38LA_QIVQeztCh2UYgjtEAAYASAAEgJeavD_BwE&gclsrc=aw.ds. Accessed 4 April 2022.

2 While a number of poverty alleviation NGOs do explicitly aim to put the social rights, such as Article 25, more firmly on state agendas, some argue at the same time that the relationship between rights and development is not straightforward. In referring to Ingram's (2018) recent analysis later in this Conclusion, I suggest some potential drawbacks of a rights-based approach.

3 For further readings, in addition to the perspectives suggested in Chapter 3, excellent recent analyses of indigenous peoples' contestations of dominant conceptions of development worldwide include Magni (2017) and McNeish (2008).

4 For instance, Ashford (2007) argues, in a sense against Pogge, that the human right to basic necessities generates positive duties on the part, largely, of affluent populations of the world. While this argument may be compelling, there still seems to remain substantial room for controversy over what these positive duties imply, or what affluent citizens must do to comply with these duties.

References

Aruna, M. and Rema Jyothirmayi (2011). 'The Role of Microfinance in Women's Empowerment: A Study of the Shg Bank Linkage Programme in Hyderabad (Andhra Pradesh)', *Indian Journal of Commerce and Management Studies* 11/4: 77–82.

Ashford, Elizabeth (2007). 'The Duties Imposed by Human Rights to Basic Necessities', in T. Pogge (ed), *Freedom from Poverty as a Human Right: Who Owes What to the Very Poor*, (Oxford: Oxford University Press) pp. 183–218.

Aslop, Ruth (ed), (2004).*Power, Rights and Poverty: Concepts and Connections* (Washington: World Bank Publications).

Audet, Francois (2015). 'From Disaster Relief to Development Assistance: Why Simple Solutions Do Not Work', International Journal 70/1: 110–118.

Bateman, M. (2010). *Why Doesn't Microfinance Work? The Destructive Rise of Neoliberalism* (London: Zed Books).

Bateman, M. and H. J. Chang (2012). 'Microfinance and the Illusion of Development: From Hubris to Nemesis in 30 Years', *World Economic Review* 1: 13–36.

Buchanan-Smith, Margaret and Simon Maxwell (1994). 'Linking Relief and Development: An Introduction and Overview', IDS Bulletin, 25/4: 2–16.

Cornwall, Andrea and Karen Brock (2005). 'What Do Buzzwords Do for Development Policy? A Critical Look at 'Participation', 'Empowerment' and 'Poverty Reduction'', *Third World Quarterly* 26/7: 1043–1060.

Deveaux, Monique (2021). *Poverty, Solidarity and Poor-Led Social Movements* (Oxford: Oxford University Press).

Food Security Information Network. (2022). 'Global Report against Food Crises 2022'. Available at: https://www.fao.org/3/cb9997en/cb9997en.pdf. Last accessed: 02.03.23.

Food Security Information Network (2022). 'Press Release: Global Report on Food Crises Reveals Scope of Food Crises as Covid-19 Poses New Risks to Vulnerable Countries'. http:www.unicef.org/turkiye/en/press-releases/global-report-food-crises--reveals-scope-food-crises-covid-19-poses-new-risks. Last accessed: 22.02.23.

Fox, Carolina (2017). 'In the Mind, the Household or the Market? Concepts and Measurement of Women's Economic Empowerment', World Bank (Working Paper) 8079. Available at: http://documents.worldbank.org/curated/en.436011496234827185/pdf/WPS8079.pdf. Accessed 6.12.22.

Grugel, Jean (2009). 'Do Rights Promote Development?' *Global Social Policy* 9/1: 79–98.

Honneth, Axel (1997). 'Recognition and Moral Obligation', *Social Research* 64/1, The Decent Society (Spring): 16–35.

Hulme, David (2010). *Global Poverty: How Global Governance is Failing the Poor* (London: Routledge).

Ingram, David (2018). *World Crisis and Underdevelopment: A Critical Theory of Poverty, Agency and Coercion* (Cambridge: Cambridge University Press).

Khan, I. U. (2021). 'WFP Calls for Urgent Aid as Millions of Afghans Face Starvation'. Available at https://www.aljazeera.com/news/2021/8/24/wfp-food-aid-afghanistan-starvation-taliban/. Accessed 4.12.22.

Klugman, Jeni, Lucia Hanmer, Sarah Twigg, Tazeen Hasan, Jennifer McClearly-Gills, and Lucien Santamanin (2014). *Voice and Agency: Empowering Women and Girls for Shared Prosperity* (New York: World Bank Publications).

Little, David (2019). *The Paradox of Wealth and Poverty: Mapping the Ethical Dilemmas of Global Development* (New York: Routledge).

Magni, Giorgia (2017). 'Indigenous Knowledge and Implications for the Sustainable Development Agenda' *European Journal of Education*, 54/4 (Education for People, Prosperity and the Planet: Can We Meet the Sustainability Challenges?'): 437–447.

McNeish, John Andrew (2008). 'Overview: Indigenous Peoples' Perspectives on Poverty and Development', in R. Eversole, John Andrew McNeish, and Alberto

D. Cimadore (eds), *Indigenous Peoples and Poverty: An International Perspective* (London: Bloomsbury), pp. 229–239.

Narayan, Deepa (ed). (2002). *Empowerment and Poverty Reduction: A Sourcebook* (Washington, DC: World Bank).

Pogge, T. (2005). 'Real World Justice', *The Journal of Ethics*, 9: 29–53.

Pogge, Thomas (2007). 'Severe Poverty as a Human Rights Violation', in T. Pogge (ed), *Freedom from Poverty as a Human Right: Who Owes What to the Very Poor?* (Oxford: Oxford University Press), pp. 11–53.

Pogge, Thomas (2007). 'Are We Violating the Human Rights of the World's Poor?' in D. Kinley (ed), *Human Rights: Old Problems. New Possibilities* (London: Edward Elgar Publishing), pp. 40–72.

Prugl, E. (2017). 'Neoliberalism with a Feminist Face: Creating a New Hegemony at the World Bank', *Feminist Economics* 23/1: 30–53.

Saefullah, Ku Kurnianwan (2019). 'The Failure of Financial-Economic Policies to Reduce Global Poverty', in L. Jan Slikkerveer, G. Baourikis, and K. Saefullah (eds), *Integrated Community Development* (Dordrecht: Springer), pp. 67–90.

Rubenstein, Jennifer (2007). 'Distribution and Emergency', Journal of Political Philosophy, 15/3: 296–320.

Sumner, A., Eduardo Ortiz-Suarez, and Chris Hoy (2020). 'Precarity and the Pandemic', WIDER Working Paper 2020/77 (June 2020).

Taylor, Charles (1994). 'The Politics of Recognition', in A. Gutmann (ed), *Multiculturalism: Examining the Politics of Recognition* (Princeton: Princeton University Press), pp. 25–74.

Taylor, M. (2004). 'Responding to Neoliberalism in Crisis: Discipline and Empowerment in the World Bank's Development Agenda', in P. Zaremba (ed), *Neoliberalism in Crisis, Accumulation and Rosa Luxemburg's Legacy* (Research in Political Economy, vol. 21, Bingley: Emerald Group Publishing), pp. 3–30.

Valensi, Giovanni (2020). 'Covid-19 and Global Poverty: Are LCDs Being Left Behind?' *The European Journal of Development Research* 32: 1535–1557.

Wilkinson, I. and A. Kleinman (2016). *A Passion for Society: How We Think about Human Suffering* (Berkeley: University of California Press).

World Bank (2000). *World Development Report 2000/2001: Attacking Poverty* (NY: Oxford University Press).

Young, Iris Marion (2006). 'Responsibility for Global Justice: A Social Connection Model', *Social Philosophy and Policy*, 23/1: 102–130.

Young, Iris Marion (2010). 'Responsibility and Global Labour Justice', in G. Ognjenovic (ed), *Responsibility in Context* (Dordrecht: Springer), pp. 53–76.

Index

For Product Safety Concerns and Information please contact our EU
representative GPSR@taylorandfrancis.com
Taylor & Francis Verlag GmbH, Kaufingerstraße 24, 80331 München, Germany

www.ingramcontent.com/pod-product-compliance
Ingram Content Group UK Ltd.
Pitfield, Milton Keynes, MK11 3LW, UK
UKHW022355190926
475702UK00015B/2303

* 9 7 8 1 0 3 2 4 3 8 2 0 7 *